Can Hunger be Defeated?

Can Hunger be Defeated?

Advancing Food Security in South Asia

edited by

Stefan Mentschel

YODA PRESS
79, Gulmohar Enclave
New Delhi 110 049
www.yodapress.co.in

This publication is sponsored by the Rosa Luxemburg Stiftung with funds of the Federal Ministry for Economic Cooperation and Development of the Federal Republic of Germany. This publication or parts of it can be used by others for free as long as they provide a proper reference to the original publication.

ISBN 978-93-82579-72-4

Editors in charge: Ishita Gupta and Tanya Singh
Typeset by Jojy Philip
Printed at Replika Press Pvt. Ltd.
Published by Arpita Das for YODA PRESS, New Delhi

Contents

Preface

Stefan Mentschel and Neha Naqvi

When the Congress-led government of Prime Minister Manmohan Singh introduced the National Food Security Act in 2013, the international media termed it the largest social welfare scheme in the world. Experts opine that it is by far one of the most comprehensive legislations on the Right to Food in the world as the bill gives two-thirds of India's 1.3 billion people the legal right to a uniform quantity of food grains at a fixed price. In concrete terms this means that more than 800 million Indians are guaranteed at least five kilograms of rice, wheat or millets at 3 Rupees, 2 Rupees and 1 Rupee per kilogram, respectively. Effectively this amounts to approximately 25 kilograms of rice, wheat or millets per month per family (assuming an average family size of five). Additionally, roughly 20 million of the poorest households receive an extra 10 kilograms of food grains, amounting to 35 kilograms altogether.

Eight years earlier, in 2005, Singh's Government had already introduced another massive social welfare scheme, the Mahatma Gandhi National Rural Employment Guarantee Act. It was created to provide legal entitlement to a hundred days of employment, every year, for every rural household in the country at minimum wage. It was primarily seen as a social protection measure for the most vulnerable people in rural India, by way of providing employment opportunities. Employment is meant to be provided within a fortnight of the demand for employment being made. If the government is unable to provide employment, an unemployment allowance is meant to be provided to job-seekers who demand employment. The programme now covers the entire country and has emerged as the largest employment programme in the world.

Food and employment are just two areas in which support schemes have been put in place. According to Biraj Patnaik, the former Principal Adviser to the Supreme Court of India on the Right to Food, India has a plethora of social welfare programmes covering entire populations across sectors. Apart from food and employment, these include schemes related to health, education, and social assistance such as pensions for the elderly and the disabled. He states that overall, there are nearly 70 centrally sponsored programmes supported financially by the Central Government in New Delhi and many others that are paid out of state and local budgets. The total budget outlay of the Central Government for the social sector stands at around 2 per cent of the GDP and the total spending in these sectors (including the contribution of the states) is approximately 7 per cent of the GDP.

However, despite all of these social welfare schemes, ground realities in India speak an entirely different language. Close to a third of the population is living below the official poverty line, according to Government reports. United Nations data reveals that where sanitation is concerned, more than half of 'open defecations' in the world on any given day are happening in India, and only a third of the population has access to a private toilet. Moreover, malnutrition and hunger persist in the country. According to a study from 2012, the child malnutrition rate in India was 42 per cent at the time. Unfortunately not much has changed since. India is still the country with the largest number of under-nourished children in the world. It is ironic that chronic malnutrition persists despite the fact that India is supposed to have achieved self-sufficiency in food grain production and has mostly been a net exporter of food, over the past few decades.

These glaring contradictions form the backdrop to this book. Disparity in terms of access made us want to reflect on possible reasons why social welfare schemes are often unable to reach the people they are intended for. We were inspired to take a closer look at ground realities in different parts of India, in search for answers. This combines ground reports from four distinct areas in India—namely Bundelkhand that lies partly in the states of Uttar Pradesh and Madhya Pradesh, Maharashtra in the West of the country, Odisha in the East and Assam in the North East—as well as political analysis on Social Protection, Food Security and Food Sovereignty. For the reports, our authors travelled to specific villages, speaking with people on the ground about their experiences with and expectations of certain social welfare schemes and the deep seated consequences of an inequitable struggle with poverty. Flowing from this, the analytical pieces were framed by fellow experts in their fields, to help place these observations in context.

In this vein, Achyut Das makes the case for a multi-pronged approach to policy changes, grounding his views in the lived experiences of Adivasi communities in Odisha. He identifies the many levels on which action needs to be taken in this particular context, in order to improve food security, assure sustainable livelihoods and provide ecological securities. He advocates for the rigorous analysis of relevant legislations, programmes and practices. Asking that national food production programmes not be permitted to evade scrutiny, he requests the reviewing of agriculture technologies applicable to Adivasi land in particular. His suggestions underscore the fact that agriculture needs to be both nutrition-focused and gender-sensitive when taking into account planning and implementation processes. This ground report underlines the need for people-centric formulations, ones that bear witness to Adivasi knowledge systems that have flourished for years.

Flowing from this in some respect, Rajeev Khedkar's report from Maharashtra further charts out exclusion, by recording the experiences of Dalit and Adivasi communities confronted with widespread malnutrition. The research points towards strategies that could serve to strengthen awareness building mechanisms around the long-term effects of malnutrition. The author also makes the case for the protection of forest rights in the context of the Adivasi people, providing evidence for why and how this will impact their ability to secure traditional livelihoods. He also seeks to underscore reasons for mobilising civil society in order to optimally implement government schemes, especially in remote villages.

India's North-Eastern state of Assam finds Amarjyoti Borah locating his study across different villages in the Morigaon district. He chose to focus on the region on account of its exposure to extreme environmental changes in the last few years. He describes an increase in floods around the Brahmaputra river, a spike in instances of soil erosion and the consequences of increasingly erratic rain patterns in the area. The report examines the impact this has had on local farmers, most of whom don't have access to irrigation facilities nor agricultural machines. Providing concrete examples from four different villages, he illustrates both the challenges being faced and efforts to adapt to and survive harsh circumstances. The study lays emphasis on reasons why state supported programmes tend not to deliver in ways that meet ground realities in the Morigaon district. The author explores the obstacles preventing farmers from accessing benefits they are entitled to. He also brings to light how changing weather patterns in the area attest to global climate change, describing the devastation they wreak at the local level. An assessment of how local populations view the support programmes on offer are summarised, followed by an overview of some of the more important social policies that come into play.

In Bundelkhand, Bharat Dogra writes about a region consisting of 13 districts in Central India that regularly experience extreme forms of hunger and malnutrition. 2016 saw the situation worsen on account of an extensive drinking water crisis and a serious shortage of animal fodder. In his account, a sharp decline in the availability of cereals, wheat, rice, pulses and milk products—complicated by withering livestock—is recorded as having significantly contributed to farmer suicides recorded. The chapter further proceeds to examine the realities of exploitation and inequality that when coupled with the inadequacies of governance contribute to the breakdown of food security. The report also sheds light on how gender, age, caste and class interact with these realities.

Anchoring these experiences in theory is Debal Deb's analytical piece 'Opposing the Enclosure of Land, Seeds and Knowledge Commons'. The author reflects upon the fact that despite the confluence of many decades of experiences with indigenous land rights struggles and food rights movements around the world, the many definitions of Food Sovereignty appear to fall short of the basic tenet of access to food. Key terms examined include *sustainability*, *autonomy*, and *ecological systems*. Among other aspects explored, the chapter approaches food sovereignty as both a reaction to and an intellectual offshoot of older concepts such as the Right to Food and Food Security. It alludes to a fundamental operational difference between the two ideas and locates this variance in the mode of production.

In 'Social Protection and Food Security – A Comparative Study of South Asian Countries', Praveen Jha relies on large-scale databases and secondary sources to argues that the impact of public provisioning on social protection measures, if effectively leveraged, could reap immediate and long term benefits in the realm of hunger eradication, reducing malnutrition and food insecurity. The paper proceeds to map the trends in hunger, malnutrition and other indicators of food and nutrition security across regions in South Asia. The author draws insights from select initiatives with respect to social protection schemes and policies. Detailing achievements as well as gaps in policy frameworks, the chapter offers vital information promoting Food Security in the region.

The final chapter of the book is Harsh Mander's thoughtful and detailed analysis on 'Advancing Food Security in India—

The National Food Security Law and its Aftermath'. The focus of his writing examines a four-and-a-half-year long, journey with India's historic National Food Security Act, 2013 (NFSA), that—as mentioned—initially inspired us at Rosa Luxemburg Stiftung to compile this book. Harsh Mander's text follows the Act from initiation to its passage, and reflects on the status of its implementation. The design of India's legal and policy framework for the right to food is recognized for its rich, well-documented debates that unfold in the public domain over many years. Government actors, law makers, activists, scholars and other citizens each have a hand in shaping it. The paper spends some time on these debates—particularly ones that went into the provisions of the NFSA. It outlines the choices and decisions that were made, tracing the process of implementation by the central and state governments in the first two-and-a-half years of its becoming law. The author provides an overall evaluation of the law, its implementation with respect to the social and economic rights guaranteed to food insecure populations in India by its Parliament.

With this said, it is our hope at Rosa Luxemburg Stiftung that putting together this book will be a step towards placing voices from the ground and policy analysis connected with Food Security and Food Sovereignty, at the same table. That in so doing, we invite dialogue, continue conversations and renew our collective commitment to research and activism on a subject that remains achingly relevant—involuntary hunger and its human cost.

Food Sovereignty

Opposing the Enclosure of Land, Seeds and Knowledge Commons

DEBAL DEB

Dr Debal Deb is the founder of Vrihi, which is the largest non-governmental folk rice gene bank in India, and of Basudha research farm, Odisha, where more than a thousand rice land-races are conserved and agroecology is demonstrated. He has 30 years of experience in research related to agroecology, ecological economics, development studies, human ecology, biodiversity conservation etc. He is an internationally known scientist who has received several fellowships and published more than 80 articles for renowned national and international journals and platforms.

Introduction

In 1974, too much rain in Bangladesh resulted in flooding and subsequent devastation of rice crops. The shortfall in rice production caused a steep rise in the food price, which disentitled the rural people from their food access resulting in famines in different parts of the country. The same year the World Food Conference of the Food and Agriculture Organization (FAO) of the United Nations was established, with the goal to address world hunger in light of the famine in Bangladesh. The term 'food security' was used in this conference to denote the 'availability at all times of adequate world food supplies of basic foodstuffs to sustain a steady expansion of food consumption and to offset fluctuations in production and prices.'[(1)] U.S. Secretary of State Henry Kissinger made an extremely aspirational declaration, calling for an end to hunger in ten years. Although this has not been achieved, the term 'food security' has been used in all food policy discourses around the globe.

In 1983, the FAO redefined food security as a matter of both physical and economic access of all people to food.[(2)] Enough food is produced to feed everyone, yet a significant proportion of the developing world remains hungry,[(3; 4)] owing to disentitlement of the poor to adequate food. In his classic analysis of the 1943 Bengal Famine, Amartya Sen showed that lack of purchasing power of the poor, as opposed to actual food availability deficit, was the cause.[(5)] This analysis influenced the UN and other institutions to acknowledges that the problem is not the supply of food that is in shortage, but rather access to food.[(6)] This has caused a shift from viewing hunger as a product of scarcity to hunger as a matter of security. The FAO also recognizes that hunger is linked to poverty and that 'agricultural growth involving smallholders, especially women, will be most effective in reducing extreme poverty and hunger when it increases returns to labour and generates employment for the poor.'[7]

This economic approach to food security recognizes that variability and uncertainty of the market prices is a major threat to food security. The FAO group of experts, for example, primarily blames speculation on the market as the culprit for price swings that cause destabilization, and calls for multilateral rules to control market when food is no longer cheap, not just when prices are too high, in order to protect importing countries.[8] Their view on establishing food security is purely economic and political, calling for a concerted effort of all nations to come together in consensus on protecting prices of food globally for those who cannot afford such unpredictability in the market. Although this is an important aspect, it still leaves out a lot of factors, such as people who do not have access to food regardless of market conditions. While many countries today depend on the 'free' market, proposing the need for price controls demonstrates a flaw in reliance on markets for distribution of food. Clearly, 'free' market, unaccompanied by governmental action, cannot solve the problem of food insecurity, as the market is inefficient in distributing food and ensuring access.

Another problem with depending on market policies that safeguard prices to help with food security issues is that it still leaves people dependent on external conditions to provide access to food and primarily focuses on protecting importing countries. Such policies only support commodity crops, as opposed to subsistence crops. Focusing on commodity price policies alone does not account for distribution or access to food.

This economic approach to food security, based on marketing of food crops and price control, also misses the fact that the 'success' of industrialized agriculture in increasing crop yields has masked negative externalities, with environmental and health problems that have been well-documented[9; 10] and evaluated in terms of their cost.[11; 12] The latest UN report estimates an annual death toll of 2,00,000 from agricultural pesticides exposure.[13] Industrial agriculture has also truncated genetic diversity of all major crops, leading to severe uncertainty of food production in the face of climatic vagaries.[14] Focus on conventional food security thus loses sight of the environmental and health impacts of industrial food production systems, undermines the overall well-being of producers and consumers, and fails to address the ecological unsustainability of the globalized fossil fuel-intensive food production system. Focusing on increased food production is therefore not sufficient to ensure food and nutritional security of any country. 'What is important is who produces the food, has access to the technology and knowledge to produce it, and has the purchasing power to acquire it.'[15]

The conceptual movements for food security and food sovereignty emerged in response to, and challenge, the prevailing industrial agriculture. The ideas of food sovereignty have evolved since the 1940s, with a growing understanding of the political and ecological aspects of food production and distribution. A description of the evolving concept of food sovereignty requires a retracing of the history of industrial capitalism and how it captures the agriculture and food systems, which we will discuss in the following sections.

Capitalist Growth and the Origin of Modern Food Insecurity

William Kapp, one of the founders of ecological economics, famously characterized the modern growth economy as a system of 'unpaid costs'.[16] Today, we know this all too well—heavy metals in children's bloodstreams, the disappearance of the Arctic sea ice cover, the melting of the Siberian permafrost—and subsequently, the Canadian permafrost, massive garbage dumps in the oceans, agro-toxic overload in our soil, water and food, the spill-out of fatal radioactivity from the Jadugoda mines to Chernobyl and Fukushima.

The whole motive for economic prosperity—since the global conquests that began in 1492—has been to treat all fruits of nature as a 'free gift'. Both classical and neoclassical economics consider creation of value only from human labour applied to the fruits of nature. Thus, a tree's ecological services are free, and have no value, until it has been felled and sawn into timber; fish of the sea are 'free'—of no value, until they are caught with net or fishing hook. The economy grows only when these 'free' products of nature are harvested and 'produced' by human labour, creating 'value' in the process. The cost of 'production' consists only of the cost of materials required in the production and the cost of labour involved. All other costs—the depletion of the quality of the environment or health hazards—are what Arthur Pigou described as 'incidental uncharged disservices', which are paid by society, the public in general.[(17)] This economy sees humans as free to act, as if economic production/consumption is somehow exempt from thermodynamic and other critical natural laws. It is this ecologically empty vision that has generated the sustainability conundrum.

Neoclassical economic growth is thus predicated on 'conquests' of nature. This conquest is achieved by the employment of technology to sequentially exhaust the stock of natural resources in order to maximize profit.[(18)] The capitalist expansion is achieved by means of (1) mapping and codifying natural resources; (2) simplifying and homogenizing nature within the sphere of production; and (3) extracting as much resource material and generating profit as quickly as possible, for the lowest possible capital expenditure. 'Taken together, these interwoven projects—creating "economies" of rationalization, control, and speed—have combined to do something more than facilitate high-profit primary production complexes. They have worked to reduce the costs of production for capital as a whole.'[(19)]

Forests were replaced in the 19th century with monoculture plantations of hardwood trees for railway and ship building; in the following centuries with rubber, eucalyptus and oil palm; and today, the forests, including Reserve Forests in India, are de-notified and cleared for highways, factories and mines. Since the 1950s, industrialization of marine fishery has reduced the entire marine fish stock to ten per cent within a period of just 50 years—'not just in some areas, not just for some stocks, but for entire communities of the large fish species from the tropics to the poles.'[20] The accessible stock of natural oil has been depleted, the peak oil phenomenon at the onset of the 21st century has exposed the unsustainability of our fossil fuel-based civilization. The vacuous Green Revolution of the 1960s, and the non-revolution in agricultural biotechnology of the late 20th century show the unsustainability of industrial agriculture more cogently.[4; 18; 19]

FOOD INSECURITY: OPPORTUNITY FOR CAPITAL INVESTMENT AND GROWTH

Industrialization of agriculture in Europe and America in the 19th century resulted in export of crops and livestock for food and fibre from country to town across vast distances. Unidirectional flow of biomass from the farm fields became imperatively intensive with growing international trade in crops. Some leading agronomists on both sides of the Atlantic voiced their concern about the declining soil fertility, and urged that municipal wastes be ploughed back into agriculture as organic manure. In *The Natural Laws of Husbandry*, Liebig insisted that farm productivity could be sustained if 'all the solid and fluid excrements of the inhabitants of towns' were returned to the country farms, which had generated the supply of agricultural produce for the town.[21] Marx, who was thoroughly acquainted with the advances in soil chemistry and the works of leading agronomists of his time (including Liebig's), deplored the industrial exploitation of the soil:

> Large-scale industry and large-scale mechanised agriculture work together. If originally distinguished by the fact that the former

> lays waste and destroys principally labour power, hence the natural force of human beings, whereas the latter more directly exhausts the natural vitality of the soil, they join hands in the further course of development in that the industrial system in the country-side also enervates the labourers, and industry and commerce on their part supply agriculture with the means for exhausting the soil.[22]

Although factory production of fertilizers was initially slow to spread in Europe, by the first decade of the 20th century, Europe's agriculture was completely industrialized and suffused with synthetic fertilizers. Knowledge of agricultural chemistry was profitably utilized in the service of capital, resulting in accelerating depletion of soil nutrients: '…all progress in increasing the fertility of the soil for a given time is a progress toward ruining the more long-lasting sources of that fertility.'[23] With the expansion of the agrochemicals market, industrial growth enveloped agriculture, whose development was foisted on a mechanical view of agriculture—a view that endorsed what Sir Albert Howard called the 'NPK mentality':

> The factories engaged during the Great [First World] War in the fixation of atmospheric nitrogen for the manufacture of explosives had to find other markets, the use of nitrogenous fertilizers in agriculture increased. Until today the majority of farmers and market gardeners base their manorial programme on the cheapest forms of nitrogen (N), phosphorus (P) and potassium (K) on the market. What may be conveniently described as the NPK mentality dominates farming alike in the experimental stations and the countryside. Vested interests, entrenched in time of national emergency, have gained a stronghold.[24]

Since the late 1940s Southern governments perceived the problem of poverty and hunger as paramount. To overcome the endemics of hunger, governments of ex-colonies took recourse in the industrial and agricultural development, as prescribed by neoclassical economics. The issue of hunger has been the prime motive in all ex-colonies for embracing the manifold development strategies from the late 1940s onwards.[25] The strategies of national governments to ensure food security have since ranged from food procurement through centralized distribution system, food fortification and supplementation, nutrition education and comprehensive national food and nutrition planning, to fertilizer factories, the Green Revolution, land reform and international food aid.

Soon after World War II, the World Bank (WB) and the International Monetary Fund (IMF) became the official guides and purveyors of national and international development policies. Upon the Bank's policy recommendations (and admonitions), industrial growth promotion, earning foreign exchange by export, and enclosure of the commons became the three conspicuous programmes of all national development agenda in the South. [18] In the 1960s, in the face of rising political discontent and social unrest throughout the Third World, and the spectre of communism in the First World, the development theory added emphasis on agricultural modernization. Increasing food production became an additional priority for the South.

Agricultural modernization entails industrialization of the means of agricultural production, transfer of capital and expertise from the North to the South, and a flourishing agri-business. The objective of agricultural development is the production of cheap food and cheap labour in the South, to make capital investment more profitable. In the 1960s, development economics began to consider peasants and small farms as potential capital-generators.[25]

The agricultural modernization projects in the South were driven by both the Malthusian fear of hunger and the logic of industrial expansion to create and capture the global food market.[18] Aside from population control programmes, the Green Revolution was the most important part of this campaign for development, which the World Bank, the Rockefeller Foundation and the Ford Foundation designed in a bid to stave off the risk of a communist revolution in the Third World. The Green Revolution constituted a new form of land commercialization in the South—'a ruthless form of "land reform" (i.e. land appropriation and enclosure of the rural commons) that was legitimated by reference to Malthusian population tendencies.'[(26)]

The Green Revolution opened a vast market for operation of giant multinational companies (MNCs) in the South. Clearly, the scope of garnering profits lay in three related fields: seeds, fertilizers and pesticides. Seeds of high input-responsive crop varieties (wrongly termed 'high yielding varieties' or HYVs) were sold to farmers as part of a package of agricultural development. Most of the HYV seed firms are also the leading chemical firms—Sandoz, Pioneer Hi-bred, Cargill, Volvo, ICI, Monsanto, Syngenta, Dekalb-Pfizer, BASF, and Bayer, whereas only six are traditionally seed producers. After the take-over of Monsanto, Bayer is the largest producer of PCBs (polychlorinated biphenyls) and at the same time, the world's largest seed corporation.

The agricultural modernization drive has escalated over the past few decades. Neoliberal policies—characterized by deregulation, privatization, cut-backs of essential services, tax benefits and subsidies to industry—have sought to consolidate the global food system, and led to a corporate-controlled supply of both the materials of food production and the food products, based on industrial production and marketing of seeds and agrochemicals, and processed food grains. In this modern, internationalized industrial agriculture, food production is de-linked from the specificities of local ecosystems, social relations and food cultures.[(27)]

This system of globalization and industrialization has received endorsement and support from the World Bank, national governments, think tanks and universities. These institutions have created what Haas calls an 'epistemic community'[(28)] for designing global food security. These institutions also put forth a semiotics of yield efficiency, productivity, economies of scale, trade liberalization, free markets and 'feeding the world', all of which are purported to build food security for the global population. These terms help to forge the societal consensus, and a scientific legitimacy, needed to gain control over the agrarian production relations to (re)orient them toward the needs of industrial agriculture and profit-taking.[29] This product of the epistemic community of agricultural development is pivoted on the neoliberal policy that is divorced from a social commitment to solve the problem of the poor's entitlement to food[3]. In its pursuit of short term crop yield increase, agricultural modernization by industrialization and internationalization neglects the issues of the impacts of modern agrochemicals and agro-biotechnology on soil and biodiversity[14; 30; 31; 32] and human health.[33; 34]

The new supply of exogenous seeds, machinery, deregulated market logic and the merger of seed business with chemicals industry and transgenics research impose a knowledge monoculture that destroys all local and traditional knowledge systems. Beginning with the Green Revolution in the 1960s, agricultural modernization has destroyed the traditional systems of sustainable agriculture and food systems. The huge repertoire of crop genetic diversity, created and maintained in the farmers' hands, has disappeared from the farm fields, while a part of this genetic wealth is preserved in a few national and international gene banks for developing new varieties. These gene banks are also open to seed researchers for 'gene mining'—selecting and using specific genes for unique agronomic characters for developing new varieties, which are aggressively promoted, at the behest of the national agricultural institutions, to replace all local landraces. The new 'miracle varieties', developed from hybridization and genetic manipulation of several landraces, serve to propel the seed and agrochemical industry, as these new crop varieties cannot thrive on marginal farm conditions, and must rely on adequate supply of industrial fertilizers, pesticides and irrigation.

The aggressive campaign for promoting HYVs has resulted in the disappearance of thousands of indigenous crop landraces, thereby destroying food security of the farmer.[35] Unlike these farmer landraces, selected by generations of farmers for adaptation to local soil, topographic and climatic conditions, the modern cultivars (cultivated varieties) rely heavily on extraneous 'inputs' of industrial agrochemicals and massive supply of water for irrigation. Application of synthetic fertilizers causes rapid soil erosion and compaction, reducing the natural fertility of soil, which the farmer seeks to recover by pumping an ever-increasing dose of fertilizers, until the soil becomes saline and unproductive. This is exactly what has happened in Punjab—India's Green Revolution capital. In this mode of agriculture, production is focused on food for profits, rather than fulfilling basic nutritional needs.[(4)]

A second policy approach, in line with the Washington Consensus, is that the food market is liberated, and left to the control of private businesses. Under the democratic commitment, the state agrees to provide a minimal quantity of food grains to the poor on subsidy, through the infrastructure of public food distribution system (PDS), which the governments increasingly aim to privatize under the neoliberal regime. Food for the PDS or rationing is procured from the federal food stock (e.g. Food Corporation of India's grain stores), which crucially depends on the seasonal harvest of food crops. The maintenance of the stock is a point of rationale for the governments to import foods on deregulated tariff and subsidies, to the decline of the sale price of the same foods for the domestic farmer-producers. Failure to sell at a competitive price leads to distress sale by the producer, and entrenches the disentitlement and hunger of the farmer households.

Despite notorious corruption and disposal of poor-quality grains in the PDS in India, all rural and urban households were entitled, until 1997, to PDS. This façade of welfare disappeared in 1997. In a bid to reduce public expenditure on food subsidies, as stipulated by the IMF and World Bank loan agreements, the government of India introduced a new 'targeted PDS', which categorized the population above and below poverty line (APL and BPL), with lower food prices for the latter. In subsequent years, the sale price of food grains was raised, leading to a widening gap between the government's minimum support price for procurement of grains from farmers and the off-take price at ration shops. This generated the paradoxical state of India exporting food while fostering hunger in the country. As fewer and fewer people could afford to pay the food price, the difference in the unconsumed grain quantity added to the 'excess' food stocks in the storehouses of Food Corporation of India, and this difference persisted over years:

> In the years from 1997 to 2004, this difference exceeded 100 million tonnes, half the annual production of the country. This generated the shameful anomaly of India exporting large quantities of food (often contributing to cattle-feed in the EU), even as hundreds of millions of people went hungry within the country...a significant proportion of deserving poor households were wrongly excluded from access to food. The inevitable result was a significant rise in malnutrition in many parts of the country....[36]

Thus, the PDS was made to fail, and this failure became a justification of both the establishment of the food market and its liberalization.

However, it is imperative to understand that even in the absence of corruption and negligence with quality, the PDS is unlikely to ensure entitlement to adequate food and nutrition, because neither subsidized food nor direct payments can solve the root cause of poverty and food disentitlement—the lack of entitlement to the food producing habitats, and the disintegration of the community rights over land use. The food security discourse, pivoted on the 'food dole' approach, was challenged in the 1990s because, while it speaks to everyone's right to food, it says nothing about who produces what, how it is produced or where it is produced.[37]

ENCLOSURE AND FOOD INSECURITY

Food security is intimately contingent on the land where food is produced. With the advent of industrial growth and market expansion, all the food producing habitats are usurped by industry, either to monopolize food production, or to manufacture more profitable commercial products in the food producing space. The causal linkage between the enclosure of food producing habitats and hunger is seldom articulated in literature dealing with food security.

Throughout human history, wild lands—forests, grasslands and wetlands—have served as a source of substantial quantities of food. The wild lands not only provide all the diet items for hunter-gatherers and pastoralists, but also for the settled agriculturist societies, who supplement their cultivated food crops with uncultivated plant foods (wild mushrooms, tubers, leafy vegetables, edible flowers and fruits) gathered from the wild. Thus, wild lands function as important food producing habitats[38] for the people who are intimately dependent on their proximate ecosystems for survival.

Dispossession of food producing habitats—village woodlands, pastures, agricultural lands, swidden forests and wetlands—entails disappearance of food security for the 'ecosystem people' who are largely dependent on the wild lands for food and livelihood. Dispossession incidents historically occurred mainly during and after military conquests or invasions, and sometimes from oppression by a feudal overlord. However, expansion of capitalism, beginning in the 18th century in England, evoked a legislative mechanism that legitimized and precipitated the process of large scale, country-wide, systematic state enclosure of the commons and dispossession of the peasant farmers and pastoralists,[23; 39]—a process that became a model for all subsequent land grabs in other countries.

The livelihood consequence of the disappearance of the commons is evident from the hideous ecological impacts of European-style land uses in their colonies. In India, as elsewhere in Asia, people traditionally used to gather free goods from forests and water bodies, which were communally managed and used. The rural commons like tanks, forests and pastures used to serve as stores of resource reserves and contributed to rural equity.[40] The English East India Company's administrators considered all these commons as unproductive. By turning village tanks and wells into private property, British legislation closed previous free public access to water for irrigation and drinking purposes, as well as aquatic food organisms. Consequently, water scarcity became a problem for the poor who did not hold colonial land-deeds.

In conformity with the prevailing English utilitarian concept of nature to be exploited for the benefit of civilization, wild lands with no private ownership were considered 'wastelands' and 'a bar to the prosperity of the Empire'.[41] In the early decades of colonial rule, forested terrains were a sign of backwardness of a country, while human settlements and agricultural landscapes were signs of progress and civilization. Clearing these wastelands for cultivation was a priority task of the Company, which instituted the *Bazé Zameen Daftar* (Wastelands Department) and *Bazé Zameen* regulation in 1788, which prohibited landholders from making rent-free land grants. This restriction, however, resulted in food scarcity for the poor, who no longer had access to wild foods to supplement their diet in the lean seasons. Furthermore, this regulation also caused a slump in agricultural recovery after the 1770 famine.[18]

Unlike the previous episodes of piecemeal, locally negotiated enclosure, by and large restrained by moral economies—which preserved part of the commons that had sustained social order and livelihoods of the 'ecosystem people'[42]—the European parliamentary form of enclosure in the 18th century mobilized state power to usurp the rural land for capital accumulation, expunging the remnants of the commons and communal institutions.[23; 43] This process was accompanied by several other transformations, such as the intensification of land use; the forcible extension of market economy and the creation of wage labour; and the penetration of urban capital in the countryside.[44]

This process created a new category of poor as migrant vagabonds and beggars, who became entirely devoid of food entitlement and security. The 'commoners' were 'first forcibly expropriated from the soil, driven from their homes, turned into vagabonds, and then whipped, branded, tortured by laws grotesquely terrible, into the discipline necessary for the wage system.'[23] The enclosure of the commons not only decimated the natural wealth of biodiversity, but also brought about unprecedented hunger, oppression and strife for the indigenous people in the colonies. The hordes of the dispossessed peasants formed the reserve army of the proletariat, waiting to sell their labour in a factory. As Marx put it:

> ...the historical movement which changes the producers into wage-workers, appears, on the one hand, as their emancipation from serfdom and from the fetters of the guilds.... But, on the other hand, these new freedmen became sellers of themselves only after they had been robbed of all their means of production, and of all the guarantees of existence afforded by the old feudal arrangements.[23]

The components of the 'old feudal arrangements' were the common woodlots and pastures in Europe, while in the pre-colonial and pre-industrial societies in Asia, Africa, Australia and the Americas, the community resource management systems conserved village ponds, community pastures, community forests and even agricultural lands managed by reciprocal labour exchange among neighbours.(18) The enclosure and disappearance of these commons engendered endemic poverty and food disentitlement of the dispossessed. In this English model of enclosure of the rural commons and coercive dispossession of land, replicated in all post-colonies that follow the industrial development route, parliamentary acts regularize and normalize enclosure, especially in regions where the retention of the traditional modes of land use and traditional community ownership of land prove resistant to marketization.(18; 45; 46; 47)

The drive for enclosure of the commons was directly inherited from the drive for privatization of resources. With the onset of capitalism, the Western land tenure system entitled the colonizer to clear 'unoccupied' wild lands, 'because clearance is evidence of tenure'.[48] Thus, in early colonial periods in the New World, immigrant European settlers were given titles to as much frontier land as they could clear. In British India and Burma, frontier areas like the Sundarbans and eastern Himalayan foothills were cleared by settlers who thereby obtained legal titles to the land for rice cultivation and tea plantation. The colonial concept of 'wastelands' ran roughshod over the 'social meanings' of land to the natives of all pre-colonial states, and brought an abrupt end to traditional land rights by enclosures. All protests and rebellions against the enclosure of the commons were quelled by military oppression, leading to massacres, dispossession and eviction of the indigenous peoples.

Violence was not the only means of converting indigenous commons into private property, but it played a part in several wars and insurgencies—as in the series of tribal uprisings against the British colonial enclosure of the hills and forests, which constituted principal food producing habitats. In India, some of the milestones of indigenous discontent are the uprisings and insurrections of the Tamar (1795), Bhumij (1798–1799), Munda (1819–1820), Paik (1817), Bhil (1818–1831), Santal (1955–1956), Kharia (1860–1880) Kairwar (1871), Munda (1895), Sardari (1859–1895), and the Oraon (1915–1920). All of these revolts were quelled by ruthless massacres and eviction of the indigenous people from their ancestral lands.[(38)] These ecosystem refugees supplied the army of labour for agriculture and industry, both geared to generate revenue for the empire.

Colonial enclosures, indigenous uprisings and the hegemony of European political economy constituted a common feature of the European colonial expansion. Throughout the colonial history, the transformation of land ownership from commons to private property swept all parts of the world where European empires were built. Assaults on the commons have continued, even after independence of the ex-colonies, often justified with reference to notions of development and progress. In Peru, for example, the government laid out plans to open up the rainforest for exploration of oil and gas companies, in order to increase the gross domestic product (GDP). Such proposals would obviously result in accelerating climate change both by extracting fossil fuels and by destruction of the Amazonian rainforest. In opposition to this plan, Amazon-dwelling indigenous groups organized into the Interethnic Association for the Development of the Peruvian Rainforest (AIDESEP), which is committed to sustainable development. The AIDESEP used nonviolent direct action to halt the granting of concessions to the oil companies. In response, the Peruvian police killed many protesters on the World Environment Day of 2009. Peruvian President Alan Garcìa subsequently compared AIDESEP to a dog that is not gnawing a bone, yet jealously guarding it from others who could get nourishment from it. He argued that the indigenous people failed to make full use of the forest resources, and prevented the country from developing—an argument that every government in the South upholds, whenever there is resistance to enclosure.(47)

Invasion, conquest and enclosure of the habitats of the 'natives' of the entire Old as well as the New World were justified from the progressivist perspective because the indigenous peoples supposedly had neither the intelligence nor capability to transform wilderness into civilized habitats.(18) (see Box 1) Beginning in the early 17th century, the English employed the Lockean logic that rights to property should go to those who could 'improve' it, or produce the most from it in commerce to justify expropriation of land both from the village commons in England and from conquered peoples in the colonies.

From the 1950s onwards, development economists prescribed 'development projects' to make all common lands economically productive. The World Bank and IMF advised national governments to improve the land use to facilitate industrial growth—building river dams, factories, and thermal and hydroelectric power plants—each of which entailed state take-over of the commons such as rivers, village forests, pastures and ponds. The World Bank provided loans to the poor countries chiefly for agricultural development, which included mammoth irrigation projects and the Green Revolution technology, which initiated the process of what Kloppenburg[52] calls 'accumulation by dispossession' of the seed commons. Subsequently, the IMF, DFID and foreign industrial investment in infrastructure development—highways, urbanization, and power projects—and necessitated usurpation and enclosure of the remaining patches of the commons in the tribal hinterlands of Africa and Asia. The inevitable consequence of all these development projects is the creation of millions of development refugees, who were stripped of their livelihood and food security overnight. The autonomy of the entire rural economy and cultural life was destroyed in order to propel the economic growth engine.

Box 1:
The Western Legacy of the Logic of Land Appropriation

The argument of stupidity and/or incapability of the indigenous people to 'utilize' their own resources has always been the perennial developmentarian argument to justify the appropriation of indigenous habitats since the early days of colonial occupation of lands. In fact the assumption of idiocy of the non-European people is a legacy of Herbert Spencer (1895), who believed, 'The intellectual traits of the uncivilized…are traits recurring in the children of the civilized.' Harvard Professor Louis Agassiz wrote in his 10 August 1863 letter to Lincoln's Inquiry Commission: Blacks were 'indolent, playful, sensuous, imitative, subservient, good natured, versatile, unsteady in their purpose, devoted, affectionate, in everything unlike other races, they may but be compared to children, grown in the stature of adults while retaining a childlike mind.'[49] American President Andrew Jackson shared a similar conviction some decades earlier.[50]

> They have neither the intelligence, the industry, the moral habits, nor the desire of improvement which are essential to any favorable change in their condition. Established in the midst of another and a superior race, and without appreciating the causes of their inferiority or seeking to control them, they must necessarily yield to the force of circumstances and ere long disappear.

Based on this presumption of the inherent incapacity of the non-European people to 'develop their own lands', European colonists had the right to invade and occupy lands that they deemed had remained 'empty', 'wastelands', or 'unused', or at best 'unproductive'.[18] The US President Theodore Roosevelt found natural justice in grabbing of the Native Americans' homelands, for 'this great continent could not have been kept as nothing but a game preserve for squalid savages.'[50] Indeed, the colonial ideology had 'an extraordinary capacity to invert causation' and hold the Natives responsible for many of the problems created by colonial incursions:

> It was a similar inversion which enabled imperial powers, having invaded and conquered much of the continent, to present Africans as essentially violent and themselves as peaceful. Thus African hunting methods in which snares and traps might be used were condemned as cruel and wasteful— like those of the unlanded poacher in Britain.[51]

ENCLOSURE IN THE 21ST CENTURY: LAND GRAB AND SEED PATENTS

All the past and current events of enclosure intervenes in the spheres of production and social reproduction, and not only in the realm of consumption but also regarding social ordering and processes of subjectification.[53] Production and accumulation is obviously linked to the enclosure of common land and other material resources. However, it is also necessary to recognize the concomitant articulation of enclosure to underlying strategies of proletarianization of producers in the pre-capitalist production systems, creation of a labour surplus, market expansion, social normalization also deserves articulation. While these dynamics do not usually respond to a preconceived, fully articulated plan, the intrinsic logic of accumulation and concentration of wealth orients the land use norms in a particular direction so that a pattern of procedural regularities and effects emerges out of a set of variegated territorial agencies.(44)

The recent wave of land grabs is not only associated with the appropriation of natural and rural habitats under the influence of urban centres, but also has a direct impact on urban agglomerations themselves. Their legal and managerial procedures are used in the creation of special economic zones for industrial operations, high-class housing developments, tourism complexes and infrastructural networks.(44; 54) The industrial commodification of nature and the disintegration of the commons have led—and lead everywhere—to the rapid erosion of the resource base of the ecosystem people, driving them to cities as development refugees.(18)

Today, *ex novo* formations of enclosure for the expansion of industrial capital rely more consistently upon state apparatuses to capture resistant non-capitalist productive spaces. This appropriation of these 'non-capitalist' food producing spaces truncates food production from the enclosed lands, and creates endemic hunger in the wake of development in the captured areas. Large numbers of development refugees evicted from these enclosed habitats add to the reserve army of wage labourers for industry.

> The nature of the commons under seizure conditions enclosure's interrelation with those apparatuses: material commons—land, resources and the like—require legal mobilizations of enclosure to re-spatialize codes of possession and property; social

commons—e.g. collective appropriations of public space—necessitate police deployments of enclosure to discipline spatial behaviour, and so forth[44]

Today's global phenomenon of land grab is identified as 'the latest spatial fix of a crisis-prone system',[55] which entails the penetration of governments and private firms and investment banks—in several countries in Africa,[56] Asia,[54;36] Latin America[57] and the former Soviet Eurasia.[58] In all these countries, the state functions as the facilitator of the industrial development process, 'ranging from the implementation of investment-friendly legal and fiscal frameworks, to active involvement through expropriation and eminent domain, to the building of support infrastructure and other projects.'[44] As was the case with English enclosures, the dispossession of the commoners by legalized coercion and police terror lubricates the penetration of capital into pre-capitalist/non-capitalist societies that lack formal land rights or include forms of communal tenure.[57]

As was the case in the past, commoners, squatters in traditionally vacant public land and expropriated smallholders, or those outcompeted by big operators are the direct victims of land grab. In these new experiences, accumulation by displacement and de-peasantization, are, however, not matched with a parallel process of the creation of industrial labour force. Although a common feature of the land grab is associated with promises of jobs for the dispossessed, a majority of the dispossessed is not absorbed in the factory or the mining industry, for which the commons was destroyed.[59; 60]

Alongside the corporate land grab for urbanization, the biological realm has been increasingly commoditized, through a process of accumulation by dispossession.[52] Seed corporations are now appropriating the crop seeds, so far considered the common pool resource of all humans. With the first patents on living organisms in the 1980s, capitalism ventured into the hitherto unvanquished territory, by exclusive private ownership of the global commons of life forms and the knowledge commons. Not only the new transgenic hybrids, a large number of heirloom crop varieties and seeds are also brought under the realm of corporate intellectual property rights (IPR), facilitating biopiracy patents on diverse indigenous plants and folk knowledge.[61] Just as the enclosure of the common lands was legitimized in the previous centuries with new laws, today's patents on life—capitalism's last frontier—are also facilitated by WTO/TRIPS and a cascade of national intellectual property laws and international treaties over the past few decades.

With the progress of agricultural development, the interests of the seed business and agrochemicals industry increasingly converge, leading to (a) merger of agribusiness companies, and (b) expansion of the agrochemical corporation into the seed sector. The new seeds, agrochemicals, and machinery are all marketed by MNCs, upon huge subsidies from national governments. The ownership of global seed supply has become increasingly concentrated. The top ten seed multinational companies control more than half of the global seed supply. Among them, Monsanto and DuPont, took 20 per cent and 15 per cent of the world's total seed market share in 2014 respectively, ranking first and second. On December 11, 2015, the first merger was announced between Dow AgroSciences and DuPont. Soon afterward, in 2016, ChemChina announced its acquisition of Syngenta, and Bayer announced the takeover of Monsanto.[62] With such mergers and takeovers, the top five transnational companies control more than 60 per cent of the global proprietary seed supply.

Capitalism against Food Sovereignty

Geared to successively monetize, extract and exhaust resources for profit, industrial capitalism cannot allow room for food sovereignty. Because both production and distribution of foods outside the centralized market and the monetization system is anathema to capitalism, autonomy of the farmer households over their own foods cannot be attained within the ambit of capitalism. The private seed industry, which was born only during the Green Revolution era, has now matured to spread all over the globe, to annihilate all traditional systems of food production and distribution, in two fundamental ways.

Firstly, the capitalist appropriation of the materials of production—primarily, the seeds—means the termination of the producer's ownership and authority over the seeds. In all traditional societies, open-source ownership of seeds precludes any scope of seed patent, UPOV (and similar) registrations, and other forms of exclusive right to seeds. For this reason, seed industry promotes the private IPR regime in order to abolish the traditional open-source seed ownership and production system altogether.

Secondly, open exchange of seeds among farmers opposes commoditization and monetization of the seed and genetic materials, which the seed industry aggressively seeks to monetize, and transform into a new capital. Seeds and genetic materials, as parts of nature, are viewed in industrial capitalism as 'natural resources' that can be mined, usurped and tagged with a price. Seeds from hybrids and transgenic technology thus become 'value-added' products, whose prices are elevated by capital investment in proprietary technology, protected by the IPR laws, especially in the countries that are WTO/GATT signatories.

The seed market, established with the advent of the Green Revolution, is now strengthened by the IPR in breeders' varieties and seeds, squarely to annihilate the traditional usage of non-proprietary, open-source landraces and seeds. Furthermore, the seed industry has already established a stringent system of the seed IPR to prohibit any sale, donation or exchange of the proprietary seeds from the 'beneficiary' client to any other 'third party' farmer, without explicit permits and legal fees to the 'first party'—the industry. Freedom of exchange and use of the seeds for both artisanal and commercial food production is thus obviated.

In essence, the capitalist mode of quantitative economic growth decimates all the means of sustainable food production and distribution. By engendering and fostering a popular faith in unending quantitative growth, capitalism seeks to perpetuate the myth of prosperity for all from 'development'—including agricultural development—predicated on commoditization and marketing of both the materials and means of food production as well as food products. Thus, the Green Revolution model, showcasing the statistics of partial and short-term increase in cereal output,[18; 63] endorses the disempowerment of smallholders and peasants, manufacture and sale of agrochemicals, increasing corporate control of seeds, and privatization of water for irrigation.[18; 52] The Green Revolution brought around increased cereal output but statistics conceal the dark side of agricultural development—the loss of non-cereal crop diversity from monocultures of cereals, the extinction of the thousands of folk crop varieties, the depletion of farm fauna, the poisoning of food, and the disentitlement of peasants and small farmers. The loss of crop genetic diversity, in combination with declining soil fertility, and rising cost of 'inputs', deepens the imperilment of food security on marginal farms. More fundamentally, agronomic growth data conceal the fact that food production enhancement has failed to improve entitlement of the poor, and to ensure food sovereignty of both the farmer household and the nation, by making them crucially reliant on the external supply of 'inputs'. The Green Revolution hyperboles create a comfortable fantasy world in which consumers are assured of never-ending prosperity. This fantasy world also swallows the producers—the poor farmers—who abandon their traditional knowledge and skills, to become consumers of proprietary agrochemicals and seeds.[18]

FROM FOOD SECURITY TO FOOD SOVEREIGNTY

As discussed in the opening section, the mainstream identification of the linkage of food access to poverty reduction sharpened the need of sustained economic growth, and legitimized industrialization of agriculture and integration of local production systems into markets as the best means to eliminate hunger.[8] The WB and FAO recommendations of agricultural modernization to increase crop yields and price control have directed national food policies until the 1980s. However, market deregulation and the allowing of unrestrained corporate control of seed and food market, beginning in the 1990s, have enhanced hybrid seeds and agrochemicals supply on the one hand, and undermined the PDS on the other. In the widespread faith in technological silver bullet solution to the food security problem, however, the issues of distributive justice, and more specifically, of resource entitlement to the poor, take a back seat in the mainstream technocratic discourse. Agricultural institutions continue to stress on enhancing food crop productivity as the solution to food security. Mainstream crop breeding and agronomic research is engaged in harnessing biotechnology to increase food production in the face of declining availability of land and water,[64] and agricultural modernization is the prevalent international and national policy objective.

As a guideline to national policies to ensure food availability to the poor, the FAO introduced the concept of food security. The term 'food security' was first mentioned in the 1943 Hot Springs, Conference of Allied governments, which led to the creation of the FAO. Much later, the 1974 World Food Summit, held in the context of worsening food scarcities in the global South, forged the definition of 'food security',[1] as cited in the opening page of this treatise. This definition of food security focused on countries rather than on the household or individual level. Over the next two decades, the FAO added additional elements to its definitions, including 'access' for all people, food safety, and cultural preferences.[65] In the expanded definitions too, countries and nations as a whole remain as the focus of food security, rather than households. Food security is thus conceived of as an outcome of top-down statutory policy of implementing selected technocratic solutions to the problem of food scarcity. Agricultural modernization to ensure adequate food production, state-controlled PDS, and minimum support price for procurement of food from farmers, are considered necessary for building food security for the country.

Parallel to this statutory and institutional approach, the alternative approach to food security was proffered by an expanding group of environmental activists, who considered 'organic' methods of food production as a means to food and health security. While the statutory agricultural institutions always sought to silence the opponents of the Green Revolution by negating the possibility of organic agriculture to feed the burgeoning world population, organic farming 'activists' argued for the liberation of farmers from the dual trap of pesticides and debt, which they incur for the costly agrochemicals. Organic agriculture would, they argued, free the farmers from the dependency on industrial agrochemicals and corporate seeds for their own food, ensuring food security for the peasant household. The official acknowledgement of the failure of the Green Revolution to yield benefit on marginal rain-fed farms and to poor smallholders[66] also convinced many governments of the South to support organic agriculture. India drafted its Organic Agriculture Policy in 2005, and a few recent schemes (such as the National Agricultural Development Project, launched in 2014) to promote organic agriculture, to reduce dependence on chemical inputs.

Although the biodynamic and 'organic' agriculture movement were born in the early 1900s in Germany and Britain, the great thrust for 'organic food' movement in the global North rose in the wake of Rachel Carson's classic *The Silent Spring*.[67] In the South, the environmental critique of agricultural modernization highlighted the environmental and health impacts of agrochemicals and the social disruptions caused by the Green Revolution. The growing critique of industrial agriculture, and the international concerns with the hazards of pesticides, prompted many governments to proscribe or restrict a range of pesticides in agriculture. The 'organic' food movement swelled in the North from the 1960s onward, influencing policy makers and the state departments of agriculture and environment in various countries. The 'organic movement' as Reed (2010) shows, spread as a social movement to promote zero-chemical, ecological farming principles, and organic food as a choice for health-conscious consumers.[68]

In all countries, including in the industrialized North, farmers are increasingly shifting toward 'organic farming', in order to reduce their reliance on corporate supply of agrochemical inputs. However, in the course of their shift toward or 'least external input sustainable agriculture' (LEISA), agroecology movements in different countries (e.g. La Via Campesina in Mexico and Farmer-to-Farmer Agroecology Movement [MACAC] in Cuba) show that either enhanced food production or 'zero-chemical input' is not enough for sustainability in agricultural production, as long as the farmers remain dependent on the farm implements, fossil fuel-based economy, and on the external market for sale of their produce.[15; 69] The consumption of fossil fuel in mechanized farms and for transport of these implements and food make the industrial system inherently unsustainable, 'organic' method of cultivation notwithstanding. Moreover, food sovereignty cannot be attained in a policy environment that allows land grab and fosters agribusiness subsidies. The focus on 'organic' food—primarily in response to the urban consumer demands for healthy, non-toxic food—tends to ignore the importance of ecological complexity of the food production system, and the political implications of the requirement of access to land for peasants. Farmer's entitlement to food producing habitat (the land), and their sovereignty over the material of production (seeds) and the means of production (the implements and manure), as well as their autonomy over their farm produce, are essential for agricultural sustainability and food justice. This was articulated, for the first time, in the Havana Declaration of Food Sovereignty (2001):

> Food sovereignty recognizes agriculture involving peasants, indigenous peoples and fishing communities with links to the territory; primarily oriented towards the satisfaction of the needs of the local and national markets; agriculture whose central concern is human beings; agriculture which preserves, values and fosters the multifunctionality of peasant and indigenous forms of production and management of rural areas.
>
> ...This implies, as well, the recognition of autonomous control of their territories, natural resources, systems of forms. In this sense, we support the struggles of all of the indigenous peoples and peoples of African descent in the world, and demand full respect for their rights. Food sovereignty further implies the guarantee of access to healthy and sufficient obligation for national governments and the full exercise of civil rights.

The food sovereignty movement has further evolved from the growing realization that the current food crisis is not due to any deficit in the farmers' ability to produce food, but due to (a) food speculation and stocking that transnational food corporations and investment funds engage in, (b) the global food injustices, implying creation of islands of overconsumption amid the ocean of poverty, where peasants do not have money to buy adequate food, and/or lack land on which to grow it, and (c) eco-destructive policies like the promotion of agrofuels that devote farm land to feeding automobiles. The key to ending hunger is not just production of sufficient food, but 'how we grow it'—and, 'It is here where the corporate agribusiness model of large-scale industrial monocultures is failing us, and where peasant-based sustainable farming systems based on agroecology and Food Sovereignty offer so much hope.'(70)

Although the eco-political notion of food sovereignty is more radical and comprehensive than the FAO definitions of food security, some of the definitions of 'food security' developed in the 1980s and early 1990s seem to contain the seeds of the currently accepted notions of agroecology and food sovereignty. For instance, Solon Barraclough defined food security as:

> Sustained and assured access by all social groups and individuals to food adequate in quantity and quality to meet nutritional needs. A food system offering food security should have the following characteristics: (a) capacity to produce, store, and import sufficient food to meet basic food needs for all groups; (b) maximum autonomy and self-determination (without implying autarchy), reducing vulnerability to international market fluctuations and political pressures; (c) reliability, such that seasonal, cyclical and other variations in access to food are minimal; (d) sustainability such that the ecological system is protected and improved over time; and (e) equity, meaning, as a minimum, dependable access to adequate food for all social groups.[71]

In this definition, such terms as 'autonomy and self-determination', 'sustainability', protection of 'the ecological system', and 'equity' are the key concepts in food sovereignty. Interestingly, the early definition of food sovereignty, given in the 1996 statement of La Vía Campesina at Rome World Food Summit also focuses on countries:

> Food sovereignty is the right of each nation to maintain and develop its own capacity to produce its basic foods respecting cultural and productive diversity. We have the right to produce our own food in our own territory. Food sovereignty is a pre-condition to genuine food security.[64]

Notably, this early definition of food sovereignty echoes the FAO definitions of food security in its focus on countries, rather than on households and local communities of peasants and indigenous people. Parallel to a nation's political sovereignty, food sovereignty of a nation is prerequisite to its food security.

Box 2: Milestones in the Evolution of the Food Sovereignty Framework

1996

Food Sovereignty: A Future Without Hunger. La Vía Campesina's 1996 Statement by the NGO Forum to the World Food Summit.

2001

Our World is Not For Sale. WTO: Shrink or Sink. Our World is Not for Sale Network.

Final Declaration of the World Forum on Food Sovereignty, Havana, Cuba.

Priority to Peoples' Food Sovereignty. La Vía Campesina.

Sale of the Century? People's Food Sovereignty. Part 1 – the Implications of Trade Negotiations. Friends of the Earth International.

Sale of the Century? People's Food Sovereignty. Part 2 – a New Multilateral Framework for Food and Agriculture. Friends of the Earth International.

Food Sovereignty in the Era of Trade Liberalisation: Are Multilateral Means Feasible? Steve Suppan, Institute for Agriculture and Trade Policy.

2002

Food Sovereignty: A Right for All. Political Statement of the NGO/CSO Forum for Food Sovereignty. Rome, Italy.

Statement on People's Food Sovereignty: Our World is Not for Sale. Cancun, Mexico.

2003

What is Food Sovereignty? La Vía Campesina.

Towards Food Sovereignty: Constructing an Alternative to the WTO's AoA. International Workshop on the Review of the AoA, Geneva, Switzerland.

Trade and People's Food Sovereignty. Friends of the Earth International.

How TRIPS Threatens Biodiversity and Food Sovereignty. Hyderabad, India.

Statement on People's Food Sovereignty: Our World is Not for Sale. Cancun, Mexico.

2005

Food Sovereignty: Towards Democracy in Localised Food Systems. Michael Windfuhr and Jennie Jonsen, FoodFirst Information and Action Network (FIAN), FIAN International.

2006

Agrarian Reform and Food Sovereignty: Alternative Model for the Rural World. Peter Rosset, University of California - Berkeley/Global Alternatives.

2007

Final Statement of the Nyéléni Forum on Food Sovereignty. Sélingué, Mali.

2011

Representatives from 34 European countries met in Krems, Austria to plan for a European movement for Food Sovereignty.

The 2001 Havana Declaration clearly mentioned the right to food for everyone, and recognized the right of the communities of peasant farmers, fishers and indigenous people to fulfil their food requirements and to uphold their cultural identities. Nevertheless, it indicated the duty and responsibility of the governments to foster and safeguard food sovereignty of people of all ethnicities and occupations. The 'nation' was however replaced with 'peoples, communities, and countries' in 2002, with the Rome +5 Summit and the formation of the International Planning Committee (IPC) for Food Sovereignty, where a large number of food rights organizations, including Vía Campesina, had met. Finally, the 2007 Nyéléni Declaration confined the sovereignty rights to 'peoples':

> The right of peoples to healthy and culturally appropriate food produced through ecologically sound and sustainable methods, and their right to define their own food and agriculture systems. It puts the aspirations and needs of those who produce, distribute and consume food at the heart of food systems and policies rather than the demands of markets and corporations.

The concept of 'food sovereignty' draws on a rich set of ideas and practices related to many local movements to assert their land rights and food rights, alternative food networks and the localization of economies as a defence against globalization. Food sovereignty, and concomitantly, agroecology, profess reduction of 'food miles'; creation of direct marketing arrangements, local farmers' markets, and local sourcing for restaurants and institutions such as schools, universities, hospitals, nursing homes and prisons, and maintenance of food gardens for all households and schools. The Cuban model of *organoponis* and farmer markets have informed and inspired these strands of food rights movements.

The Food Sovereignty movement has evolved on the basis of a common framework that allows diversity of food cultures and food systems, and takes the specificity of each different place into account (i.e. the right of all countries and peoples to define their own policies). Over a series of meetings and exchange visits, organized by La Via Campesina (LVC) in the 1990s, peasant leaders from the Americas, Asia and Europe identified their common problems and common enemies from beyond national borders, and realized the urgency to struggle together. They found that they all had severe doubts concerning the concept of food security, and through a process of dialog over several years developed 'food sovereignty' as a banner for a joint movement.[37; 72; 73]

The framework emerged from the internal dialogues in LVC in the early 1990s, and was further elaborated at the International Forum for Food Sovereignty hosted by LVC in Nyéléni, Mali in 2007, to which LVC invited international movements of indigenous people, fisher folk, women, environmentalists, scholars, consumers and trade unions for a giant *diálogo de saberes* (dialogue among different knowledge systems). Martínez-Torres and Rosset believe that this continuous and expansive *diálogo* also accelerated the recent shift toward the promotion of agroecology as an alternative to the so-called Green Revolution in many contemporary rural social movements.[73]

The Nyéléni Declaration defines Food sovereignty as 'the right of peoples to healthy and culturally appropriate food produced through ecologically sound and sustainable methods' (see above). This definition implies that food sovereignty is coterminous with sustainable agriculture and food system, which is captured in the principles and practices of agroecology.[74; 75] Maintenance of biological diversity at species and genetic levels and nutrient cycling mechanisms are global principles that are common to all agroecosystems and therefore essential in the design of sustainable agricultural systems.

Sustainable food production systems, or biodiverse farms based on agroecology involves not merely the absence of synthetic agrochemicals, but also an increasing integration of all components of agroecosystem—from soil microbes to large wildlife and farm animals. Thus, sustainability of food production in face of environmental vagaries is contingent on the richness of biodiversity in the species, functional group and genetic levels on farm.[74; 75] Genetic diversity of crops constitutes built-in insurance against hazards of diseases and pests.[35] Agroecology, based on species and genetic diversity of crops and non-crop plants and animals, provides insulation from external factors such as disturbed supply of seeds and inputs, interest rates on credit or price fluctuations.

There is little scope of adapting the industrial agroecosystems to changing patterns of rainfall, temperatures and extreme weather events.[76; 77] By contrast, agroecology ensures the use of combinations of crop species and landraces that are adapted to local soil and environmental conditions.[35; 78] For example, salt tolerant folk rice landraces are most suitable for cultivation as a strategy for adaptation to Climate Change-induced salinization of coastal farmlands, while drought tolerant landraces are appropriate for inclusion in an adaptive strategy for rice production in areas facing frequent spells of drought.[14; 35] A combination of different crop landraces are known to be a key to effective reduction of pest and pathogen outbreaks,[14; 79] and multiple cropping, involving crop rotations are a proven strategy of ensuring food security in the face of climatic vagaries.[14; 76] The use of ecologically-based food production strategies that are attuned to landscape heterogeneity may represent a robust path to increasing the productivity, sustainability and resilience of agricultural production while reducing undesirable socioenvironmental impacts.[80]

The principal components of agroecology[74; 75; 81] that contribute to food sovereignty, are:

(a) adequate economic returns to farmers;
(b) long-term maintenance of natural resources and productivity;
(c) minimal adverse environmental impacts;
(d) optimal production with minimal (ideally, zero) external inputs;
(e) satisfaction of human needs for food and income;
(f) provision for the social needs of farm families.

There exists a large body of evidence that agroecology, after conversion from industrialized agriculture, can attain all these goals.[75;82] A recent meta-analysis indicates that agroecology-based farms are likely to give lesser crop output, yet greater yield stability and more resilience to environmental vagaries than any modern farms based on agrochemical inputs.[83] While a few studies report lower crop yield in agroecological farms in the initial years, this feature is not universal. Rather, yield of rice and many vegetables may be considerably higher in agroecological than chemicalized farms.[83] In particular, agroecological systems involving locally adapted crops in marginal environmental conditions yield much more than any modern crop varieties.[14]

In addition to the explicit allusion to agroecological principle of food production, the Nyéléni Declaration reiterates the Havana Declaration's opposition to corporate appropriation of food systems:

> It offers a strategy to resist and dismantle the current corporate trade and food regime, and directions for food, farming, pastoral and fisheries systems determined by local producers and users. Food sovereignty prioritizes local and national economies and markets and empowers peasant and family farmer-driven agriculture, artisanal-fishing, pastoralist-led grazing, and food production, distribution and consumption based on environmental, social and economic sustainability. Food sovereignty promotes transparent trade that guarantees just incomes to all peoples as well as the rights of consumers to control their food and nutrition. It ensures that the rights to use and manage lands, territories, waters, seeds, livestock and biodiversity are in the hands of those of us who produce food. Food sovereignty implies new social relations free of oppression and inequality between men and women, peoples, racial groups, social and economic classes and generations.... There [must be] genuine and integral agrarian reform that guarantees peasants full rights to land, defends and recovers the territories of indigenous peoples, ensures fishing communities' access and control over their fishing areas and eco-systems, honors access and control by pastoral communities over pastoral lands and migratory routes...

Most remarkably, this Declaration also incorporates the eco-socialist tenet of intergenerational rights: 'It defends the interests and inclusion of the next generation.' Indeed, this clause draws on the indigenous ecological ethic that converges with the ecological economic principle of maintaining undiminished welfare for future generations.

The Havana and Nyéléni Declarations, taken together, thus broadened the concept of food sovereignty to address the concerns not only of farmers but also of fishers, pastoralists, consumers and indigenous people, and the addition of issues of inequality and oppression among people. Wittman et al. affirm that it effectively moved food sovereignty 'beyond the perspective of producers and production.'[84] They conclude that: 'after Nyéléni, there was no doubt that we were now talking about a global food sovereignty movement that clearly understood the challenges ahead' (*ibid.*). The food sovereignty concept has emerged to draw on local knowledge, and liberate the food system from reliance on both corporate and state agencies. The movement has also helped solidify national and international coalitions beyond LVC. Key pillars in the construction of food sovereignty for LVC have been, as reaffirmed in Nyéléni, agrarian reform, the defense of land and territory, the defense of national and local markets, and agroecology.[70; 73]

CONTRADICTIONS AND TASKS AHEAD

In spite of the confluence of many decades of experience from indigenous land rights struggles and food rights movements across the globe, the multiple definitions of Food Sovereignty render the term somewhat unwieldy. Firstly, the conceptual difference between the definitions of 'food security' and 'food sovereignty' is not unbridgeable. Despite many claims that the two notions are in a 'global conflict', characterized by 'fundamental antagonisms',[85] or that the two construe a 'conflict between models',[37] an examination of the historical legacy of these terms shows these two definitions are not diametrically opposed, except for their policy implications. The FAO definitions endorse national governments to adopt effective policies to ensure adequate food production and entitlements to the population, and to take regulatory measures to check 'price fluctuations'. By contrast, food sovereignty describes the rights of each household to produce and consume food of their choice, and an option to produce, sell and exchange food in local farmers' markets without external institutional and market influences. This right is the most basic food right, but there are other rights declared in the different versions of food sovereignty.

Even when all the definitions of food sovereignty are juxtaposed, the basic tenet of access to food for all is shared between the two ideas. Edelman suspects the two are appreciably agreeable. Indeed, as discussed above, some of the key terms like 'sustainability', 'autonomy', and 'ecological systems' are variously described in the definitions of both food security and sovereignty. Conversely, in the LVC statement of 1996, the unit of sovereignty is the nation, converging with the FAO's food security definitions.(65)

A closer examination of the food sovereignty idea reveals that 'food sovereignty is both a reaction to and an intellectual offspring of the earlier concepts of the "right to food" and "food security"',(86) and that there is a fundamental operational difference between two ideas, in the mode of production. Food sovereignty is entirely committed to agroecology for food production, while food security does not pose any such conditionality, although FAO has several documents that appreciate and endorse agroecology. A prominent instance is an FAO (2015) document which examines the efficacy of agroecology in providing adequate food and nutrition for the poor.(81)

A second difficulty is with the very term 'sovereignty', which poses a problem to identify the sovereign entity. Who is the sovereign? The individual household? The community of peasants or fishers who produce food? A village where farmer-producers and consumers freely exchange goods between each other in pre-industrial social formation? A network of villages inhabited by indigenous peasants, fishers, and graziers? The nation state? Clearly, the sovereignty of the producer household is apt to be violated whenever an industry usurps a commons, with legislative support to the land grab. Food sovereignty movements demand that the government ought to stop all conversion of food producing lands for industrial purposes, in which case, the state is the purveyor of sovereign rights to individuals.

Thirdly, food sovereignty definitions do not clarify the size of the production farm or the scale of production. As Edelman points out,

> Food sovereignty advocates rarely consider what sort of regulatory apparatus would be needed to manage questions of firm and farm size, product and technology mixes, and long-distance and international trade. 'Food sovereignty' implies limits on all of these. Who would enforce those limits?[(65)]

Edelman highlights a fourth empirical hurdle in governance terms, in that the food sovereignty's demand for autonomy of the producer and farmer market contradicts the demand for stringent state command and control of food market. The Havana Declaration demanded an 'immediate end to dishonest practices that establish market prices below production costs and provide subsidies for production and exports', and called for the integration of 'the goals of nutritional well-being into national food policies and programs, including local productive systems.' Both these demands imply the role of the state in framing an agrarian policy, and in maintaining a legislative control over the food market.

Certainly, both the autonomy of the peasant and a democratic state agrarian reform, controlled by peasant organizations, 'as an efficient public policy to combat poverty' are possible, but the limits of the state's jurisdiction and the extent of the producers' autonomy need to be empirically explored in ground details.

Indeed, Cuba demonstrates an exemplary agrarian reform that allows liberation of agricultural production from industrial inputs, supports local farmer markets, strengthens peasants' autonomy, and gives credence to the consumer's choice of food.[87] This model has variously been replicated in parts of Brazil and a few other Latin American nations.[27; 88; 89; 90] Yet, the spread of these food sovereignty practices in other Southern countries is extremely difficult in their respective governmental regimes, as the state agrarian and industrial development policies, ostensibly influenced by corporate hegemony (especially in promoting proprietary transgenic seeds, and supporting industrial encroachment of forests, wetlands and village commons) directly conflict with the grassroot needs and demands of peasants for autonomy of food production and marketing.

Over the past few decades, various forms of alliances between small producers and consumers have created local food markets in several municipalities in Europe, Canada, the US, Korea and Australia. Alongside a growing awareness of the need and efficacy of food production without synthetic agrochemicals, mark a hopeful transition toward attaining the goals of food sovereignty. While the spread of Transition Towns in the UK, Spain, France, Australia and a few places in the US have already translated some of the food sovereignty objectives into practice, the apathy of the institutional left in the South towards this evolving global movement restricts the scope of agroecology to break the shackles of industrial agriculture, and to reinstate the commons in the hands of indigenous communities. LVC and similar alliances of peasants and indigenous peoples, sustain the hope of resolving the internal conflicts and theoretical contradictions within the food sovereignty movement, and create a global model of liberatory mode of production, equitable distribution and responsible consumption of food.

REFERENCES

1. United Nations Organisation. (1975). *Report of the World Food Conference* (Rome 5–16 November 1974). New York.
2. Food and Agriculture Organisation of the United Nations. (1983). *World Food Security: A Reappraisal of the Concepts and Approaches*. Director General's Report. Rome.
3. Lappé, F.M., J. Collins and P. Rosset. (2015). *World Hunger: 12 Myths*. New York: Grove Press.
4. Reiff, D. (2015). *The Reproach of Hunger: Food, Justice, and Money in the Twenty-First Century*. New York: Simon & Schuster.
5. Sen, A. (1981). *Poverty and Famines: An Essay on Entitlement and Deprivation*. Oxford: Clarendon Press.
6. Food and Agriculture Organisation of the United Nations. (2013). *The State of Food Insecurity in the World 2013. The Multiple Dimensions of Food Security*. Rome. Available at http://www.fao.org/docrep/018/i3434e/i3434e.pdf
7. Food and Agriculture Organisation of the United Nations. (2012). *The State of Food Insecurity in the World 2012*. Rome. Available at http://www.fao.org/docrep/016/i3027e/i3027e.pdf
8. Prakash, A. (Ed.) (2011). *Safeguarding Food Security in Volatile Global Markets*. Rome: Food and Agriculture Organisation of the United Nations. Available at http://www.fao.org/docrep/013/i2107e/i2107e.pdf
9. Pesticide Action Network. (2010). *Communities in Peril: Global Report on Health Impacts of Pesticide Use in Agriculture*. Penang, Malaysia.
10. Köhler, H.R. and R. Triebskorn. (2013). Wildlife ecotoxicology of pesticides: Can we track effects to the population level and beyond? *Science* 341: 759–765.
11. Pretty, J., C. Brett, D. Gee, R. Heine, C.F. Mason, J.I.L. Morison, H. Raven, M. Rayment and G. van der Bijl. (2000). An assessment of the total external costs of UK agriculture. *Agricultural Systems* 65: 113–136.
12. Tegtmeier, E.M. and M.D. Duffy. (2004). External costs of agricultural production in the US. *International Journal of Agricultural Sustainability* 2: 1–20.

13. United Nations Human Rights Council. (2017). *Report of the Special Rapporteur on the Right to Food.* UN Human Rights Council. Doc. A/HRC/34/48. Available at http://www.fao.org/publications/card/en/c/d1f541b5-39b8-4992-b764-7bdfffb5c63f/
14. Deb, D. (2017). Folk rice varieties, traditional knowledge and nutritional security in South Asia. In G. Poyyamoli (Ed.), *Agroecology, Ecosystems, and Sustainability in the Tropics.* (pp. 112–128). New Delhi: Studera Press.
15. Pretty, J.N., A.D. Noble, D. Bossio, J. Dixon, R.E. Hine, F.W. Penning De Vries and J.I. Morison. (2006). Resource-conserving agriculture increases yields in developing countries. *Environmental Science and Technology* 40: 1114–1119.
16. William Kapp, K. (1950). *The Social Costs of Private Enterprise.* New York: Schocken Books.
17. Pigou, A.C. (1952). *The Economics of Welfare.* (4th edition). London: Macmillan.
18. Deb, D. (2009a). *Beyond Developmentality: Constructing Inclusive Freedom and Sustainability.* London: Earthscan/Routledge.
19. Moore, J.W. (2015). Putting nature to work. In C. Wee, J. Schönenbach, and O. Arndt (eds), *Supramarkt: A micro-toolkit for disobedient consumers, or how to frack the fatal forces of the Capitalocene.* (pp. 69–117). Gothenburg: Irene Books.
20. Myers, R.A. and B. Worm. (2003). Rapid worldwide depletion of predatory fish. *Nature* 423: 280–283.
21. Liebig, Justus von. (1863). *The Natural Laws of Husbandry.* New York: D. Appleton, p. 261.
22. Marx, K. 1894 (1959). *Capital.* Vol. 3. Moscow: Progress Publishers, p. 813.
23. Marx, K. 1887 (1954). *Capital.* Vol. 1. Moscow: Progress Publishers, pp. 475, 669, 688.
24. Howard, A. 1940 (2000). *An Agricultural Testament.* New Delhi: Research Foundation for Science Technology and Ecology, p. 18.
25. Escobar, A. (1995). *Encountering Development: The Making and Unmaking of the Third World.* Princeton: Princeton University Press.
26. Foster, J.B. (2002). *Ecology against Capitalism.* New York: Monthly Review Press, p. 149.

27. van der Ploeg, J.D. (2008). *The New Peasantries. Struggles for Autonomy and Sustainability in an Era of Empire and Globalization.* London: Earthscan.
28. Haas, P.M. (1992). Introduction: epistemic communities and international policy coordination. *International Organization* 46: 1–37.
29. Rosset, P.M. and M.E. Martínez-Torres. (2012). Rural social movements and agroecology: context, theory, and process [online]. *Ecology and Society* 17(3), 17. Available at http://www.ecologyandsociety.org/ vol17/iss3/art17/
30. Annetta, R., H.R. Habibi and A. Hontela. (2014). Impact of glyphosate and glyphosate-based herbicides on the freshwater environment. *Journal of Applied Toxicology* 34: 458–479.
31. Mahmood, I., S.R. Imadi, K. Shazadi, A. Gul and K.R. Hakeem. (2016). Effects of pesticides on environment. In K.R. Hakeem et al. (eds), *Plant, Soil and Microbes.* (pp. 253–269). Cham, Switzerland: Springer.
32. Sandor, M., T. Brad, A. Maxim, V. Sandor & B. Onica. (2016). The effect of fertilizer regime on soil fauna. *Bulletin UASVM Agriculture* 73 (2)/2016.
33. Richard, S., S. Moslemi, H. Sipahutar, N. Benachour, and G.E. Seralini (2005). Differential effects of glyphosate and roundup on human placental cells and aromatase. *Environmental Health Perspectives* 13: 716–720.
34. Paz-y-Miño, C., M.E. Sánchez, M. Arévalo, M.J. Muñoz, T. Witte, G.O. De-la-Carrera, and P.E. Leone. (2007). Evaluation of DNA damage in an Ecuadorian population exposed to glyphosate. *Genetics and Molecular Biology* 30: 456-460.
35. Deb, D. (2009b). Valuing folk rice varieties for agroecology and food security. *Bioscience Resource.* Commentary. Available at http://www.independentsciencenews.org/un-sustainable-farming/valuing-folk-crop-varieties/ Last accessed 26 October 2009.
36. Shrivastava, A. and A. Kothari (2012). *Churning the Earth: the Making of Global India.* New Delhi: Penguin/Viking.
37. Martínez-Torres, M.E. and P.M. Rosset. (2010). La Vía Campesina: The birth and evolution of a transnational social movement. *Journal of Peasant Studies* 37(1): 149–175.

38. Deb, D. (2014). The Value of Forest: an ecological economic examination of forest people's perspective. In T. Fenning (ed.), *Challenges and Opportunities for the World's Forests in the 21st Century*. (pp. 123–159). Heidelberg/New York: Springer. Also see Deb, D., K. Kuruganti, V. Rukmini Rao and S. Yesudas. (2014). *Forests as Food Producing Habitats: An exploratory study of uncultivated foods and food & nutrition security of Adivasis in Odisha*. Bhubaneswar: Living Farms.
39. Alden Wily, L. (2012). Looking back to see forward: The legal niceties of land theft in land rushes. *Journal of Peasant Studies* 39(3/4): 751–775.
40. Davis, M. (2002). *The Origins of the Third World: Markets, States and Climate*. Corner House Briefing 27. Dorset: The Corner House, pp. 27–28.
41. Ribbentrop, B. von. (1900). *Forestry in British India*. Calcutta: Government Press.
42. Gadgil, M. and R. Guha. (1992). *This Fissured Land*. Delhi: Oxford University Press.
43. Turner, M. (1984). *Enclosures in Britain, 1750–1930*. London: Macmillan.
44. Sevilla-Buitrago, A. (2015). Capitalist formations of enclosure: space and the extinction of the commons. *Antipode* 47 (4): 999–1020.
45. Thompson, E.P. (1991). *Customs in Common: Studies in Traditional Popular Culture*. London: Merlin Press, pp. 170, 173–174.
46. Homans, G.C. (1969). The explanation of English regional differences. *Past and Present* 42(1): 18–34.
47. Wall, D. (2014). *The Commons in History: Culture, conflict and ecology*. London/Cambridge, MA: MIT Press.
48. Pearce, David. (1998). *Economics and Environment: Essays on Ecological Economics and Sustainable Development*. Cheltenham, UK: Edward Elgar, p. 183.
49. Cited in Gould, S.J. (1996). *The Mismeasure of Man*. (Revised edn.). New York: Norton, p. 48.
50. Cited in Diamond, J. (1992). *The Third Chimpanzee: The Evolution and Future of the Human Animal*. New York: WW Norton, p. 309.
51. Beinart, William. (1990). Empire, hunting and ecological change in southern and central Africa. *Past and Present* 128: 162–86.

52. Kloppenburg, J. (2010). Impeding dispossession, enabling repossession: Biological open source and the recovery of seed sovereignty. *Journal of Agrarian Change* 10(3): 367–88.
53. Vasudevan, A, C. McFarlane and A. Jeffrey. (2008). Spaces of enclosure. *Geoforum* 39(5): 1641–1646.
54. Levien, M. (2012). The land question: Special economic zones and the political economy of dispossession in India. *Journal of Peasant Studies* 39(3/4): 933–969.
55. McMichael, P. (2012). The land grab and corporate food regime restructuring. *Journal of Peasant Studies* 39(3/4): 681–701.
56. Makki, F. (2014). Development by dispossession: Terra nullius and the social-ecology of new enclosures in Ethiopia. *Rural Sociology* 79(1): 79–103.
57. Borras S.M., J.C. Franco, S. Gómez, C. Kay and M. Spoor. (2012). Land grabbing in Latin America and the Caribbean. *Journal of Peasant Studies* 39(3/4): 845–872.
58. Visser O. and Spoor, M. (2011) Land grabbing in post-Soviet Eurasia: The world's largest agricultural land reserves at stake. *Journal of Peasant Studies* 38(2): 299–323.
59. Araghi, F. (2009). The invisible hand and the visible foot: Peasants, dispossession, and globalization. In A.H. Akram-Lodhi and C. Kay (eds) *Peasants and Globalization: Political Economy, Rural Transformation, and the Agrarian Question*. (pp. 111–147). London: Routledge.
60. Li, T.M. (2010). To make live or let die? Rural dispossession and the protection of surplus populations. *Antipode* 41(s1): 66–93.
61. Shiva, V. (2000). *Stolen Harvest: The Hijacking of the global Food Supply*. Cambridge, MA: Southend Press.
62. Zhang, J. (2017). Summary and analysis of mergers between global seed companies in 2016. *AGROPAGES Annual Review* (February 2007): 40–42. Available at http://news.agropages.com/News/NewsDetail---21186.htm
63. Evenson, R. and D. Golin. (2003). Assessing the impact of the Green Revolution, 1960 to 2000. *Science* 300: 758–762.
64. Marris, E. (2008). Water: more crop per drop. *Nature* 452: 273–277. Available at http://www.nature.com/news /2008/080319/full/452273a.html

65. Edelman, M. (2014). Food sovereignty: forgotten genealogies and future regulatory challenges. *Journal of Peasant Studies* 41(6): 959–978.
66. Food and Agriculture Organisation of the United Nations (2002). *World Agriculture Towards 2015/2030: Summary Report*. Rome, p. 57. Available at http://www.fao.org/3/a-y3557e.pdf
67. Carson, R. (1962). *The Silent Spring*. Boston, Mass.: Houghton-Miffin.
68. Reed, M. (2010). *Rebels for the Soil: The rise of the global food and farming movement*. London: Earthscan.
69. Vaarst, M. (2010). Organic Farming as a development strategy: who are interested and who are not? *Journal of Sustainable Development* 3(1): 35–50.
70. La Vía Campesina. (2010). Sustainable peasant and family farm agriculture can feed the world [online]. *Vía Campesina Views* No. 6. Available at http://viacampesina.org/downloads/pdf/en/paper6-EN-FINAL.pdf
71. Barraclough, S.L. (1991). *An End to Hunger? The Social Origins of Food Strategies*. London and Geneva: Zed Books, United Nations Research Institute for Social Development, South Centre, p. 1.
72. Desmarais, A.A. (2007). *La Vía Campesina: Globalization and the power of peasants*. London: Pluto Press.
73. Martínez-Torres, M.E. and P.M. Rosset. (2014). Diálogo de saberes in La Vía Campesina: food sovereignty and agroecology. *Journal of Peasant Studies*. [online] DOI: 10.1080/03066150.2013.872632
74. Altieri, M.A. (2015). *Agroecology: Key Concepts, Principles and Practices*. Penang, Malaysia: Third World Network.
75. Gliessman, S. (2015). *Agroecology: The Ecology of Sustainable Food Systems*, 3rd edition. Boca Raton/New York: CRC Press.
76. Altieri, M.A., C.I. Nicholls, A. Henao and M.A. Lana. (2015). Agroecology and the design of climate change-resilient farming systems. *Agron. Sustain. Dev.* 35: 869-890.
77. Rosenzweig, C. and D. Hillel. (2008). *Climate Change and the Global Harvest: Impacts of El Nino and Other Oscillations on Agroecosystems*. New York: Oxford University Press.
78. Altieri, M.A. and P. Koohafkan. (2008). *Enduring Farms: Climate Change, Smallholders and Traditional Farming Communities*. Penang, Malaysia: Third World Network.

79. Zhu, Y.Y., H.R. Chen, J.H. Fan, Y.Y. Wang, L. Yan, J.B. Chen, J.X. Fan, S.S. Yang, L.P. Hu, H. Leung, T.W. Mew, P.S. Teng, Z.W. Wang, & C.C. Mundt. (2000). Genetic diversity and disease control in rice. *Nature* 406: 718–722.
80. De Schutter, O. (2010). Report submitted by the Special Rapporteur on the Right to Food. UN General Assembly. Human Rights Council, Sixteenth Session, Agenda item 3 A/HRC/ 16/49.
81. Food and Agriculture Organisation of the United Nations. (2015). *Agroecology for Food Security and Nutrition*. Proceedings of the FAO International Symposium (18–19 September 2014). Rome. Available at http://www.fao.org/3/a-i4729e.pdf
82. Gliessman, S. and M. Rosemeyer. (2008). *The Conversion to Sustainable Agriculture: Principles, Processes and Practices*. Boca Raton/New York: CRC Press.
83. Reganold, J.P. and J.M. Wachter. (2016). Organic agriculture in the twenty-first century. *NaturePlants* 2: 1–8.
84. Wittman, H., A. Desmarais, and N. Wiebe. (2010). The origins and potential of food sovereignty. In H. Wittman, A.A. Desmarais and N. Wiebe (eds), *Food Sovereignty: Reconnecting Food, Nature & Community*. pp. 1–14. Halifax, N.S.: Fernwood Publishing.
85. Schanbacher, W.D. (2010). *The Politics of Food: the Global Conflict between Food Security and Food Sovereignty*. Santa Barbara, CA: Praeger, p. ix.
86. Fairbairn, M. (2010). Framing resistance: International food regimes and the roots of food sovereignty. In H. Wittman, A.A. Desmarais, and N. Wiebe, (eds.) *Food Sovereignty: Reconnecting Food, Nature & Community*. pp. 15–32. Halifax, N.S.: Fernwood Publishing.
87. Levins, R. (2008). *Talking about Trees: Science, Ecology and Agriculture in Cuba*. New Delhi: LeftWord.
88. Rosset, M., B. Machín Sosa, A.M. Roque Jaime, and D.R. Ávila Lozano. (2011). The Campesinoto-Campesino agroecology movement of ANAP in Cuba: social process methodology in the construction of sustainable peasant agriculture and food sovereignty. *Journal of Peasant Studies* 38(1): 161–191.
89. Meybeck, A. and S. Redfern (eds). (2016). *Sustainable Value Chains for Sustainable Food Systems*. Proceedings of workshop of the FAO/ UNEP Programme on Sustainable Food Systems (Rome, 8–9 June

2016). Rome: Food and Agriculture Organisation of the United Nations. Available at http://www.fao.org/3/a-i6511e.pdf

90. Chappell, M.J., H. Wittman, C.M. Bacon, B.G. Ferguson, L.G. Barrios, R.G. Barrios, D. Jaffee, J. Lima, V.E. Mendez, H. Morales, L. Soto-Pinto, J. Vandermeer and I. Perfecto. (2013). Food sovereignty: an alternative paradigm for poverty reduction and biodiversity conservation in Latin America. *F1000 Research* 2: 235 (doi: 10.12688/f1000research.2-235.v1)

Social Protection and Food Security

A Comparative study of South Asian Countries

Praveen Jha

Dr Praveen Jha is Professor at the Centre for Economic Studies and Planning at the School of Social Sciences of Jawaharlal Nehru University in New Delhi, India. His main areas of research and teaching are Political Economy of Development with particular reference to Labour, Agriculture, Natural Resources, Public Finance, Education and History of Economic Thought. He has published more than 70 articles in renowned journals and edited volumes and has been commissioned for papers by institutions such as the Food and Agriculture Organisation, United Nations Development Programme, National Foundation of India and many more.

INTRODUCTION

Issues pertaining to food (in)security and persistent hunger as a result of inadequate income and lack of access to sufficient and safe food have been important in policy discourses for quite some time and are matters of serious concern in several developing countries. It is evident from a variety of sources including the latest Global Hunger Index Report (2016)[(1)] that the South Asian region, along with Sub-Saharan Africa, performs particularly poorly in these respects.[(1)] Although there has been some improvement over the years, the pace of progress is very slow and calls for immediate policy attention, both for adequate public provisioning and plugging the loopholes in implementation.

As already mentioned, these issues have been at the centre of contemporary academic as well as policy discourses. An important feature of the recent literature is that it widely recognizes the critical role of social protection policies in combating hunger, poverty and inequality to realize some of the most fundamental human rights.[(2; 3; 4; 5)] Well-designed and effectively implemented social protection policies have contributed significantly in several countries in breaking the vicious cycle of poverty and vulnerability. Of course, these work particularly well in synergy with overall policy architecture of inclusive growth that boosts domestic demand and facilitates structural transformations of national economies.[(5)]

It may be useful to recall here that the definition of food security given by the World Food Summit 1996 has become a standard benchmark in discussions on the subject: Food security means that *all people at all times have access to sufficient, safe, nutritious food to maintain a healthy and active life*. This definition obviously takes into account both physical and economic access to food in order to meet people's dietary needs as well as their preferences. It is clear from this definition that apart from the availability and affordability of adequate quantities of nutritious food, supplementary infrastructure for absorption (e.g. water and sanitation, medical care, relevant knowledge etc.) should be in place to ensure food security of a nation. In other words, this seemingly simple definition is both conceptually and operationally extremely complex, as is often acknowledged in the contemporary development discourses.[1; 6; 7]

However, in much of the empirical and policy literature, adequacy of average supply of calories is seen as the core indicator of the availability or unavailability, of food, and by implication of the existence of food security or insecurity. Going beyond this indicator, recent literature has also tried to examine a number of other relevant and measurable co-relates. For instance, as per the 2015 report of the State of Food Insecurity (SoFI) by the UN's Food and Agriculture Organisation (FAO), the relevant indicators and correlates include: physical access (including infrastructure like roads and rail), economic access as well as indicators of vulnerability and shock, like the purchasing power of the masses at the lower end of the social ladder and domestic food price indices.[8] These indices include, among others, the import dependency ratio, the percentage of irrigated arable land, the volatility of domestic food prices, the per capita food production variability and the share of food expenditure of the poor. The other obvious indicators influencing food and nutrition security are the access to sanitation facilities and safe drinking water. Further indicators such as the depth of food deficit and Prevalence of Food Inadequacy (PoFI) are also important for measuring outcomes.[8]

The relevant literature clearly demonstrates that in spite of the rate of increase in global food production, which is consistently higher than the rate of the growth of the global population, there is a crisis of food security in many countries in the developing world.[7; 8] This obviously requires a careful analysis of the contemporary global food system in general. In particular, it also requires an investigation into the role of international trade, finance capital and multinational corporations, responsibilities and functioning of the national and sub-national governments. Other relevant themes of investigation include the role of development agencies; class, caste, race and gender; size of farming, control over agriculture, and access to and provisioning for social protection measures. It has also been acknowledged that the fiscal space of the countries is intimately linked to the adequate provisioning and effective implementation of social protection measures for the intended beneficiaries.

While acknowledging the complexity of causal correlates of extreme hunger and malnutrition, the primary objective of the present paper is to map and analyze the relevant evidence for public provisioning (expenditure) on social protection measures and incidence of hunger (inadequacy of dietary energy) in selected countries of South Asia. While doing so, it also engages with important issues relating to the effectiveness of different types of social protection interventions and strategies that exist and their outcomes in addressing the larger question of hunger and malnutrition. Before proceeding further, it would be pertinent to dwell briefly on the methodology and data used in this paper.

Methodology and Data Sources

This paper is primarily based on well-known, large-scale databases and other secondary sources including country specific case studies. The core claims of the paper are that the impact of public provisioning on social protection measures, if successfully and effectively implemented, could be crucial in reaping the immediate and long term benefits in eradicating hunger as well as reducing malnutrition and food insecurity.

Major sources for data in this paper are the State of Food Insecurity (SoFI), a report by the FAO (2015),[(8)] the World Social Protection Report of 2014 by the UN's International Labour Organisation (ILO),[(9)] the World Bank's International

Comparison Programme database on World Development Indicators, the Global Hunger Index (GHI) Report 2016,[1] as well as the Global Nutrition Report (GNR) of 2015.[10] Estimates of social protection expenditure, Prevalence of Food Inadequacy (PoFI), Prevalence of Undernourishment (PoU), values of GHI or Gross Domestic Product (GDP) per capita* have been either taken from the above noted sources or compiled using the data given therein. PoFI measures the percentage of the population that is at risk of not receiving the food required for normal physical activity. Therefore, it also includes those who cannot be considered chronically undernourished, but are likely to have insufficient access to food. Therefore, PoFI is anew, less conservative measure of food inadequacy in the population. In contrast, PoU is an estimator of chronic food deprivation—in other words hunger—which expresses the probability that a randomly selected individual from the population consumes an amount of calories that is insufficient to cover her/his energy requirement for an active and healthy life. This indicator is calculated as an average of three years' figures. More details on the methodology for computing the PoU are given in the State of Food Insecurity in the World report of 2013.[11]

In Table 9 in Annexure A, average social protection expenditure (as per cent of GDP) has been computed taking into account shares of social protection expenditure for the period since 1990 to the latest available year. The average of such shares for respective regions and countries have been computed based on the share

* GDP per capita is based on purchasing power parity (PPP), where GDP is converted to international dollars using purchasing power parity rates. An international dollar has the same purchasing power over GDP as the USD has in the United States. GDP at purchaser's prices is the sum of gross value added by all resident producers in the economy plus any product taxes and minus any subsidies not included in the value of the products. It is calculated without making deductions for depreciation of fabricated assets or for depletion and degradation of natural resources. GDP per capita data are in constant 2011 international dollars.

for 1990, 1995, 2000, 2005, 2007, 2009, 2010–11 and 2012–13 depending on the availability of data. Similarly, the average (since 1990 to the latest available year) GDP per capita has been computed for our sample. Using the SoFI report of 2015 by the FAO, it is possible to track changes in most of these indicators and dimensions.(8) The country specific trends are presented in the tables in the annexure. It should be clear even from a cursory look at these tables that most of the developing countries, particularly in South Asia and Sub-Saharan Africa, tend to perform poorly with respect to the select indicators; the next section provides a relevant sketch of the select countries.

The subsequent parts of the paper will be as follows: the second section maps the trends of hunger, malnutrition and other indicators of food and nutrition security across different regions and in selected countries of South Asia. The trends and patterns of public provisioning on social protection measures and their empirical association with hunger and malnutrition for the South Asian region are mapped in the third and fourth sections. The section that follows draws some insights from a couple of major initiatives with respect to social protection schemes and policies, particularly relevant for reducing hunger and malnutrition in the region. The sixth section concludes the paper, highlighting the achievements as well as gaps with respect to the overall policy framework that may be vital in promoting food security, combating hunger and malnutrition.

MAPPING HUNGER AND FOOD SECURITY IN SELECTED COUNTRIES OF SOUTH ASIA

Before we come to some of the important findings based on the SoFI reports, a couple of words with respect to 'hunger scores' emerging from the GHI reports may be of some interest. At the outset, it may be noted that in Tables 1and 2 in Annexure A, the GHI score for 2000 was 30.0 and it declined to 21.3 in 2016, thus indicating a reduction of 29 per cent in 16 years. For interpretation, higher GHI scores imply higher levels of hunger. Scores between 20.0 and 34.9 points are considered indicators of serious hunger and malnutrition, therefore the overall scores suggest some in-access to food in different regions of the world. However, despite this development the situation remains serious in the regions of Sub-Saharan Africa and South Asia where the GHI scores were 30.1 and 29.0 respectively in 2016. In contrast, the GHI scores for East and Southeast Asia, Near East and North Africa, Latin America and the Caribbean, Eastern Europe and the Commonwealth of Independent States range between 7.8 and 12.8, and represent low or moderate levels of hunger (Table 1, Annexure A). It is also worth highlighting that a number of countries in South Asia, namely Nepal, Afghanistan, Bangladesh and India, had a GHI reduction of more than 25 per cent between 2000 and 2016. In contrast, Pakistan and Sri Lanka did not perform as well (Table 2). However, it may be noted that the methodology employed by IFPRI has invited a few serious questions and several researchers prefer to use the FAO reports to track the dynamics of hunger and malnutrition. Without getting into these methodological contestations, here we have used the data produced by the FAO for our analysis.

As far as the findings with respect to hunger and malnutrition from the SoFI report are concerned, either the PoU or PoFI can be used as valuable markers to get a sense of inter-temporal and cross-country performance. As indicated at the outset, in this paper we consider the latter as more appropriate compared to the former measure because PoFI covers a larger range of people who suffer inadequate access to food. The PoFI data shows that during the period of 2012 to 2016, Afghanistan and Pakistan scored more than 30 per cent which means around one-third of population of these countries suffers from inadequate nutrition. Whereas Sri Lanka, Bangladesh and India scored 29.0, 26.0 and 24.3 per cent respectively, Nepal had the best score in our sample, which is 13.6 per cent. If we look at the percentage decline in 2014–2016 compared to scores of the regions and respective countries in 2000/2002, it is noticeable that substantial progress has been achieved by Nepal (55.1 per cent) followed by Afghanistan at a (34.1 per cent) and Sri Lanka (23.5 per cent). The performance of Asia as a whole at 25 per cent is close to the world average of 23.3 per cent as seen in Table 3.

Within this overall trend of food inadequacy the FAO data shows that the South Asian region had approximately 274 million undernourished persons in the period from 2000 to 2012. This estimate increased to 281 million undernourished persons between 2014 and 2016. This rising trend was also reflected in India where the undernourished population increased from about 190 million in 2012 to almost 195 million in 2016. In Pakistan it increased from 38.1 million to 41.4 million, in Bangladesh it remained almost stagnant at 26.3 million and in Afghanistan it rose by 0.3 million over the same period as shown in Table4. As far as undernourishment as a proportion of the total population is concerned, Table 5 shows that almost 27 per cent in Afghanistan, 22 per cent each in Pakistan and Sri Lanka, 16.4 per cent in Bangladesh and 15.2 per cent in India are undernourished. This shows a declining trend from 1990–1992 onwards, even though the rates of decline have stagnated between 2012 and 2016. The same is true of the per capita availability of food, or the depth of food deficit which is measured through kilocalorie (kcal) per capita per day as per the standard defined by the FAO. As shown in Table 5a, this index shows an overall decline from 169 kcal in 1990–1992 to 114 in 2014–2016 for South Asia. The average deficiency is 127 kcal between 1990 and 2016. The highest average deficiency is observed in Sri Lanka (226kcal) followed by Afghanistan (187kcal), Pakistan (171kcal), Bangladesh (141kcal) and India (122kcal). But if we look at the sub-period between 2012 and 2016, the average per capita kcal in the region has declined by 2kcal. As seen in Table 5a this decline is a result of the regional unevenness where no country except Afghanistan has seen a significant rise and India and Sri Lanka have seen a considerable fall in the per capital kcal availability.

The most vulnerable are the large number of children and mothers who bear the brunt of food inadequacy. Due to inadequate food and nutrition for mothers, one child out of six is born with a low birth weight in developing countries, and annual incidence of under-five mortality in these countries is as high as 45 per cent (Table 6). While looking at performance of indicators of nutritional status of children under five years of age for selected countries in South Asia, it has been observed that the under-five stunting percentage ranges between 36 to 45 per cent. The latest available data shows that child malnutrition declined in countries of the region, both with respect to 'stunting' and 'wasting', which are important indications of nutritional deficiencies and lack of access to food (Table 6). In Bangladesh, India, Nepal and Afghanistan the stunting is between 36 to 41 per cent, whereas 'wasting' (which shows acute food shortage) is between 9.5 and 15.1 per cent. India figures only a little better than Pakistan in terms of both stunting and wasting and Sri Lanka is the best performing in terms of reduction in stunting and child mortality. Thus, as Table 6 shows, the challenges for South Asia are immense in terms of reduction of malnutrition and these can only be met with adequate policy support.

Another indicator for assessing the prevalence of food inadequacy is the incidence of anaemia among children under five years of age. This shows that both women and children do not receive enough nutritious food and that policy support is crucial. Graph 1 shows that anaemia amongst children under five years of age declined between 1900 and 2011. But the rate of decline is the slowest in Pakistan followed by India; leading to an alarmingly high incidence of 61 and 59 per cent for these two countries respectively. It is indeed a disturbing fact that hunger and its related diseases lead to loss of one child in every ten seconds in India.

Graph 1: Anaemia among Children Under Five Years 1990 and 2011

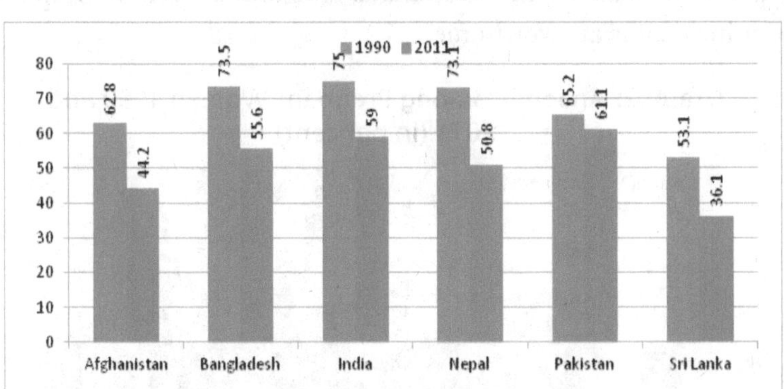

Source: Compiled from the base data given in Food Security Indicators, 2016, FAO, available at http://www.fao.org/economic/ess/ess-fs/ess-fadata/en/#. V2zlvrh97IU, accessed on 24 June, 2016.

Further, hunger and malnourishment has its own social-physical-economic geography. For instance, among India's so called 'Scheduled Castes' (SCs) and 'Scheduled Tribes' (STs), who are relatively worse off, hunger and malnutrition are particularly high. Likewise, 60 per cent of the world's hungry population are women and it is indeed a shocking statistic that 50 per cent of pregnant women in developing countries lack access to adequate dietary care which is possibly a major contributor to the large number, 240 thousand, of annual maternal deaths from childbirth.(12)

For the selected countries, the highest reduction of anaemia among pregnant women from 1990 to 2011 was reported by Sri Lanka (37 percentage points), followed by Nepal (26 percentage points), Afghanistan (11 percentage points) and Bangladesh (ten percentage points). The performance by India and Pakistan is reported to have worsened over the same period by three percentage points. In other words, there has been an increase of prevalence of anaemia among pregnant women in 2011 compared to 1990. On the whole, the rate of progress in reducing anaemia among pregnant women in these select countries since 1990s is hardly impressive. The latest available figures as seen in Graph 2 for incidences are worrisome.

Graph 2: Anaemia among Pregnant Women 1990 and 2011 (in per cent)

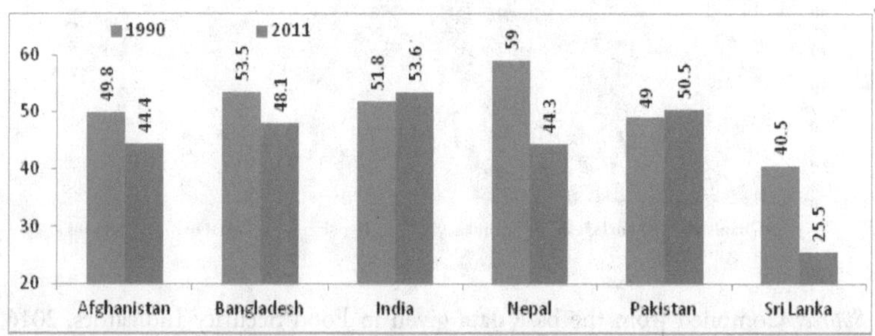

Source: Compiled from the base data given in Food Security Indicators, 2016, FAO, available at http://www.fao.org/economic/ess/ess-fs/ess-fadata/en/#.V2zlvrh97IU, accessed on 24 June, 2016.

Given that there are some obvious correlates which impact food and nutrition outcomes, a quick glance at some of these may be of some help. It is obvious that countries in the region have to go a long way in providing and facilitating sufficient food and nutrition security to their citizens. It has been argued that much of the worst performance of nutritional outcomes, especially for women and children, are linked to behavioural patterns, cultural and religious beliefs as well as inadequate scope and reach of public provisioning of nutritional support. For instance, the percentage of infants less than six months old who were exclusively breastfed in Pakistan and India were 38 per cent and 46 per cent respectively. This underscores the religious and cultural norms as well as pointing to the low level of awareness and female education. Furthermore, the percentage of vitamin A deficiency among pre-school children is reported to be highest in Afghanistan and Pakistan (47 per cent) followed by India (45.5 per cent), Nepal (38 per cent) and Bangladesh (30 per cent) as shown in Tables 6 to 8 in the Annexure.

This data again points out that public provisioning has to be inclusive, integrated and multi-sectoral and should aim at a life-cycle approach, covering sectors ranging from poverty alleviation, to employment guarantees, to infrastructure facilities and agriculture practices. Moreover, WaSH-programmes (Water, Sanitation and Hygiene) and, above all, the improvement of education and health facilities must be achieved, while a minimum basic social security has to be guaranteed.

The minimum requirement of antenatal care coverage is one of the basic factors that can help to improve the nutritional status of women and children. The state of antenatal coverage in the South Asian region is very dismal as shown in Table 7. In Afghanistan it is as low as 15 per cent and it is 25 per cent for Bangladesh. In India and Pakistan it is 37 per cent. Sri Lanka performs the best with a reported coverage of 93 per cent in 2006. The nutritional status of mother and child is also linked to the age of the woman who gives birth. It has been reported that almost 26 per cent in Afghanistan, 22 per cent in India and eight per cent of women in Pakistan give birth to a child before the age of 18, thus increasing the vulnerability of women and children to malnutrition.

But both the age of marriage as well as access to antenatal care are closely related to the educational status of women as they determine the overall awareness and improvement in the status of women. As Table 7 shows, female secondary education (by gross enrolment rates) is very low in these selected countries. As a case in point, only 38 and 32 per cent of female students enrolled (gross) in secondary education in Afghanistan and Pakistan, respectively. This reflects the power of social and cultural institutions that determine the access women have to basic nutritional requirements.

Finally, another factor closely linked to the nutritional status of women and children is access to safe drinking water and improved sanitation facilities. As shown in Table 7 the percentage of population who have access to improved sources of water in countries like Sri Lanka, India, Pakistan and Nepal are more than 90 per cent, however, the same is not true for Afghanistan (55.2) and Bangladesh (86.2) whose level of access to safe drinking water is far lower than the South Asian Region average of 92 per cent. Similarly, Table 7 also shows that the rate of progress with respect to access to safe drinking water is uneven across the region with countries like Afghanistan and Pakistan performing poorly.

Further, Table 7 shows that the percentage of the population with access to improved sanitation between 2000 and 2014 is 47 per cent for the region as a whole. The highest improvement can be seen in Nepal (104 per cent) followed by Pakistan (67 per cent), India (54 per cent) and Afghanistan (36 per cent). The point to underscore here is that adequate provisioning for and access to improved sanitation facility would not only result in improved nutritional outcomes, but also contribute towards economic well-being of the household by increasing income and reducing out of pocket expenditure on health services.

The preceding discussion has very briefly identified some enabling core factors that impact food security and the nutritional status. Apart from the ones mentioned above, other factors which may improve food and nutrition security are the availability of arable land particularly equipped with irrigation, per capita food production, and the supply variability as well as infrastructure like road and rail connectivity. Essentially, the status of all these enabling factors is either quite poor or has not received adequate attention in the policy-making process. Hence, there is an urgent need for adequate public provisioning to enable a larger part of the population to access these basic services which could help promote well-being of many. In the next section, an attempt has been made to quantify public provisioning for social protection and its association with better food and nutrition outcomes.

TRENDS IN PUBLIC PROVISIONING FOR SOCIAL PROTECTION MEASURES

Though the terms 'social protection' and 'social security' are often used interchangeably in contemporary discourses, this paper will adhere to using the term 'social protection'. In a very basic sense, social protection refers to government measures or public actions to address socially unacceptable deprivations and vulnerabilities. Its obvious components would include (social) insurance, assistance and inclusion. In academic discourses the notion of social protection has conceptually been a complex and open-ended one, as is evident from the history of the concept.[3; 5] At the most basic level, social protection is organically connected with the competing visions of development, the associated deprivations and the policy to address the same. The conception put forth by the ILO is a good operational benchmark for assessing social security policies. The ILO's Social Security (Minimum Standards) Convention of 1952 established worldwide-agreed minimum standards for all nine branches of social security. These branches are: medical care, sickness benefit, unemployment benefit, old-age benefit, employment injury benefit, family benefit, maternity benefit, invalidity benefit, and survivor's benefit. Further, the ILO has extended its social security definition by adding 'general protection against poverty and social exclusion' into the existing nine branches of social security.[13]

Apart from the ILO's definition, there are also other international classifications which define the scope of social protection. These are outlined by institutions such as the European Commission of the European Union, the Organisation for Economic Co-operation and Development (OECD) and different UN institutions. However, all the branches of social protection defined by these international organizations have been covered by the ILO's extended social security definition. For the ILO, social protection is a term that denotes *protection* against economic and social distress caused by a fall in income resulting from old age, sickness and employment injury, maternity and temporary unemployment, or the death of relatives. However, there is also substantial literature that makes a strong case for adding the provisions of *promotional* support to the provisions of *protective* coverage in a vision of social protection.[14]

Based on such conceptions, there have been several policy dialogues, globally and regionally, to chart a broad roadmap and to highlight elements that need to be prioritized towards the goal of broad-based social security provisioning. The well-known Copenhagen Declaration and Programme of Action by the World Summit for Social Development in Copenhagen in 1995, which was reaffirmed through the 2000 UN Millennium Declaration for Reduction of Poverty, was such an exercise. At the 2010 UN Summit on the Millennium Development Goals, the idea of a universal 'social floor' was introduced, based on the recognition of the fact that it is possible to eradicate poverty and provide social security for all.[15]

In many countries, both in the developing and the developed world, social protection has come to mean a wide variety of schemes and programmes, usually taken up by the state for the benefit of the public at large, or the poorer sections whose basic entitlements are yet to be provided. As hinted earlier, social security in contemporary discourses takes into account both *protective* and *promotional* aspects, and thus there are many constitutive elements that make up the picture of social security.[5] Hence, for policy priorities with respect to social protection, one needs to clearly state the norms, needs and requirements in a particular context and at a specific socio-economic conjuncture. In other words, depending on the specificities on the ground, one can think of an appropriate menu from a wide spectrum of policy options like infrastructure, education, health and sanitation, insurance and safety nets or public works programmes, which may be better suited and effective in the given context.

Social protection policies have to be seen in the context of the age and skill profile of the population. It has been observed that the aging population (over 65 years of age) in these select countries ranges from five per cent in Afghanistan to eighteen per cent in Sri Lanka. As shown in Table 8, the percentage of skilled attendants at birth ranges from 34 per cent to 99 per cent. In other words, almost all babies born in Sri Lanka, but only around one-third of those born in Bangladesh were attended by skilled personnel. On a similar count, density of nurses and midwives per 1000 population are much higher in Sri Lanka compared to the other countries in the South Asia Region.

With respect to total public social protection expenditure (including health expenditure) as a proportion of the GDP, it is quite clear that developing regions tend to do comparatively little on this front. As Table 9 shows, Africa's total public social expenditure stands at 5.1 per cent, which is less than one-fifth of the share of Western Europe, which stood at 26.7 per cent of GDP in 2010–2011. The same table shows that the world average of public social protection expenditure increased from 5.8 per cent in 1990 to 8.6 per cent in 2010–2011. However, it is clear that both within developed and developing regions there are significant variations.

While looking at the share (per cent) of public expenditure and investment on a few important dimensions of public social protection across various regions, it has been observed that the share of public social protection expenditure for the elderly, as per cent of GDP, shows a wide range. The two ends of the range are Sub-Saharan Africa (1.1 per cent) and Western Europe (11.1 per cent). The world average stands at 3.3 per cent. Similarly, the share of social benefits for persons of active age (excluding general social assistance) ranges from 0.3 per cent to 5 per cent with the world average share at 1.5 per cent as shown in Table 10. In fact, the story for all components of social protection is roughly the same.

The overall expenditure on social protection as represented by Table 11 shows that within South Asia, Sri Lanka spent 4.8 per cent of its GDP as an average share between 1990 and 2010–2011 for social protection, followed by India, Nepal, Bangladesh and Pakistan with 2.0, 1.9,1.6 per cent and 0.9 per cent respectively. In most countries in the region, the first decade of the 2000s stands out for poor performance in terms of public provisioning for social protection. This clearly shows that the social provisioning has been negatively affected by the recent neoliberal policies of contemporary South Asian governments.

The inadequate space for social provisioning is also affected by the GDP and the per capita income. Within South Asia, the average GDP per capita varies from 6,513 USD in Sri Lanka at the top to 1,479 USD in Afghanistan at the bottom. The average GDP per capita in India and Pakistan were reported to be 3,163 USD and 3,803 USD respectively. In Bangladesh, it stood around 1,940 USD and 1,664 USD Nepal in the same period as shown in Table 12. Within the countries of South Asia, there seems to be a wide variation as well as a low level of income at the same time, which partly contributes to inadequate space for public provisioning of social support programmes. Many times it has been argued that low levels of income constrains the countries from adequately provisioning for social protection measures. But it is worth highlighting that there are countries that have prioritized their public purse and adequately provisioned for social protection measures, even with low levels of per capita income.

Public Provisioning for Social Protection and Prevalence of Food Inadequacy: The Interlinkages

This section examines the relationship between social protection expenditure, GDP per capita and PoFI. It lends strong support to the claim that countries that prioritize social protection expenditure are able to address the problem of hunger and malnutrition to a large extent. The following three indicators were taken into account: the share of social protection expenditure,* the GDP per capita, and the prevalence of food inadequacy. Of course, one size cannot fit all and much more careful country-specific examinations of the above noted and other variables in tackling hunger and malnutrition are needed. As already stated before, *food security has several dimensions and indicators, its correlates are manifold, the cause-effect relationships are quite complex and ought not to be reduced to a simplistic framework. However, the preliminary exercise suggests that adequate public provisioning for social protection measures seems to play a critical role in countries which have addressed one of the most basic human needs like food security.*

It is important to highlight that—except Sri Lanka—Nepal had the highest social protection expenditure with 1.94 per cent of the GDP. But Nepal's PoFI score was only 21.5, which is one of the lowest in South Asia. Table 13 confirms this conclusion and shows that Nepal not only has the lowest PoFI, but also the lowest GDP per capita in the region. Another important aspect is that Nepal has one of the highest social protection spending, but the correlation between low GDP per capita and low levels of PoFI is not a general trend. As it can be seen in Table 13, Sri Lanka has a high share of social protection expenditure on average and higher GDP per capita, but the average score for PoFI is still worst among the selected countries. The reasons for such an unevenness in PoFI scores may be a result of a number of other reasons such as the political and economic context, social structure and class-caste inequalities, which need a careful examination as well.

These results can be compared with similar conclusions by Jha and Acharya,(5) which show that modest levels of social protection

* The average total social protection expenditure (as per cent of the GDP) has been computed taking into account shares of social protection expenditure for the period since 1990 to the latest available year. The average of such shares for respective countries have been computed based on the share for 1990, 1995, 2000, 2005, 2007, 2009 and 2010–11, depending on the availability of data.

below five per cent of the GDP do not necessarily lead to low GHI scores. Countries with modest levels of social expenditure but relatively good GHI scores, such as Mexico and Morocco (both with a GHI score of nine), Peru (GHI score of sixteen), China (GHI score of eighteen) and Vietnam (a GHI score of twenty), illustrate this. It is also important to note that low levels of per capita income are not necessarily major constraints in the provisioning of social protection. For instance, the same study by Jha and Acharya reported that there are 35 countries which have an annual per capita income of USD 5,000 or less, and only a few of these are able to spend five per cent or more of their GDP on social protection measures. In contrast, there are other countries with higher per capita incomes but lower levels of social protection expenditure—around three per cent or less of the GDP. This clearly indicates that even a country with low level of per capita income could prioritize their respective annual budgets towards social protection measures, which could reduce hunger and malnutrition in the long run.

Finally, with respect to the relationship between per capita income and PoFI, it is true that higher levels of per capita income support lower levels of hunger. This is evident from various existing studies. However, in our sample Sri Lanka has a relatively high level of per capita income but also a high score for PoFI, and it requires a careful examination.[(5)] Another important point to stress is that countries can address hunger and malnutrition effectively through high levels of social protection expenditure, even though they have lower levels of per capita income. This is, for example, the case in Nepal. It has been pointed out in the study by Jha and Acharya, that countries like Ghana, Nigeria, Armenia, Guyana and Vietnam have been able to reduce hunger and malnutrition with high levels of expenditure on social protection.

The diversity of trends presented above shows that the reduction of hunger and malnutrition is influenced by a complex of factors, some of which are interrelated to each other and require careful in-depth examination. The success and failure of social protection programmes can be attributed to multiple reasons and the ground reports in this book illustrate some of these complex linkages. However, we can identify some general trends as well: The first concerns the way in which social protection programmes address inequalities and take particular care to reduce the social and economic distance between vulnerable groups and the more affluent citizens. Vulnerability may itself be defined in terms of the age, gender and ethnicity. For example, it is quite clear that girl children, elderly and women face discrimination in terms of access to food all over the world. There are also historically deprived social groups who have been subjected to oppression and who suffer from severe malnutrition in all its complex aspects.(15) Further vulnerability to hunger also arises from livelihood insecurity and unemployment. In order to minimize the impact of these vulnerabilities, it is important to have programmes that particularly address these aspects. Some good illustrations of this aspect are the *Bolsa Familias* Programme of Brazil and the Child Grants Programme in South Africa, which particularly target the malnutrition of poor families and vulnerable sections. The recent legislation on the Right to Food and the earlier Rural Employment Guarantee Act in India are also designed to reduce such vulnerabilities.

The second factor influencing the success or failure of social protection programmes is their priority in budgetary allocations. This does not only mean that the overall budgetary allocation is satisfactory, but also that per capita allocation is sufficient to provide access to food. For example in South Africa, the old age pension scheme provides an amount of ZAR 900 to all elderly people, which is sufficient to provide access to food.(7) But in India, the old age pension and the widow pension schemes are far below the desired levels of per capita allocations and thus do not provide a sufficient support structure for access to food. Similarly the lack of expansion of infrastructure for the public distribution system

(PDS) of food in India is another reason for its limited success.[6] Hence, the level of budgetary allocations are an important determining factor in the success or failure of the programmes.

The third important issue to be considered is the overall coherence of social protection programmes. By this we mean a comprehensive social protection policy which provides coherent inter-linkages between different sectors and schemes to achieve the strongest impact. The need to provide a social protection floor for workers in informal employment is particularly significant in this regard, especially as the degree of informalization seems to have increased manifold during the neoliberal globalization.[7; 16] The lack of such integrated policies is detrimental to the functioning of specific programmes, as they are not supported or supplemented by schemes that ensure the overall wellbeing of vulnerable sections.

Finally, social protection has to be seen in the overall macro-economic context. It is well known that in the *dirigste* era, the state was committed to provide social welfare in order to maintain the aggregate domestic demand within the national economy. As a recent report of the ILO (2014) notes, social protection is also important to provide income security to the working masses.[10] But the outcomes of social protection policies across the world are quite uneven. Whereas 80 per cent of the working poor were covered by social protection in Europe in 2014, only 17 per cent in Asia and eight per cent in Africa got social protection. For South Asia, this coverage stagnated at less than ten per cent. This was largely because the neoliberal states of these countries have disassociated themselves from the project of providing comprehensive social protection.[5] The next section draws a couple of lessons from a few major schemes and programmes to illustrate the interlinkages between these four factors.

SOCIAL PROTECTION PROGRAMMES AND SCHEMES, SOME ILLUSTRATIONS

In this section we look at a couple of case studies which show that well-designed and adequate provisioning for social protection measures can be effective in reducing hunger and food inadequacy, if other related measures are in place. The impact on hunger can be gauged directly or in terms of the indirect effect of social protection expenditure. As several examples from countries like South Africa and Brazil show, universal social protection programmes with adequate allocation of resources can have an extremely positive impact on food security.[7] Some of the following examples from South Asia illustrate some of these points as well.

India: Food entitlement under the Right to Food Legislation

India's public distribution system (PDS) is the world's largest government supported distribution network, with 498 thousand fair price shops nationwide, that serve approximately 160 million households. From these fair prices shops, the entitlement of cereals alone ranges between 25–35 kg per household per month. Soon after the launch of the economic reforms in the early 1990s, there was a considerable weakening of PDS. However, there have been signs of recovery in the recent years and in some states of India the system as a whole seems to be working very well and there are many evidences to suggest that it has been instrumental in poverty alleviation. For instance, a recent paper by Dreze and Khera (2013) finds that between 2004–2005 and 2009–2010, the PDS reduced the average poverty-gap index of rural poverty from 22 per cent to 18 per cent. In the same period, the performance of states with a relatively well functioning PDS has been even more impressive. For example Tamil Nadu and Chhattisgarh reduced the said gap from 83 to 61 per cent and 57 to 39 per cent, respectively. We may also note that prior to the neoliberal economic reforms of the

1990s, India had a universal PDS scheme and the present targeted PDS scheme created serious problems.[6; 16]

Another contentious issue is the debate on cash transfers versus transfers in kind for the provisioning of food. As a recent survey shows, a large majority of the respondents (and particularly women) expressed a strong preference towards transfers in kind in all states, except in those with poorly performing PDS schemes.[17] The debate on kind versus cash is a contentious one as different countries and contexts can provide substantial evidence to support either argument. Instead of simply focusing on this binary opposition, a satisfactory answer can perhaps be found if the variables of context, services, overall programme design and infrastructure for implementation are taken into account as well. In other words, infrastructure, coverage, transparency, extent of entitlement, simplicity of delivery mechanisms, *inter alia*, are critical causal factors for a particular mode of provisioning of social protection. Incidentally, a recent cross-country and cross-income study by the World Bank [19] reports that provisioning of food in cash or kind is just one of the many factors that impact nutrition. Structural factors and institutional prerequisites also play crucial roles in achieving the desired outcomes.

A frequent critique of India's PDS is that of leakages. At least a part of these can be resolved with technical fixes, improved delivery mechanisms and expansion of the PDS network. For instance, the leakages for rice and wheat came down from 55 per cent to 35 per cent between 2004–2005 and 2011–2012 due to improvements in the delivery system. During the same period, the percentage of households accessing PDS almost doubled from 23 per cent to 44.5 per cent,[19] thus showing the importance of a properly functioning PDS infrastructure.

India: Supplementary Food and Nutrition through School Meal Programme

Supplementary meal and nutrition programmes can be very effective in tackling children's malnutrition and adequate spending on infant and early childhood care is extremely critical for physical and mental health. Medical evidence shows that negligence in early childhood care leads to irreversible damage in later years. There are examples of outstanding successes in this regard, even in developing countries. Supplementary food and nutrition programmes not only 'reduce hunger and improve food security, particularly for children but also provide incentives for girl children to attend school. School feeding does increase the food consumption of learners, and many programmes have also improved learners' micronutrient status'.[20] In this context, India's Integrated Child Development Services (ICDS) and Mid-day Meal schemes have drawn considerable attention for both appreciable and problematic reasons. In some parts of the country both the programmes have been greatly successful whereas in several states their implementation remains quite inadequate.

India: The Mahatma Gandhi National Rural Employment Guarantee Scheme and the Right to Employment

The Mahatma Gandhi National Rural Employment Guarantee Scheme (MGNREGS) of 2005 aimed at enhancing livelihood security by giving at least 100 days of guaranteed wage employment annually to every household whose adult members are willing and capable of doing manual work. It is indeed the largest public employment programme in the world, providing work for 50 million rural households, where nearly one in every three rural household has benefitted from the scheme.[21] Through this provisioning 1.21 billion of person-days of employment were generated in 2013–2014. Out of the beneficiaries, 40 per cent belonged to marginalized groups of so-called 'Scheduled Castes' and 'Scheduled Tribes', and 56 per cent of the total people covered were women. It is often argued that gender sensitive social assistance programmes are likely to achieve greater impact on household food security because of 'women's dominant role as food producers and care workers within families'.[21] In this light, the MGNREGS has provided millions of women with work and income support to sustain their families and children and to improve their access to food.

Bangladesh: Community-led Integrated School Nutrition Programme

The community-led Integrated School Nutrition Programme in Bangladesh was rolled out with the primary objective of reducing malnutrition by distributing calorie-rich, culture-specific food among primary school children. It also focused on reducing hunger and micronutrient deficiencies and increasing school enrolment and attendance, especially for poor children. Hot-cooked meals have been served to approximately 18,000 of the most vulnerable primary school children on every school day in 45 schools in urban slums in Dhaka and in some rural communities in the districts of Trishal and Mymensingh. The Ministry of Primary and Mass Education and other development partners established the provisioning of meals through cluster kitchen model. They deliver nutritious hot-cooked meals, made from locally grown commodities, to vulnerable children and integrate the community into the programme as well. Mothers' clubs were formed to manage and monitor the programme and the initiative has proved to be cost effective. Moreover, the programme has integrated key elements of community services such as gender empowerment, WaSH and de-worming in its implementation.

Pakistan: Pension and Social Security Scheme

There have been a number of legislations in Pakistan which cover basic needs like medical care, housing, education and nutrition and also include cash benefits. Some of these are the Workmen's Compensation Act of 1923, the Sindh Maternity Benefit Act of 1929, the Punjab Maternity benefit Act of 1943, the West Pakistan Maternity Benefit Ordinance of 1958, the Provincial Employees Social Security Ordinance of 1965 and the Employees

Old Age Benefits Act of 1976. The latter provides benefit to almost 202,000 people, with a budget of PKR 948 million in the fiscal year of 2001–2002. Out of this, PKR 747 million is spent on payment of old age pension, PKR 187 million is allocated towards survivor pension, PKR 8 million is allocated towards payment of invalidity pension and PKR 6 million is spent on old age grants. Though this allocation indicates the commitment and priorities of the Government of Pakistan towards ensuring social support for the elderly, there are several problems with the implementation of the scheme, like the scale of coverage, amount of pension and the modalities relating to access by the elderly. Nonetheless this programme helps to improve the nutritional security of the elderly population.

Sri Lanka: The *Samurdhi* Social Protection Programme

Sri Lanka has been one of the best performing countries in the South Asian region as far as poverty reduction and health outcomes are concerned. These outcomes have been achieved through a widespread social safety programme by the name of *Samurdhi* which addresses basic livelihood and other needs of the poor and socially vulnerable people. The programme comprises of multiple components including the subsidy or the cash transfer programme, the social security programme and the nutrition programme—all designed to achieve the short term objective of reducing the vulnerability of low income families. Monthly cash transfers depend on the size of the family. Until the end of 2014, the maximum amount given to a family under this subsidy program was LKR 1500, while the minimum was LKR 210. However, these amounts were increased twice in 2015, once in January and again in April.[22] Moreover, there are programmes for micro-finance and livelihood development geared towards the long term objective of poverty reduction.

But the impact of the *Samurdhi* programme had serious problems as well, partly because of flawed targeting. The study by Tilakratna and Jayawardana shows that only 47.4 per cent of the poor received the benefits of targeted cash transfers in 2009–2010, and more that 80 per cent of the people receiving livelihood support were not poor. So even though the improvement of health and nutrition outcomes is attributed to the *Samurdhi* Scheme, its role in Sri Lanka's success is quite limited. Hence one might conclude that the programme needs to become universal in order to reach those who are really in need.

Nepal: The Universal Pension Scheme

Nepal is one of the best examples for a universal, non-contributory pension scheme for the elderly above 70 years of the age. The scheme was introduced after the constitutional reforms in 1995 and provided a pension to all people over the age of 75 years. At that time, the social protection of the state was ten per cent of Nepal's GDP. However, in the early 2000s, the government decided that the age of eligibility for universal pension would be reduced from 75 years to 70 years. It also decided that all widows over the age of 60 would get a pension. The cash amount transferred to each individual was increased from LKR 250 to LKR 500 between 1995 and 2008. The entire expenditure for social services constituted 25 per cent of the total GDP of the country. The benefits are disbursed through the district development councils.(23) By 2014, about 720 million elderly and about 250 million widows had benefited from the old age pension scheme, which constituted a major part of the elderly population of Nepal.

The scheme itself marks an important step in ensuring that the vulnerable elderly population gets access to food. The scheme increased the self-reliance and income security of the elderly, who are otherwise dependent on their family members. In this sense, universal pension schemes are an important mechanism to improve the accessibility to food. Consequently, the proportion of people suffering from hunger came down from 47 to 22.5 per cent between 2000 and 2010, despite the fact that Nepal had the lowest per capita income in the entire region in this period.[24] The Nepalese example also shows that even in low income countries, social protection commitments can be fulfilled if they are prioritized by the sitting government.

The examples illustrated above lead to three broad conclusions. Firstly, it is seen that success rates of programmes are conditioned by their universal coverage and that targeted programmes have not fared very well. Despite its success, the *Samurdhi* Programme in Sri Lanka suffered from flawed targeting and the PDS in India became weaker once it was transformed into a targeted system after the economic reforms. Secondly, the allocations for social protection programmes are not necessarily linked to GDP growth. The example of Nepal illustrates how low per capita income is not a deterrent to public expenditure on social security. Thirdly, the decentralization of decision making and involvement of local communities has been important to attain success, as seen in the case of Bangladesh. Some of these conclusions are expanded in the concluding observations.

CONCLUSION

The analysis in this paper shows that there are complex relationships between food security, per capita income and the position of selected countries with respect development indicators. Nevertheless, in almost all the cases presented here, there is a strong positive correlation between public provisioning for social protection and lower levels of food inadequacy. A country with better and wider public provisioning to various branches of social protection, promotion and security could go a long way in addressing the concerns of food (in)security, hunger and malnutrition. The major policy challenge confronting most developing countries—and especially the selected countries in this study—is to devise appropriate strategies for protecting the vulnerable sections of population.

It has been stated in a lot of the contemporary literature that limited national public finances are a major constraint to providing social protection for the vulnerable, labouring populations. It has also been argued that high informality results in challenges to expanding social protection coverage. Hence there is a need for promoting community initiatives that reduce the cost of targeting and ensure broad transparency.[(4)]

While some of these arguments may have a certain relevance especially with respect to the need for a new political contract for implementation of social protection, this chapter also demonstrates that such a generalization is not valid for all cases. The case studies cited show that even countries with low levels of per capita income can address the problem of food (in)security by higher levels of social protection expenditure, particularly for the vulnerable sections of the population. In terms of explaining outcomes relating to food security, it seems robust to argue that a broad package of policies, prioritizing social protection and directly targeted programmes to support food availability through public distribution systems, supplementary feeding programmes or wage entitlements through public works programme can achieve a lot. However, it is important to take into account the questions of adequacy resources, appropriate policy designs as well as institutions and governance and structures created to effectively deliver the relevant services. Lessons can be learnt from the success stories in this regard, particularly based on programmes like Challenging the Frontiers of Poverty Reduction in Bangladesh, Zero Hunger in Brazil, MGNREGS in India, the Child Support Grant in South Africa and the *Samurdhi* Scheme in Sri Lanka.

It is important to stress that in most developing countries, the biggest concern with respect to public provisioning towards social protection is securing adequate fiscal or expenditure space through appropriate policies. Contrary to the view that countries with low GDP cannot create such a space, we would argue that even at low levels of income, like for example in Nepal, it is possible to mobilize adequate resources for the provisioning of social protection measures. Either conceptually or historically, there is no reason to believe that a country needs to wait to reach relatively high levels of per capita income before it can make adequate progress in social protection. At the end of the day, it is the political economy of a country, inclusive politics and progressive policies which can facilitate a transition to greater fiscal space and higher allocation for social protection.

As it happens, during the period of the so-called economic reforms, most developing countries experienced serious stress in expanding the scope of their fiscal space, which is evident from their tax-to-GDP or expenditure-to-GDP ratios.(7) Thus, an obvious challenge is to wage united struggles for increasing the fiscal spaces in order to extend the coverage of social protection. There is no dearth of instruments, but the real challenge is to use creative means of organizing the working classes to force states to adopt appropriate policy measures.

ANNEXURES

Table 1: Region-wise Global Hunger Index Score

Regions	*1992*	*2000*	*2008*	*2016*
Developing World	35.3	30.0	26.2	21.3
Africa South of the Sahara	47.9	44.4	36.3	30.1
South Asia	46.4	38.2	35.3	29.0
East and South East Asia	29.4	20.8	17.0	12.8
Near East and North Africa	18.3	15.9	13.8	11.7
Eastern Europe and Commonwealth of Independent States	NA	14.1	9.3	8.3
Latin America and the Caribbean	17.2	13.6	9.6	7.8

Note: Not Available

Source: Collated from the data given in the Global Hunger Index Report, 2016.

Table 2: GHI Scores of Select South Asian Countries since 1990

Country (with data from)	*1992 (1990-1994)*	*2000 (1998-2002)*	*2008 (2006-2010)*	*2016 (2011-2016)*	*Percentage point decline in 2016 from 2000*
Afghanistan	49.3	52.4	39.2	34.8	34
Bangladesh	52.4	38.5	32.4	27.1	30
India	46.4	38.2	36	28.5	25
Nepal	43.1	36.8	29.2	21.9	40
Pakistan	43.4	37.8	35.1	33.4	12
Sri Lanka	31.8	27	24.4	25.5	6

Source: Collated from the data given in the Global Hunger Index Report, 2016.

Table 3: Country's Score for Prevalence of Food Inadequacy (In per cent)

Country	*1990-92*	*2000-02*	*2008-10*	*2012-14**	*2014-16**	*Percentage point decline in 2014-16 over 2000-02*
World	25.8	21.9	19.1	17.4	16.8	23.3
Developing Countries	31.7	26.1	22.6	20.4	19.6	24.9
Asia	32.6	26	22.9	20.3	19.5	25.0
Southern Asia	32.8	27.2	25.6	24.8	24.5	9.9
Afghanistan	36.9	55.5	35.3	34.4	36.6	34.1
Bangladesh	41.2	30.6	26.7	26.9	26.0	15.0
India	33.1	26.5	25.4	24.6	24.3	8.3
Nepal	31.6	30.3	18.6	13.6	13.6	55.1
Pakistan	32.8	31.0	29.8	30.2	30.5	1.6
Sri Lanka	42.1	37.9	34.6	31.2	29.0	23.5

Source: Compiled by authors from the base data given in Food Security Indicators, 2016, FAO, available at http://www.fao.org/economic/ess/ess-fs/ess-fadata/en/#. V2zlvrh97IU, accessed on 24 June, 2016.

Table 4: Number of People Undernourished (in Millions)

Regions/ Sub-regions/ Countries	*1990-92*	*2000-02*	*2005-07*	*2010-12*	*2011-13*	*2012-14**	*2013-15**	*2014-16**
Southern Asia	291.2	272.3	319.1	274.2	276.3	279.5	280.9	281.4
Afghanistan	3.8	10.0	8.3	7.1	7.3	7.7	8.1	8.6
Bangladesh	36.0	27.7	24.3	26.5	26.8	27.0	26.8	26.3
India	210.1	185.5	233.8	189.9	191.0	193.1	194.1	194.6
Nepal	4.2	5.2	4.1	2.5	2.3	2.2	2.2	2.2
Pakistan	28.7	34.4	38.1	38.3	39.2	40.0	40.8	41.4
Sri Lanka	5.4	5.7	5.9	5.3	5.2	5.1	4.9	4.7

Source: Compiled by authors from the base data given in Food Security Indicators, 2016, FAO, available at http://www.fao.org/economic/ess/ess-fs/ess-fadata/en/#.V2zlvrh97IU, accessed on 24 June, 2016.

Table 5: Prevalence of Undernourishment (in per cent)

Regions/ Subregions/ Countries	*1990-92*	*1999-01*	*2004-06*	*2009-11*	*2010-12*	*2011-13*	*2012-14**	*2013-15**	*2014-16**
Afghanistan	29.5	45.2	35.2	24.7	24.3	24.4	25.1	26.0	26.8
Bangladesh	32.8	23.1	17.1	17.2	17.3	17.3	17.2	16.9	16.4
India	23.7	17.0	21.2	15.7	15.6	15.4	15.4	15.3	15.2
Nepal	22.8	22.2	17.0	10.2	9.2	8.5	7.9	7.7	7.8
Pakistan	25.1	22.4	24.7	21.7	21.8	21.9	22.0	22.0	22.0
Sri Lanka	30.6	29.9	29.5	26.0	25.3	24.6	23.8	22.9	22.0

Source: Compiled by authors from the base data given in Food Security Indicators, 2016, FAO, available at http://www.fao.org/economic/ess/ess-fs/ess-fadata/en/#.V2zlvrh97IU, accessed on 24 June, 2016.

Table 5a: Depth of Food Deficit (kcal/caput/day)

Regions/ Subregions/ Countries	*1990–92*	*1998–00*	*2004–06*	*2009–11*	*2010–12*	*2011–13*	*2012–14*	*2013–15*	*2014–16*	*Average (1990–92 to 2014–16)*
Southern Asia	169	131	150	117	116	115	116	115	114	127
Afghanistan	202	309	224	151	149	151	158	166	173	187
Bangladesh	247	189	116	120	121	122	122	120	116	141
India	165	120	152	112	111	110	110	110	109	122
Nepal	149	157	111	64	58	53	50	49	51	82
Pakistan	179	159	188	166	167	169	170	171	172	171
Sri Lanka	228	265	266	230	224	217	209	200	192	226

Source: Compiled by authors from the base data given in Food Security Indicators,2016, FAO, available at http://www.fao.org/economic/ess/ess-fs/ess-fadata/en/#.V2zlvrh97IU, accessed on 24 June, 2016.

Table 6: Prevalence of Stunting and Under-Five Mortality Rate Across Countries in South Asia since 1990s

Country	*Prevalence of wasting in children under-5 years (%)*				*Prevalence of stunting in children under-5 years (%)*				*Under-5 mortality rate (%)*			
	1990–94	*1998–02*	*2006–10*	*2011–15*	*1990–94*	*1998–02*	*2006–10*	*2011–15*	*1992*	*2000*	*2008*	*2015*
Afghanistan	11.4	13.5	8.9	9.5	51.1	54.7	51.3	40.9	16.8	13.7	11.0	9.1
Bangladesh	16.1	13.8	17.5	14.3	71.5	54.0	43.2	36.4	13.2	8.8	5.6	3.8
India	20.0	17.1	20.0	15.1	61.9	54.2	47.9	38.7	11.9	9.1	6.6	4.8
Nepal	12.5	14.2	12.6	10.5	61.6	57.1	49.3	37.4	12.7	8.1	5.1	3.6
Pakistan	17.5	15.5	13.3	21.4	54.5	41.5	40.6	45.0	13.4	11.2	9.6	8.1
Sri Lanka					29.7	18.4	18.3	14.7	2.1	1.6	1.2	1.0

Source: Compiled from the data given in the Global Hunger Index Report, 2016.

Table 7: Indicators of Nutritional Status of Select Countries in South Asia

Country/Indicators	*Afghanistan*	*Bangladesh*	*India*	*Nepal*	*Pakistan*	*Sri Lanka*
Year, vitamin A deficiency in preschool-age children (%)	2013	2013	2013	2013	2013	2013
Vitamin A deficiency in preschool-age children (%)	47	30	45.5	38	47	6
Year of most recent estimate, Exclusive Breastfeeding (EBF) of infants <6 months	NA	2014	2005	2014	2013	2006
Exclusive Breastfeeding (EBF) of infants <6 months (%)	NA	55	46	57	38	76
Year, Minimum Acceptable Diet (MAD) of 6-23 month-olds	NA	2013		2011	2013	NA
Minimum Acceptable Diet (MAD) of 6-23 month-olds (%)	NA	32		24	15	NA
Year, Minimum Dietary Diversity (MDD) of 6-23 month-olds	NA	2013		2011	2013	NA
Minimum Dietary Diversity (MDD) of 6-23 month-olds (%)	NA	38.2		28.5	22.2	NA
Year, Antenatal care (4+ visits) (%)	2010	2013	2005	2011	2012	2006

Country/Indicators	*Afghanistan*	*Bangladesh*	*India*	*Nepal*	*Pakistan*	*Sri Lanka*
Antenatal care (4+ visits) (%)	15	25	37	50.1	36.6	93
Year, Early initiation of breastfeeding (within 1 hour after birth) (%)	2011	2013	2007	2011	2013	2006
Early initiation of breastfeeding (within 1 hour after birth) (%)	53.6	44.3	40.5	44.5	18	80
Year, Severe Acute Malnutrition Geographical Coverage (%)	2012	2012	2012	2012	2012	2012
Severe Acute Malnutrition Geographical Coverage (%)	NA	9.8	11.7	4.1	0.5	11
Year, Vitamin A supplementation, full coverage (%)	2013	2013	2013	2013		2013
Vitamin A supplementation, full coverage (%)	97	97	53	99	0	92
Year, Immunization coverage DTP3 (%)	2013	2013	2013	2013	2013	2013
Immunization coverage DTP 3 (%)	71	97	72	92	72	99
Year, Iodized salt consumption (%)	2011	2013	2009	2011	2011	2006
Iodized salt consumption (%)	20.4	57.6	71.1	80	69.1	92

Country/Indicators	*Afghanistan*	*Bangladesh*	*India*	*Nepal*	*Pakistan*	*Sri Lanka*
Year, Early childbearing—births by age 18 (%)	2010–2011		2005–2006		2012–2013	2006–2007
Early childbearing—births by age 18 (%)	26		22		8	4
Year, Female secondary education enrollment rates (gross) (%), 1st of 5 most recent surveys	2013	2012	2011	2014	2013	NA
Female secondary education enrollment rates (gross) (%), 1st of 5 most recent surveys	38.26	57.19	66.29	69.07	32.21	NA
Population with access to Improved Water Sources (in per cent, 2015)	55.3	86.9	94.1	91.6	91.4	95.6
Population with access to Improved Sanitation (in per cent, 2015)	31.9	60.6	39.6	45.8	63.5	95.1

Note: Not Available

Source: Compiled from the base data given in Global Nutrition Report, 2015 (IFPRI) available at http://ebrary.ifpri.org/utils/getfile/collection/p15738coll2/id/129443/filename/129654.pdf and Food Security Indicators, 2016(FAO), available at http://www.fao.org/economic/ess/ess-fs/ess-fadata/en/#.V2zlvrh97IU, accessed on 19 February, 2017.

Table 8: Health Personals in Select Countries

Country / Indicators	*Afghanistan*	*Bangladesh*	*India*	*Nepal*	*Pakistan*	*Sri Lanka*
Total under-5 population (thousands)	4807	15202	122215	2807	21363	1881
Population >65 years (%)	5	10	11	10	9	18
Skilled attendant at birth (%)	38.6 (2010–11)	34.4 (2013)	52.3 (2007–08)	36 (2011)	52.1 (2012–13)	99 (2006–07)
Population density of health workers (per 1,000 population) density of physicians	0.27 (2013)	0.36 (2011)	0.70 (2012)	0.21 (2004)	0.83 (2010)	0.68 (2010)
Population density of health workers (per 1,000 population) density of nurses and midwives	0.50 (2009)	0.22 (2011)	1.71 (2011)	0.46 (2004)	0.57 (2010)	1.64 (2010)
Population density of health workers (per 1,000 population) density of community health workers	NA	0.33 (2011)		0.63 (2004)	0.07 (2010)	NA

Note: Figures in bracket show the corresponding year.

Source: Global Nutrition Report, 2015 (IFPRI) available at http://ebrary.ifpri.org/utils/getfile/collection/p15738coll2/id/129443/filename/129654.pdfassessed on 19 February, 2017.

Table 9: Share of Social Protection Expenditure (including Health Expenditure) in GDP (in per cent)

Regions/Sub-regions	*1990*	*1995*	*2000*	*2005*	*2007*	*2009*	*2010/11*
Africa	2.7	2.8	4.3	4.3	4.8	5.4	5.1
North Africa	4.2	4.3	5.9	6.4	8.4	9.5	9.0
Sub-Saharan Africa	2.4	2.5	3.2	3.8	3.9	4.4	4.2
Asia and the Pacific	3.4	2.8	3.5	3.0	4.1	5.3	5.3
Middle East	4.9	5.2	6.6	7.6	6.5	8.8	8.7
Western Europe	20.9	23.6	23.3	24.8	24.1	27.2	26.7
Central and Eastern Europe	12.8	15.5	14.6	16.6	16.2	19.7	17.6
Latin America and the Caribbean	8.0	9.6	10.2	11.4	12.0	13.6	13.2
North America	14.0	15.8	14.7	16.1	16.4	19.2	19.4
World	5.8	6.0	6.5	6.7	7.3	8.8	8.6

Source: World Social Protection Report 2014, International Labour Organisation, Geneva.

Table 10: Public Social Protection Expenditure by Guarantee, Latest Available Year (as per cent of GDP) regional average (weighted by total population)

Major area/region	*Social protection*	*Health care*	*Social protection for elderly*	*Social benefits for excluding general social assistance*	*General social assistance*	*Social protection for children*
Africa	4.3	2.6	1.3	0.4	0.2	0.2
North Africa	10.0	3.2	5.0	1.1	0.3	0.4
Sub-Saharan Africa	4.3	2.6	1.1	0.3	0.2	0.1
Asia and the Pacific	4.6	1.5	2.0	0.4	0.4	0.2
Western Europe	27.1	7.9	11.1	5.0	0.9	2.2
Central and Eastern Europe	17.8	4.4	8.3	3.0	1.3	0.8
Latin America and the Caribbean	13.9	4.0	4.6	2.0	2.6	0.7
North America	17.0	8.5	6.6	2.8	1.1	0.7
Middle East	11.0	2.0	3.3	1.5	3.4	0.8
World	8.8	2.8	3.3	1.5	0.7	0.4

Source: Compiled from the data given in ILO Social Security Inquiry database.

Table 11: Select Country's Share of Social Protection Expenditure in GDP (in per cent)

Country	*1990*	*1995*	*2000*	*2005*	*2007*	*2009*	*2010-11*	*Average share (1990 to 2010-11)*
Bangladesh	0.7	1.1	1.1	1.2	2.0	2.3	2.7	1.6
India	1.7	1.6	1.6	1.5	1.9	2.6	2.6	2.0
Nepal	2.0	1.2	1.7	1.5	1.8	3.1	2.3	1.9
Pakistan	1.5	0.4	0.3	0.4	0.5	1.7	1.7	0.9
Sri Lanka	5.3	6.8	4.4	5.6	4.5	3.7	3.1	4.8

Note: Not Available

Source: World Social Protection Report, 2014, International Labour Organisation, Geneva.

Table 12: Per Capita GDP-PPP (constant 2011 International USD)

Country Name	*1990*	*2000*	*2005*	*2010*	*2011*	*2012*	*2013*	*2014*	*2015*	*Average GDP Per Capita (1990 to 2015)*
South Asia	1862	2542	3160	4178	4376	4557	4775	5032	5317	3101
Afghanistan	**NA**	NA	1167	1663	1713	1899	1876	1844	1808	1479
Bangladesh	1290	1646	1937	2451	2579	2715	2843	2979	3137	1940
India	1773	2521	3213	4405	4635	4833	5090	5392	5730	3163
Nepal	1198	1540	1693	1997	2042	2115	2176	2278	2312	1664
Pakistan	3057	3502	4028	4297	4323	4380	4477	4589	4706	3803
Sri Lanka	3666	5580	6527	8563	9213	9980	10239	10642	11048	6513

Note: Not Available.

GDP per capita based on purchasing power parity (PPP). PPP GDP is gross domestic product converted to international dollars using purchasing power parity rates. An international dollar has the same purchasing power over GDP as the U.S. dollar has in the United States. GDP at purchaser's prices is the sum of gross value added by all resident producers in the economy plus any product taxes and minus any subsidies not included in the value of the products. It is calculated without making deductions for depreciation of fabricated assets or for depletion and degradation of natural resources. Data are in constant 2011 international dollars.

Source: World Bank, International Comparison Programme database, World Development Indicators

Table 13: Relationship among PoFI score, Social Protection Expenditure and Per Capita GDP.

Countries	*Average Score for PoFI (1990–92 to 2014–16)*	*Average Share of Social Protection Expenditure (1990 to 2010–11)*	*Average Per Capita GDP (1990 to 2014)*
Bangladesh	30.28	1.59	1940
India	26.78	1.93	3163
Nepal	21.54	1.94	1664
Pakistan	30.86	0.93	3803
Sri Lanka	34.96	4.77	6513

Source: Compiled by the author from the available data sources.

NOTES

1. Von Grebmer, Klaus; Bernstein, Jill; Nabarro, David; Prasai, Nilam; Amin, Shazia; Yohannes, Yisehac; Sonntag, Andrea; Patterson, Fraser; Towey, Olive; and Thompson, Jennifer. (2016). *2016 Global hunger index: Getting to zero hunger*, Bonn, Washington, DC and Dublin: Welthungerhilfe, International Food Policy Research Institute, and Concern Worldwide. Available at: http://dx.doi.org/10.2499/9780896292260.
2. Kannan, K.P. (2004). *Social Security, Poverty Reduction and Development: Arguments for Enlarging the Concept of Social Security in a Globalizing World.* Social Security Policy and Development Branch, ILO, Geneva.
3. Kannan, K.P. and Jan Breman.(Eds) (2013). *The Long Road to Social Security: Assessing the Implementation of National Social Security Initiatives for the Working Poor in India*. New Delhi: Oxford University Press.
4. Bastagli, Franseca. (2013). *Feasibility of Social Protection Schemes in Developing Countries*. London: Overseas Development Institute.
5. Jha, Praveen and Nilachala Acharya. (2016). Public provisioning for social protection and its implications for food security. *Economic*

and Political Weekly, Vol. 51, No. 18, April 2016: pp. 98–106, New Delhi, India.

6. Swaminathan, Madhura. (2000). *Weakening Welfare: The Public Distribution of Food in India*. New Delhi: LeftWord Books.
7. Jha, Praveen. (2014). *Public Provisioning for Social Protection and Agriculture: Some Implications for Food Security*. New Delhi: Centre for Economic Studies and Planning, Jawaharlal Nehru University (Mimeo).
8. Food and Agriculture Organisation of the United Nations. (2015). *The State of Food Insecurity in the World.* Rome. Available at http://www.fao.org/publications/sofi/2015/en/
9. International Labour Organisation. (2014). *World social protection report 2014/15: Building economic recovery, inclusive development and social justice*. Geneva, Switzerland. Available at http://www.ilo.org/global/research/global-reports/world-social-security-report/2014/WCMS_245201/lang--en/index.htm
10. International Food Policy Research Institute (2015): *Global Nutrition Report 2015: Actions and Accountability to Advance Nutrition and Sustainable Development*. Washington, DC. Available at http://www.ifpri.org/publication/global-nutrition-report-2015
11. Food and Agriculture Organisation of the United Nations. (2013). *The State of Food Insecurity in the World.* Rome. Available at http://www.fao.org/docrep/018/i3434e/i3434e00.htm
12. The United Nations. (2013). *The Millennium Development Goals Report*. New York. Available athttp://www.un.org/millenniumgoals/pdf/report-2013/mdg-report-2013-english.pdf. Last viewed on 8 July 2014.
13. International Labour Organisation. (2010): *World Social Protection Report: Providing coverage in times of crisis and beyond.* Geneva, Switzerland. Available at http://www.ilo.org/wcmsp5/groups/public/@dgreports/@dcomm/@publ/documents/publication/wcms_146566.pdf
14. Jha Praveen, R. Ramakumar and Nilachala Acharya. (2012). 'Social Security in India' in Zoya Hassan and Mushirul Hassan (eds), *India Social Development Report: Minorities at the Margins.* New Delhi: Oxford University Press. pp. 141–158.

15. Srivastava, Ravi S. (2013). *A social protection floor for India,* International Labour Office, ILO, DWT for South Asia and ILO Country Office for India – New Delhi: ILO, 2013.
16. Ghosh, Jayati and C. P. Chandrasekhar. (2002). *The Market that Failed.* New Delhi: LeftWord Books.
17. Khera, Reetika. (2011). 'Revival of the Public Distribution System: Evidence and Explanations', *Economic and Political Weekly*, Vol. XLVI, No. 44 & 45, pp. 36–50.
18. World Bank (2014a). 'Little Choice Between Cash and Kind in Provisioning Food', http://blogs.worldbank.org/impactevaluations/cash-king-revival-cash-versus-food-transfers-debate-guest-post-ugo-gentilini. Accessed on 9 August, 2014.
19. Himanshu (August 7, 2013), 'PDS – A Story of Changing States'. *liveMint*, New Delhi. Available at http://www.livemint.com/Opinion/TTLqU0Cg2iF4hYtJSHtMRI/PDS-a-story-of-changing-states.html
20. High Level Panel of Experts (HLPE) (2012). *Social protection for food security. A report by the High Level Panel of Experts on Food Security and Nutrition of the Committee on World Food Security*, Rome, Italy. Available at http://www.fao.org/cfs/cfs-hlpe/reports/en/
21. Government of India (2015). *Annual Report, 2014-15*, Ministry of Rural Development, New Delhi, India.
22. Tilakratna, G and S. Jayawardana. (2015). *Social Protection in Sri Lanka: Current Status and Effects on Labour Market Outcomes.* SARNET Working Paper 3. New Delhi: Institute of Human Development.
23 Bonnerjee A, and G. Kohler (2011). 'The Challenge of Food and Nutrition Security and Policy Initiatives from the South' presented at International Conference on Rethinking Development in the Age of Security and Uncertainity, 19–22 September 2011, Institute of Development Studies, Sussex.
24. Upreti, et al. (2012). *Livelihoods, Basic Services and Social Protection in Nepal*, Working Paper 7, Secure Livelihoods Research Consortium, London. Overseas Development Institute.

Hunger, Injustice and the Changing Weather

A Report from Bundelkhand

Bharat Dogra

Bharat Dogra is a freelance journalist who has been involved in several social movements and initiatives. Nearly 8000 reports and articles written by him have been published in India and abroad during the last four and a half decades.

India's high economic growth rate in the last many years has unfortunately co-existed with high levels of malnutrition and under-nutrition in many parts of the country. This is often rooted in local causes of inequalities, injustices and ecological ruin. The situation is aggravated in periods of adverse weather and disasters. In 2016, many parts of India were experiencing a serious period of hunger and malnutrition, as droughts were reported from nearly half of the more than 600 districts in the country. One such affected region was Bundelkhand in central India, comprising of 13 districts. This paper describes the seriousness of hunger in this region and analyses its causes, while also briefly discussing possible remedial actions.

The first part describes the situation in a village and relates it to the wider reality. The next introduces the region of Bundelkhand. The third part looks at the increasingly erratic weather patterns as well as deficient rainfall. This is related to climate change but the role of local factors of ecological ruin is also explained. Part four discusses local realities of exploitation and inequalities. In the next section, we examine the inadequacies of governance in general and in part six, we look at the low potential performance of the food security system in particular. The seventh part—the most detailed section—brings together all the realities described above to show how these have resulted in the serious present day hunger situation. In this context, special vulnerabilities based on gender, age, caste, class etc. are also taken into account. The final section discusses future prospects and possible remedial actions.

Hunger in a Village

Asharam was a farmer from Naugavaan village in Naraini block of Banda district. During an intensive drought, he struggled hard to save the wheat crop on a small part of his farmland. As it is, crops had been planted only on a small part of the village's farmland under the drought conditions in the beginning of 2016. These crops were now threatened by hungry farm animals too. Asharam requested his wife to give him some food so that he could go to the fields at night and guard the meagre crop. However, there was no food at home and so he had to go to the field hungry. When he returned home the next morning, he simply collapsed and died.

In Naugavaan, there are several such sudden deaths and the villagers attribute it to the combined impact of hunger, malnutrition and tensions regarding the economic crisis. A group discussion in Naugavaan village revealed an abnormally high number of deaths in recent times. The number of women who were introduced as widows was also very high. The farmers in this village have lost three crops in quick succession—the first due to excess and untimely rains and hailstorm and the next two due to prolonged drought conditions. They have exhausted all the grain stored at home. Many of them are down to eating just one meal a day, consisting of *roti* (traditional bread) and salt. Some leftovers may be consumed later. When it is possible, chutney made with a few tomatoes and chillies is prepared to go with the *rotis*. On a better day, some cheap vegetables like potatoes and aubergines are eaten in a diluted form so that the watery vegetable can be shared among more family members.

The condition is even worse in the neighbouring hamlet of Kyotra. Women here say that they are forgetting the taste of pulses, which is generally the staple source of protein for them. Due to an alarming shortage of fodder in the drought year, no milk is available either. Hence both the main sources of protein are out of reach. As farm and dairy animals are dying at an alarmingly high rate (about 100 animals died in this small hamlet of about 150 families in just two months), future prospects are also becoming grim. In fact even before the recent drought, livelihood prospects had been becoming more difficult for the people of Kyotra. The small farmers living here were never able to earn much from agriculture due to difficult terrain and uneven land.

Belonging to the Kevat community, which usually lives on river banks, the people have complemented farming with fishing and artisan work. They grow *san*, a fibre crop which they use for making ropes and related products, on the land near the river. However, the rapid depletion of the river in recent years linked to many-sided ecological ruin has not only created a shortage of water, but harmed their other sources of livelihood as well. Hence hunger and malnutrition have now become chronic in this village.

The livelihood problems have accentuated underlying governance problems. Kyotra has remained a remote and poorly-connected village without electricity, schools or nutrition- and health-centres. Several elderly and disabled persons depend increasingly on the mercy of others for their survival. They are entitled to get pension under the various schemes of the government, but these pensions reach very few of those who need them urgently. The impact of multiple, continuing deprivation is evident in families like those of 55-year-old Bhura Kevat, who has lost four family members—his wife, father and two younger brothers—in just one year.

Naugavaan with its various hamlets is just one example of the thousands of villages in Bundelkhand going through extremely difficult times. Levels of malnutrition and hunger were extremely high at the time of the author's research and increased further during the course of the year. Even if the weather had been favourable, no crop could be expected in most villages until October and November. Only a few farmers in some patches were able to plant the winter crop, which is harvested earlier in March and April. Moreover, the shortage of drinking water in many villages affected people as well as farm animals and aggravated the hunger to an intolerable level. Under such circumstances, the role of the government (and to a lesser extent also of non-government voluntary organizations) becomes very important for preventing extreme forms of hunger, malnutrition and thirst in Bundelkhand.

Of course, hunger and malnutrition exist to some extend even in normal years. A significant part of the population including the marginal farmers (i.e. those with very small holdings) and landless farm workers can neither grow adequate food nor have adequate alternative opportunities. The problem of malnutrition is generally worse among women, as they are often the last to eat in the family and generally prioritize the needs of children and men over their needs. Also, food insecurity can worsen in the weeks before the harvesting season, by when the meagre stocks have been exhausted.

However, hunger and malnutrition in Bundelkhand was a much more serious and widespread than usual in 2016. It surprises many people how hunger and malnutrition can exist despite many-sided interventions from the government in the form of rural employment guarantee schemes, special food subsidies and nutrition programmes. This is partly because of the poor implementation of the programmes, but even more so due to many-sided ecological ruin, linked to social inequalities and unjust practices by the dominant sections of society.

THE REGION OF BUNDELKHAND

The Bundelkhand region is located in the heart of India, between the Gangetic plains on the northern side and the Vindhya hills in the south. It is mainly a rural area, with nearly 80 per cent of the people living in villages. Only the city of Jhansi and the tourist towns of Orcha and Khajuraho are widely known outside of Bundelkhand. Its history is marked by remarkable achievements in water harvesting works on the one hand, and by acts of valour in opposing the colonial rule led by the famous Rani of Jhansi, on the other. Bundelkhand is spread over thirteen administrative districts in two states. Seven of these districts are in the state of Uttar Pradesh (Mahoba, Banda, Chitrakut, Hamirpur, Jhansi, Lalitpur and Jalaun) and six districts are in the state of Madhya Pradesh (Chattarpur, Tikamgarh, Panna, Datia, Damoh and Sagar). Taken together, these districts constitute the region of Bundelkhand, which spreads over 69,000 square kilometres and is inhabited by about 20 million people.

The region has been attracting frequent attention at the national level, but generally for all the wrong reasons. Firstly, there have been many instances of feudal injustice linked to the formation of armed gangs and their violence. This insecurity in villages has adversely affected development prospects. Secondly, there have been many reports of hunger, malnutrition and drinking water shortages. These in turn have been linked to frequent droughts and other adverse weather conditions such as hailstorms, floods and sandstorms.

In this deteriorating condition, governance should have been improved significantly to help the increasingly vulnerable people. Unfortunately, this did not happen and there have been many reports of corruption, careless implementation and inadequate allocations in the context of key schemes related to food security. As a result, the public distribution system of food grains, nutrition and health programmes as well as rural employment and livelihood programmes did not fulfil the expectations. High hopes arose when the government presented a special Bundelkhand package of various schemes for this region, but soon there were widespread allegations of corruption as well as careless spending all over again.

CLIMATE CHANGE AND LOCAL ECOLOGICAL RUIN

As the situation in Bundelkhand has deteriorated rapidly precisely during the time when climate change was prominent in the news, it is inevitable to attribute the adverse weather conditions in Bundelkhand to it as well. This relationship is valid, but at the same time it should not be used to divert attention from the various local aspects of ecological ruin which are clearly linked to deteriorating prospects of food security and sustainable agriculture. 'If you look at the earlier graphs of rainfall data in Bundelkhand, deficit rainfall in one year would soon be made up by a normal year. But in more recent years the tendency for several deficit years to be clustered together is evident', explains Bhartendu Prakash from *Vigyan Shiksha Kendra* (VSK), a voluntary organization working in the region.

However, Prakash stresses the importance of focusing on local, avoidable aspects of ecological ruin as well. As convenor of VSK, he coordinated a study with the Indian Institute of Technology (IIT) in New Delhi to prepare a detailed report on water resources of Bundelkhand. This report, *Problems and Potentials of Bundelkhand with Special Reference to Water Resource Base,* says: 'The situation as it stands today is extremely precarious. The forests have been thinned to near extinction and the undergrowth has stopped due to lack of moisture and shade.'[1] Calling this 'the greatest event of far-reaching consequences for Bundelkhand', the report laments its adverse impact on rainfall, rivers, groundwater recharge and soil fertility. Although this report was published in 1998, little has been done since then to counteract and the situation became even graver.

The depleted forest cover as well as the loss of traditional species of trees also had a harmful impact on food security. Several nutritious fruits, flowers, herbs and roots previously available in forests are now vanishing from the region. In normal years, this loss is felt particularly when the grain stocks of small farmers are exhausted just before the new harvest. In drought years when agricultural yield is much less, the disappearance of nutritious forest products has its worst impact. Some of the best forests of Bundelkhand flourished on hills, but they were destroyed by tree felling as well as indiscriminate mining. As the VSK report says,

> This mining flattened many hills and denuded them of forest cover, thereby disrupting the processes of interception of clouds for rainfall and infiltration of rainwater into the soil. Heavy sand mining has caused depletion and drying up of several rivers, accentuating greatly the threat from droughts.

Under these conditions, water conservation and water collection are badly needed in villages. Over the centuries, useful tanks and other rain water harvesting structures were created. But instead of maintaining and improving them with new scientific knowledge, recent decades witnessed a decay of this traditional infrastructure. This neglect led to an increasing dependence on the extraction of ground water, which resulted in a rapid lowering of the water table in many places and again aggravated the threat of droughts.

For centuries, this region had a mixed agricultural system and the farmers practised crop rotation with different plants suited to the agro-climatic conditions of Bundelkhand. They were capable of withstanding drought conditions naturally. For example, the *Kathia* variety of wheat was hardy and imbued with high nutrition and medicinal qualities. And the *Sathia* variety of rice could be ready in just 60 days, hence more capable of providing some yield in a year of difficult weather conditions. However, the neglect of these traditional crops and cropping patterns and their increasing replacement by outside varieties propagated by the so-called Green Revolution required more water and fertilizers, which proved harmful for soil quality and the water table.

The aggravation of drought conditions and people's vulnerability to adverse weather conditions are as much related to local factors of ecological ruin as they are to the wider phenomenon of climate change. Certainly, these changes have been so significant as to fundamentally disrupt the rural economy based on agriculture and animal husbandry. An inter-ministry team of the central government in New Delhi visited various parts of Bundelkhand and presented rainfall data to reveal very significant deviation from normal patterns, generally on the deficit side. Such deficit rain fall for a prolonged period of several years, as witnessed in Bundelkhand recently, is clearly different from the earlier droughts, which were limited to a much shorter time span.

However, the actual experience of farmers in several years has been even more devastating than what is suggested by the data.

This is due to increasing incidence of untimely rain: Whatever rain comes deviates from the well-established pattern to which cropping patterns are linked, thereby upsetting all the farming schedules. In 2015, for example, the well ripening winter crop of wheat, gram and mustard was abruptly destroyed completely due to heavy but untimely rains, accompanied by hailstorms at many places. This lasted from February to early April and was followed by a prolonged drought for the rest of the year. If you look at the total volume of rainfall in such a situation, it may be close to the average norm, but the uneven and untimely distribution actually makes the condition ruinous for farmers. Thus, while the *rabi* crop (winter crop) was destroyed by excess of rainfall, the *kharif* crop (summer crop) was ruined by drought. Furthermore, the next *rabi* crop could not be planted in most of the fields due to the prolonged drought. Another recent phenomenon is that rain may occur but remain restricted to a very small area. One village may receive much rain while a neighbouring village may remain entirely dry. Overall, the number of rainy days decreases and there is a tendency for the rainfall to occur over fewer days, including some of very heavy rainfall.

INEQUALITIES AND EXPLOITATION

In several villages of the Bundelkhand region, inequalities in land ownership are high. A significant part of the farmland is concentrated in the hands of a few families, while many others own very little or are completely landless. A more equitable distribution of land can certainly improve the food security of the weakest landless sections. However, the progress of land reforms has been poor except in a few areas where social activists have made sustained efforts.

+The voluntary organization *Akhil Bhartiya Samaj Sewa Sansthan* (ABSSS) made constant efforts in the Manikpur block of Chitrakut district. Gaya Prasad Gopal, the director of ABSSS said:

> When we started working here, many landless persons who had been allotted land were not aware of where exactly this land has been provided. Some were forcibly prevented from cultivating this land. In many cases, the landless workers had been reduced to working as bonded workers.

While sustained efforts for several years helped to improve the condition of indigenous people and their land rights in the Manikpur block, in many parts of Bundelkhand the denial of land rights to the weakest sections of society continues, leading to exploitation, food insecurity and hunger. During serious droughts, even some of the normally prosperous farmers face considerable difficulties. However, the business of moneylenders or *sahukars* continues to flourish as more and more people come to borrow money at extremely high rates of interest. This interest rate is often five per cent per month, but tends to go up further in situations of distress.

Raju Bhaiya, director of *Vidyadham Samiti*, another voluntary organization in Bundelkhand, said:

> In several villages, landless farm workers were forced into bonded worker type arrangements as they had not been able to return the loan taken at a very high rate of interest. Such exploitation led many of them to seek employment in distant areas as migrant workers. At the same time, the richer landowners resorted to higher mechanisation of farm work to reduce their dependence on farm workers. Consequently, there was less employment and more capital expenditure. The village community started to disintegrate and it became more difficult for all to work together for village's development and welfare.

Bhagwat Prasad from ABSSS agrees: 'On the one hand, exploitative relationships deny land and labour rights to the poor. On the other hand, such relationships make it more difficult to work together for the common good.'

During a year of normal rains and crops, a hunger death had been reported from a small village in Banda district. After the villagers reported their grievances in a group discussion, one landless worker said: 'The main question is why, if there is only enough food on the fields of just a few land users in the village, why is it not used first to combat the hunger of the village's people?'

This unjust and exploitative system is even crueller when it gets linked up with criminal groups. Some of the most powerful landowners and contractors derive a part of their power from their alignment with the notorious criminal gangs of the area. This further increases fear and insecurity in the village and creates conditions in which people's cooperation for long-term development tasks becomes very difficult.

GOVERNANCE PROBLEMS

Bundelkhand's problems have increased further due to poor governance at various levels, from policy failures to implementation problems. Bhartendu Prakash said:

> In two most important areas—water and agriculture—the technologies and development strategies propagated by the government were not consistent with the real needs of the region. The government has invested in several large dams, while the real need is for smaller water conservation projects. The most recent example for a wasteful use of funds in projects of dubious merit is the *Ken Betwa Link Project,* which aims to transfer water from a so-called surplus to a deficit river without first checking up the availability of surplus water. This project will waste scarce funds on a massive scale while messing up the water situation further, apart from causing displacement.

Braj Gopal, an expert on the water resources of the region, said:

> Such a big budget project with many serious impacts cannot be cleared at a time when important aspects have not been studies properly. There is a lot of evidence that the same budget, if reallocated for several smaller water conservation projects closely linked to the needs of villagers, will give much better results.

One initiative which was suitable for decentralized, low cost adoption in many villages was the *Mangal Turbine*. This turbine is an invention of Mangal Singh, a farmer and innovator from Lalitpur district, who also obtained a patent for it. This turbine makes it possible to lift water without any diesel or electricity just by using the power of flowing water. Hence it can help greatly to reduce the irrigation costs in many villages of Bundelkhand, as nothing more than a small river or rivulets is required close to the field. Moreover, its value is greatly enhanced in times of climate change as it holds great potential to reduce greenhouse gas emissions.

The first demonstration of the *Mangal Turbine* near Bhailoni Lodh village attracted many visitors from far and wide. Many senior experts and officials praised it and yet the innovation did not spread. Despite the attention on the turbine, the necessary support from the government never came. Mangal Singh struggled hard to spread his innovation, but he was subjected to harassment. He echoed these feelings when he said: 'Overgenerous budgets are available for those big projects from which a lot of money can be stolen, but not for the smaller projects like the one that I was trying to spread.'

Today, Bundelkhand is full of irrigation and water collection projects that were declared complete but have made very little, if any, contribution in helping farmers. Despite a lot of money being spent on these projects, there is still no adequate protection from drought. In some cases, development work already done before was declared as new work and money was collected again for it.

In contrast, when careful, well-planned work has been taken up by voluntary organizations for soil and water conservation, this has brought sustainable benefits. 'We have to learn from traditional wisdom while also adding modern scientific advances of a ridge to valley approach', explained Bhagwat Prasad. 'When we made such efforts with the involvement of indigenous people, then water could be retained in some tanks even at the time of severe drought.' The farmer Kodo Kol is a beneficiary of one such project in the Manikpur block. He said with a confident smile during the prolonged drought of 2015: 'I think that I'll still be able to get enough water from the tank we created in order to grow enough food for my family's needs.' In Chitrakut, Banda and other districts, there are several examples of farmers from the poorest communities benefiting from the watershed projects taken up by voluntary organizations. This shows what could have been achieved if the government funds had been utilized honestly and efficiently.

GOVERNMENT'S FOOD SECURITY SYSTEMS

The public distribution systems of food, the special nutrition schemes and the employment guarantee programmes are central to the government's effort to foster food security. The public distribution system had earlier been providing two grades of subsidized food grains (mainly wheat and rice) to 'below poverty line' (BPL) families and to the *antyodya* ('even poorer or poorest') households. In the first category, 35 kg food grain was provided for around 270 INR and in the second category for about 90 INR. This was substantially below the market rates. Despite leakages and corruption, many poor households benefited from this subsidy. However, many deprived families also complained that they had been left out of the food security net, while others less dependent on the subsidized food were getting it.

To improve the situation of hunger and malnutrition in the Indian countryside, the central government enacted the National Food Security Act in 2013. The act made it possible to include about 75 per cent of rural households in a single category of subsidized food beneficiaries. Through subsidization, the rates of wheat were reduced from 18 INR to 2 INR per kg and the rates of rice were reduced from 22 INR to 3 INR per kg. However, this subsidy is available only to the extent of 5 kg per family member and month. Consequently, a family of six members is entitled to get only 30 kg in one month. In a typical hard working rural family this food grain lasts only for about a week. During the remaining days of the month, they remain dependent on grains from the market where the prices keep on rising. The market price for pulses has been rising even faster, essentially making this staple source of protein out of the reach of an overwhelming majority of people.

Despite the special vulnerability of Bundelkhand, the implementation of the National Food Security Act has been delayed in the region. In the seven districts of Uttar Pradesh, the scheme officially started only as late as January 2016. However, even in the first week of February when this writer made inquiries in several villages, the subsidized wheat at the rate of 2 INR per kg reached only a very small part of the population. And even those who got these highly subsidized grains reported how the indicated number of family members in their cards had been reduced so that they were getting smaller rations than their entitlement.

The other important component of food security consists of nutrition programmes like the Integrated Child Development Services (ICDS) and mid-day meals in schools. They operate far below their potential of supplementing children's nutrition. One reason for this is corruption within the system: An ICDS worker reported on the condition of anonymity that she has to regularly give a part of her salary to her superiors in order to keep her job. Besides, there is pilferage at both programmes and the quality of the mid-day meal can be quite poor at times. But on the whole, such programmes make at least some contribution to food and nutrition security in villages, particularly in situations of serious drought. However due to budgetary problems in 2015, there were disruptions in the supply of nutritious food (*panjiri*) to ICDS centres. In particular the supply of food for adolescent girls under the empowerment programme SABLA was disrupted. Latest enquiries in early 2016 revealed that this is now being improved.

In this context, the much discussed National Rural Employment Guarantee Act (NREGA) from 2005 is obviously important as it entitles any needy villager, at least on paper, to get employment in or near the village. The authorities have a legal responsibility to provide him or her employment for 100 to 150 days in a year at the prevailing minimum wage rate. The programme has also suffered from budgetary constraints and the performance of NREGA in the Bundelkhand region has been worse compared to the Indian average.

During the period of extreme drought in 2015, inquiries revealed that NREGA work had only a marginal presence in most of the villages or did not even exist at all. During this period of acute distress, youths were constantly leaving the villages in search of work. The absence of NREGA's support during this critical period was very disappointing. It was only in early 2016 that NREGA work in several villages increased, although this expansion still did not meet the demand. Additionally, long delays in payment of wages distressed most of the workers. For example at the main NREGA work site in Nibhi village of Banda district, no payment had been made even after one and a half months. When in fact, wages should be settled within at most fifteen days. One women working at the site shared: 'We leave home hungry in the morning and work till noon when some children bring a few *rotis* with salt for us. Sometimes we just chew a few leftovers and sleep.'

Such a situations could have been avoided easily by timely payments. In the villages of Manikpur and Mau of the Chitrakut district, many people complained that payments for minor irrigation or other public works under NREGA had not been made even for the last two to three years. In Pachara village of Mahoba district, women said that they needed lighter work. This statement has to be understood in the context of hunger and malnutrition, which greatly weakened the villagers, particularly women. Urmila complained: 'We have been given the work of digging rocky land at considerable depth and then carrying soil and rocks for a long distance. If some lighter work is given and wages are paid promptly for a day's work, we'll benefit considerably.'

Drought relief works used to start soon after the declaration of drought, but now due to the NREGA scheme, no further drought relief work was done this year. Various problems with the implementation of NREGA cause difficulties and distress. In such a situation, drought relief work should be introduced in addition to NREGA work to ensure timely payments and relief to the drought-affected people. The entire food security system needs considerable improvement to cope with increasing challenges.

PRESENT DAY SITUATION OF HUNGER

All the factors mentioned above have contributed to the present day situation of extreme distress. In most villages, over 90 per cent of rural families cannot get basic, nutritionally-adequate food consisting of a main cereal (wheat *rotis* and to a lesser extent some rice) with pulses, vegetable, some milk and fruits in an adequate amount regularly. Pulses, once the staple source of proteins, have become a rare treat and the milk yield of starving dairy animals has been reduced to a trickle. So children generally do not get any milk and the inadequate supply of nutritious food from ICDS and mid-day meals is the only help.

In a normal agricultural year, all farmers have some stocks of food grains (mainly wheat and rice) and pulses (usually lentils) in their homes. These crops also provide fodder for farm and dairy animals, so that some milk is available. Often the stocks of grains and pulses don't last for the entire year, and the weeks before the new harvest are usually the most difficult. If this period of shortage is confined to just a few weeks, it can be overcome as farmers find some temporary substitutes. They eat, for example, the leaves of gram and mustard crops or of the green *bathua* (*Chenopodium album*), which grows freely as a weed and is very nutritious. However, this entire system of local food security does not exist today anymore. In the case of about 90 per cent of village households, there are no stocks of home-grown cereals and pulses.

Hence there is a near total dependency on food purchased from the market. The subsidized grains of the new food security act still reach only a small number of households and last for only a week anyway.

If a typical family of six members has to eat food in accordance with the nutrition requirements, they have to purchase 5 kg of wheat at 90 INR as well as pulses, vegetables, oil, spices and sugar adding up to around 110 INR per day. In total, at least 200 INR are needed daily in the present situation to provide the minimum of satisfactory nutrition to a family. However, this is less than the day's wage of a worker in the village or the nearest town. Sometimes even if two weak family members work together, they are not able to earn this amount. And in this frugal estimate of pulses, vegetables, oil and spices, we have not even included milk, tea-leaves or fruits.

But food is just one component of many pressing expenses. Just one serious illness or injury can lead to an expense equivalent to several days of food expenses as access to public health care is very limited in Bundelkhand. Moreover, people also live under the avoidable social burden of ceremonial and marriage expenses, which cause a lot of tension and postponement of marriages.

In such a situation, it is easy to understand why very high levels of hunger and malnutrition exist in Bundelkhand's villages. Even to sustain one's life at such a minimum level, loans have to be taken. When asked the simple question if many families in a village were indebted, the answer usually was 'almost everyone'. Some of the debts are owed to government banks (mainly rural banks), while another substantial share of loans is owed to private money lenders who charge very high interest rates.

In both cases, the repayment of loan instalments and interest payments generate a lot of tension. A family may have to cut costs further because of loan repayment, thus aggravating hunger even further. Banks may start legal proceedings against them and private money lenders generally resort to very rude methods to get back their money. In some cases, effective control of the farmer's land may pass on to the moneylender or else the debtor and his family may have to toil in bondage-like conditions. All this leads to long term deprivation and hunger.

One important coping mechanism in such difficult situations is to migrate to distant places like Surat, Rajkot, Mumbai or Delhi in search of work. Some workers who succeed in finding adequate positions are able to provide the badly needed support to their families or may even manage to add to their assets. But there are far more reports of workers having to return to their village with diseases or injuries or after being duped of their wages. Still, due to large scale deprivation, railway stations in Bundelkhand remain crowded with workers—and often their families—leaving for distant places in highly uncertain conditions. Elderly family members necessarily need to stay behind and remain highly exposed to hunger, malnutrition and even thirst, as it very hard to obtain drinking water during droughts. Kind neighbours help as much as they can, but as everyone is facing extreme deprivation, such neighbourly help may become less frequent. Hence, there is an increasing need for community kitchens to support such elderly persons. Such kitchen could be linked to the large-scale cooking already being done for mid-day meals or taken up as a separate initiative.

Women in families of migrant workers with small children and elderly members to support also face increasing difficulties for survival. The number of widows in some villages is also alarmingly high. Many of them do not receive any regular pension and even when they get some social security payments, they are very meagre. Women generally eat after all other family members and in a situation of serious food shortage, little food is left for them. Moreover, prejudices against women persist and they are often seen to be very weak. On top of this, domestic violence and unjust treatment of daughters-in-law in joint families further aggravate the situation of women.

Bundelkhand has several vulnerable communities such as the indigenous peoples *Kol* and *Sahariya* tribals or marginalized caste groups like the *Basor* and other Dalits (formerly known as 'Untouchables'). These and many other vulnerable communities have been in news repeatedly in the context of hunger and deprivation and policy measures geared specifically towards their requirements need to be developed. At the same time one must not forget that during serious droughts, even many of those households become vulnerable which usually do not suffer from hunger. For example in the *kharif* (summer) season of 2015, even these households experienced high losses when their crops shrivel and did not give any yield even though the land had been well sown.

Recent surveys undertaken by voluntary organizations like *Vidyadham Samiti*, *Swaraj Abhiyan* and *Parmarth* have confirmed very high levels of malnutrition and hunger in various districts of Bundelkhand. Children especially suffer badly in such situations, particularly when they accompany their parents in search of migrant work. Some of them have to toil in unhealthy conditions, while other children are at least admitted to school in the new areas of work, but often cannot adjust to the unfamiliar surroundings. After some time, many of them drop out of school because of poverty or the need to look after smaller children and grandparents at home.

Another serious problem is the grave shortage of fodder for animals. Much of it used to come from crop residues, but with the failure of crops there is hardly any fodder as well. As Prem Narayan, a farmers' leader from Lavkush Nagar in Chattarpur district, explains: 'Despite shortage of rain, some farmers planted the *rabi* crop in the hope that they will at least get some fodder. But the crop growth has been so retarded that even fodder availability will not be much.' The overall decline of moisture has meant that grass growth is very low. The government has provided some meagre support in the form of fodder distribution, but this is far too little to make any significant impact on the overall situation. The price of *bhusa* (dry fodder) has increased between 750 and 1,500 INR per 100 kilograms in various places and thereby almost approached the price of grain. People who cannot afford food for themselves cannot be expected to buy fodder for cattle at such high prices. So the cattle are left more or less on their own to find fodder and water. As a result, hungry and thirsty farm animals have been dying in large numbers. Mortality rates of farm animals far above the usual rates are being reported from several villages.

In addition, there are indications of human deaths significantly above the average of previous years in some villages. For instance in villages like Naugavaan and Kyotra in Naraini block, group discussions brought up many references to recent deaths and to the problems of widows. Such reports by the villagers need to be examined through more extensive surveys over a wider area. Often, the official figures are not very reliable in many places. As senior officials generally deny any hunger deaths in their locality, the Uttar Pradesh state government announced that district magistrates will be held responsible for any such deaths.

The increasing number of farmers committing suicide in recent years is another disturbing development. In many cases, it is the combination of extreme deprivation and indebtedness which drove the farmers into desperation. Their widows face a plethora of problems. Mannu Lal was a farmer of Oran village, who could not get employment after migrating to a faraway metropolitan area. When he returned home, he found his crop was destroyed, too. One morning, he climbed a tall eucalyptus tree in his courtyard and hanged himself to death before bystanders could do anything. When I visited his family some months later, his relatives and neighbours told me how despite several promises by the government, nobody provided any help to them. Most families of trauma death and suicide cases continue to face a lot of problems. Abhishek Mishra, director of the voluntary organization *Arunodya* in Mahoba district, regularly visits families of suicide victims. He explains their situation: 'At one time, hopes were raised by the government and we worked hard to collect information about those families who needed help. But most of the families were left in the lurch.'

FUTURE PROSPECTS

Although almost everyone agrees that the situation of hunger, insecurity and related distress is very serious, it does not appear that adequate preparations have been made to tackle these challenges. Normally, the harvest of *rabi* crops in April brings joy to the villages. But in 2016, this crop was only harvested in the irrigated pockets, which make up around one-fourth of the cultivated land. And even there, the yield per acre was much lower than normal. Only if weather conditions are favourable later in the year, farmers are able to grow their *kharif* crops and receive some relief around November. Therefore, the absence of home-grown food persists at least until the end of the year. Bundelkhand is known for its remorseless summer and serious drinking water shortages occur even during normal years. After the prolonged drought in 2016, scarcity became more acute and widespread. Moreover, this drought combined with a shortage of fodder for animals posed a very serious challenge, particularly as cattle mortality was already high.

To tackle this precarious situation, the government needs to implement some decisive policy reform. First, NREGA needs to be scaled up significantly, prompt payments to the workers must be ensured and the programme needs to be supported by other drought-relief projects. Second, the Food Security Act should be implemented rigorously and its reach expanded further in order to reach all those people in need. Third, plans on the village and *Panchayat* level should be prioritized to meet drinking water, food and fodder needs of farmers and their animals. Such plans prepared by the villagers themselves must be a priority under

NREGA. Fourth, all existing and potential water sources should be mapped carefully in order to optimally use the limited resources and save lives. Moreover, water storage units can be installed near bore wells so that cattle can quench their thirst. Similarly, fodder camps can be initiated. Fifth, the government needs to cooperate more closely with voluntary organizations. For example during the severe drought of 1980–1981, this worked quite successfully and they jointly implemented relief projects in the Manikpur block. Such cooperation will also contribute to a broader inclusion of the population of Bundelkhand, including people from urban areas, into relief work. Already, some voluntary organizations led by example and started seed banks in several villages to make food grains easily available to the neediest people.

However, more basic changes within the development paradigm towards equality, justice and ecological regeneration are needed for long-term sustainable development of Bundelkhand. With these basic precepts as the foundation for development, both traditional wisdom and latest scientific advances should be harnessed to find solutions which are in tune with the geographical and agro-ecological conditions of Bundelkhand. Village communities should be united on the basis of justice and equality to realize the great untapped development potential. Agro-ecological farming can be a most important component of this initiative to eliminate hunger and malnutrition.

There are already some successful examples for organic farming, natural water harvesting or sustainable soil and water conservation projects. In the Manikpur block, ABSSS successfully combined water harvesting work with land reforms. Based on VSK's experimental farming in Terahi Maafi village of Banda district, Bhartendu Prakash has been advocating organic farming in Bundelkhand for a long time. In Chattarpur district, the successful organic agriculture at Gandhi Farms provided practical alternatives and gave new hope to many farmers. Another example is Mangal Singh's device for lifting water, which can further contribute to reduce production costs and promote eco-friendly agriculture. Of course, such small efforts will have to be multiplied many times before they can make a significant impact on the entire region. Hence, these eco-friendly and justice-based principles realized on the ground need to serve as example for policy changes on the larger level.

SUMMARY

Bundelkhand, a region comprising of thirteen districts in central India, regularly experiences extreme hunger and malnutrition. In 2016, the situation aggravated further due to an extensive drinking water crisis and a very serious shortage of fodder for animals. There was a sharp decline in the availability of main cereals wheat and rice and even more so in the staple sources of protein: pulses and milk products. The mortality rate for farm and dairy animals was already way above the average rate and a significant number of farmer suicides and trauma deaths were reported. To avoid such casualties in the future, a lot of efforts must be taken now.

In Bundelkhand, hunger exists even if the weather conditions are normal. The major reasons behind it are the massive social inequalities and the prevailing injustice. However, the extreme situation of 2016 resulted from highly erratic weather for several years, culminating in a prolonged and serious drought in 2015. Such conditions have to be understood in the wider context of global climate change. But at the same time, the role of local ecological ruin caused by deforestation, indiscriminate mining and over-extraction of water must not be forgotten.

This time of crisis revealed again that the government's food security system functions much below its potential. Improvements in the food security system as well as in the overall governance of social support programmes are needed to increase their efficiency and to curb wide-spread corruption. Women, children, old and disabled people, without any support are most vulnerable, but also middle-aged household heads with family responsibilities are highly exposed to stress and are vulnerable to trauma. In the case of Dalits, most of them are not getting local work and have migrated. Despite growing consciousness and assertiveness at several places the overall condition of Dalits remain precarious and in recent years the programme of land distribution among them has not progressed at all. These vulnerable sections of the population need to be given special attention when making policy decisions.

NOTE

1. Prakash, B., S. Satya, S.N. Ghosh and L.P. Chourasia. (1998). *Problems and Potentials of Bundelkhand with Special Reference to Water Resource Base.* New Delhi: Indian Institute of Technology, Centre for Rural Development and Technology.

Agriculture, Livelihood, and Well-Being of Indigenous Communities in Odisha

Analysis and Policy Imperatives

Achyut Das

Achyut Das is a writer and activist based in Rayagada district of Odisha. He is the founder of *Agragamee* the non-governmental organization and has worked there since 1981 focussing on 'food and voice'. *Agragamee* means to ensure food security for the most vulnerable communities and to empower them with the awareness and skills to check their exploitation and to sustainably manage their natural resource base.

Introduction

Nutrition, more than anything else, indicates the state of wellbeing of people, a community and a nation. Indian populations have been exhibiting significantly high levels of under-nutrition across different ages, which has been a cause for much concern for the last decade and more. Several bilateral and multilateral efforts, as well as initiatives by the United Nations and private corporate agencies are stepping in to address this enduring problem.

India has one of the largest pre-school nutrition programmes in the world, in addition a whole series of support schemes for older age-groups. Especially vulnerable groups like adolescent girls, pregnant and lactating women as well as the elderly have also been included in the group of beneficiaries to address malnutrition. All this has been further consolidated under the National Food Security Act (NFSA). Moreover, several states have put in their resources making essential grains and pulses available at low prices universally.

The eastern state of Odisha had made rice from the Public Distribution System (PDS) universally available in the so called KBK districts of South and West Odisha, named after the Kalahandi Balangir Koraput region. The eight KBK districts are Malkangiri, Koraput, Nabrangpur, Kalahandi, Rayagada, Nuapada, Balangir and Sonepur. Before the introduction of the NFSA, they were known all over the country for their poverty and underdevelopment. But how much difference has all this made?

According to UNESCO's Global Monitoring Report 2007, 47 per cent of India's Children are malnourished.[1] As per the National Family Health Survey, 39 per cent of rural women in the age-group of 15–49 suffer from chronic energy deficiency and 58 per cent are anaemic. Among rural children in the age group between six and

35 months, 81 per cent are anaemic, 41 per cent are stunted and 20 per cent suffer from wasting. The complex Human Development Index of 2014, also underlines India's dismal position at 130 out of 188 countries, behind many of our Asian neighbours, such as Malaysia, Thailand and Sri Lanka.[2]

Needless to underline that the reasons for this are manifold and complex. It became increasingly apparent that food schemes only scratch the surface of this multi-layered problem. On the other hand, agricultural production is increasingly failing to provide any kind of nutritional security to rural communities, as the spread of commercial farming has significantly reduced the arable area under food crops. Furthermore, small and marginal farmers who stick to traditional cropping are pushed to the edge of survival due to fluctuating and diminishing production. Much of agriculture in the country is unsustainable and leads to erosion and destruction of valuable agricultural land. In response, a small number of farmers in different corners of the country are taking to organic and traditional farming techniques. There is also a rising outcry against the excessive domination of the market forces, and the increasing push for genetically engineered crops. Farmer groups are also networking to counter the market forces and promote traditional seeds and agriculture, which is further driven by the consumers' awareness and demand for organic foods.

Much of this din however, does not reach the hinterlands, where farmers continue to be trapped by different oppressive forces, including seeds agents, labour traffickers, and other vested interests. While there is awareness about the dangers of excessive commercialization amongst the indigenous community, poverty, food insecurity, and an extreme paucity of choices make the indigenous farmer easy prey for different forces of exploitation.

It goes without saying that agriculture and nutrition are closely interlinked, especially in a country like India, where two-thirds of the population still live in rural areas. This makes the challenge all the bigger, as there are no easy quick-fix solutions. What could be the way out?

INDIGENOUS AGRICULTURE AND LAND USE

Agragamee's extensive and long involvement with farmers in the rural areas has underlined the lack of easy solutions. Several indigenous farmers themselves have burnt their fingers with commercial farming and are looking for alternatives now. Domburu Saunta from Dhepaguda village is one of them. He describes his experience with non-traditional crops provided by the government (Hindi: *sarkar*): 'I used to cultivate *sarkari* maize. We had to pay 1,200 Rupees for the seeds. Then, you have to pay for the fertilizers and pesticide sprays. In total one has to spend around 12,000 to 15,000 Rupees per acre (around 4,000 square metres). We don't even calculate the cost of our labour for the crop. In the first year, I got around 25,000 Rupees for my crop. However, the second year I got much less, and in the third year, I suffered a complete loss. So I have completely given up the cultivation of this commercial maize, and now I grow *ragi*, and other traditional millets. The production is less, but one does not have to suffer a loss, like I did with the maize.'

Domburu Saunta is not the only one in Dhepaguda village in Digi Gram Panchayat of Nabrangpur district who had a bad run with commercial maize cultivation. Almost everybody in the village used to cultivate maize until 2014–2015. And almost everyone has given it up now. Daimati Saunta, a local ward member, provides an explanation: 'People used to grow crops they could consume before. Then, this person who is a complete outsider came to the village and he started promoting commercial maize. He gained out of people's loss and even mortgaged their gold and silver. Now, people have lost their crop and the productivity of their land is also gone.' And she concludes: 'This man has become rich!'

Agriculture in the districts of South Odisha has become increasingly unproductive, and farmers are moving away from traditional crops. In some cases they have taken to maize, in other cases, it is eucalyptus, vegetables, fruit crops like mango and lychee or spices like ginger. In several instances, indigenous farmers lease out their lands to outsiders, who invest for coffee, cashew, black pepper, and other high value crops. The rates of distress migration have been increasing from year to year. Much of the seasonal farming is unsustainable or fetches very poor returns in the market, forcing farmers to revert back to traditional crops, like Domburu Saunta and his fellow cultivators in Dhepaguda. In several instances, people have cut down fruit orchards to revert back to subsistence cultivation.

In a programme supported by the International Fund for Agricultural Development (IFAD) for so-called tribal development in Kashipur block, extensive fruit orchards were planted, with grafted mangoes for uplands, and cashew for hill slopes. In a few years' time however, more than 90 per cent of these orchards were gone, and farmers were back to shifting cultivation and slash and burn. The lure of the commercial crops is irresistible when returns diminish in the districts mainly populated by indigenous people. Returns from such crops are a quantum jump from traditional cultivation, giving 25,000 INR and more per acre in just cash. This only compares to the first year of upland slash and burn cultivation, as the ash from the burning of heavy growth of scrub and bushes on a hill slope left fallow for six to seven years is very rich. The farmer is able to cultivate eight to 12 crops in one field, and get a bountiful return that sustains the family throughout the year. However, the subsequent year, the yield falls by more than 75 per cent, and often such uplands cannot be cultivated after two continuous years due to the erosion and leaching of the soil. Over the years, even the slash and burn areas have become barren and do not recover their scrub and vegetation for up to 10 to 12 years.

The traditional cultivation practices of the indigenous communities—also called *Adivasi* (first inhabitants)—sustained a wide variety of crops and cropping systems. They include several varieties and species of millets, including finger, fox tail and proso millets, the more common ones such as pearl millet or sorghum, and even the most exquisite varieties of scented rice, as well as the more hardy and draught resistant upland paddy and a range of pulses and oil seeds. Along with the wild fruits and roots from the forests, this provided the rich and varied diet of the indigenous people. Women were the keepers and nurturers of this form of agriculture, preserving the seeds, processing and storing the harvests, planning the daily menus, and also the selling and barter of grain in keeping with the family needs for additional requirements.

According to 'The State of the Adivasis in Odisha 2014' report, approximately 5,300 square kilometres of land in Odisha is under shifting cultivation.[3] The report points out that in its traditional form where the rotational cycles used to be long, shifting cultivation did not have an adverse impact. It is commonly understood that due to increase in the population of those dependent on it, this form of cultivation caused ecological imbalance. Most of the indigenous people also buy into the idea that increasing population is a major cause of the problem. However, the nuclear family sizes in the area is just 4 to 4.5 on average. Also the population census figures show negative growth trends for the regions, districts and communities populated by Adivasis.

The reasons are more complex than just higher population density in an extensively shifting-cultivated region. A glimpse into Adivasi history indicates that the major factor is the loss of forest cover. Even now, indigenous communities are forest dwellers. Shifting cultivation in small clearings in the middle of forests only supplemented their mainly forest-based diets, which was their major subsistence. The large-scale destruction of forests has severely affected the livelihood systems of the local communities and set into motion a downward spiral of diminishing returns. This trend has been further aggravated by land alienation and the imposition of private land tenurial systems on the traditional systems of collectively-owned territories. After independence, a complex series of changes has been set into motion in the *Adivasi* regions, which have had multiple implications for indigenous life and livelihoods.

Over the last two decades, the indigenous communities have also borne the brunt of the country's push for economic growth, at the cost of basic rights and constitutional provisions. In a state like Odisha, these communities form nearly one-fourth of the total population. And yet, they receive the least administrative attention, and programmes of development and welfare rarely impact the needs and deprivation in these regions.

Poverty is most severe in southern Odisha. While more than two-thirds of the people in this region are classified as living below the poverty line (BPL), less than one-third of those living in the north-eastern coastal areas of the state are living in such a state. It is noteworthy that districts with higher percentages of Adivasi population have higher BPL figures. The correlation of poverty and health is underscored by the overall picture of health and wellbeing of the indigenous communities. The National Family Health Survey by the central government reports the highest levels of infant mortality, neonatal mortality, child mortality and under-five mortality amongst Adivasi. The incidence of anaemia is also highest amongst Adivasi children in the age group of six to 35 months. The 2011 HUNGaMA report by the Naandi Foundation indicates that the maximum proportion of stunted, wasted and underweight children is to be found in the districts of Malkangiri, Koraput and Rayagada as poverty, food and nutrition and health are closely related.[4]

Moreover, landlessness amongst Adivasis is very high. Different studies show that the majority of Adivasi households have less than one acre of land and around one-third are completely landless. At the same time, around three thirds of the land in the districts under examination are categorized as government land. This covers almost half the forest area of the region. In effect, more than 90 per cent of the rural households have legal titles to less than ten per cent of the land.

Much of this can be attributed to the limited or biased interpretation of the existing acts. For example, the Orissa Government Land Settlement Act, 1962 (OGLSA) treats uplands as uncultivable wastelands and therefore 'objectionable' for purposes of utilizing them for agriculture.[5] The uncultivable wastelands were not to be given out for agriculture but could be settled for other purposes. Thus, the Act did not allow for the lands under shifting cultivation by indigenous farmers to be settled in their names.

The Orissa Prevention of Land Encroachment Act, 1972 (OPLEA), regulates eviction or regularization of encroachments on government land. In the case of encroachments on revenue wastelands, only landless persons were eligible for allotment of 'unobjectionable' land for agriculture.[6] The act requires formal recognition and reporting of encroachment by the revenue inspector, and for the *tehsildar* (tax inspector) to initiate due proceedings to settle the claim of the landless encroacher to 'non-objectionable' land (Section 7(a, b)). There are negligible or no incentives for these officials to settle such claims. Frequently, bribes are demanded and the people are threatened with eviction if the demands are not met. The OGLSA also allows for the land to be used for development projects, industries, state or private bodies. This can be done without the mandate of the concerned village community.

GOVERNMENT EFFORTS AND PROGRAMMES

The government has introduced a series of policies and legislations to address the complex problems of the Adivasi communities, including improving the agriculture policy, introducing the Agriculture Technology Management Agency (ATMA), and strengthening rice and maize production under the Second Green Revolution.

In 2008, the Odisha Government revised and expanded the scope of the State Agriculture Policy to cover many other aspects of cultivation. According to the government,

> The State Agriculture Policy 2008 served Odisha well, and stimulated the growth of private lift irrigation and agro industries. More than 100,000 lift irrigation points were established and the state saw the growth of many new agro-based industries. Farm mechanisation reached new heights; the number of tractors sold to the farmers increased from less than 200 tractors in 1999/2000 to more than 5,000 in 2011/2012. Odisha became the largest consumer of power tillers. A sustained and vigorous growth was maintained in agriculture.[7]

According to the government, the Agricultural Policy 2013 was another step in this direction. This policy focuses on four major areas—seeds, irrigation, nutrient and pest management as well as farm mechanization. In its paper *State Agriculture Policy 2013*, the Agriculture Department of Odisha laid out the following points.

Seeds

Recognising that seeds are one of the most important inputs to boost agricultural productivity, the state government plans a slew of measures to increase seed production. This includes the promotion and support of private seed entrepreneurs, to strengthen the Odisha State Seed Corporation, to establish seed processing plants along with storage facilities in every district and to expand seed distribution through local cooperatives. Keeping other inputs of production constant, the quality seeds alone can increase the production to the extent of nearly 20 per cent.

Irrigation

Similarly, all support is envisaged for ensuring availability of timely and adequate supply of water. The measures include immediate steps to complete on-going irrigation projects, encouraging rain water harvesting, renovation of traditional irrigation tanks and subsidies for community lift irrigation projects up to 90 per cent in *Adivasi* areas.

Integrated Nutrient and Pest Management

The integrated and balanced use of fertilizers will be encouraged. All natural and man-made sources of plant nutrients required for high agricultural productivity will be integrated besides ensuring the sound health of soil. State will endeavour to promote integrated nutrient and pest management practices in a big way through suitable programs and incentives. The State will take steps to place the necessary infrastructure to enable direct transfer of fertilizer subsidy to the farmers. The State will also take steps, using information technology, to monitor the sale of fertilizers to ensure that it is not diverted for illegal purposes. Farmers will be able to learn about the stock position of the dealers in a transparent way.

Farm Mechanization

Farm mechanization brings a significant improvement in agricultural productivity in a number of ways. The timeliness of various agricultural operations is crucial in obtaining optimal yield, which is possible only through mechanization. Second, the quality and precision of the operations are equally significant for realising higher yield. The various operations such as land levelling, irrigation, sowing and planting, use of fertilizer, plant protection, harvesting and threshing need a high degree of precision to increase the efficiency of the inputs as well as to reduce the losses. Farm mechanization also goes a long way in reducing the drudgery of agricultural operations. With mechanization, there are good chances to reduce the cost of production resulting in higher margin of profit.

Furthermore, we will look at two other initiatives introduced by the government to improve agriculture production, which are the establishment of an Agriculture Technology Management Agency (ATMA) and the Odisha Tribal Empowerment and Livelihoods Program.

Agricultural Technology Management Agency (ATMA)

Taking forward the successful pilot for extensions reforms, the central government has launched Agricultural Technology Management Agencies (ATMA) in seven states to support extension programmes in 2005 and 2006. This was subsequently revamped and expanded under the 12th Five Year Plan (2012 to 2017) to integrate the National Agriculture Research System and the various *Krishi Vigiya Kendras* (KVK). Those government institutions have the aim to strengthen district level planning using technology to reach out to the farmers. In Odisha, thirteen districts including Khurda, Koraput, Ganjam, Sambalpur, Jagatsinghpur, Balasore, Keonjhar, Mayurbhanj, Sundargarh, Dhenkanal, Bolangir, Khandhamal and Naupara have been taken under ATMA. The scheme aims at making the extension system farmer-driven, accountable to farmers and more participatory by disseminating technology through new institutional arrangements like ATMA at the district level.

ATMA guidelines mentioned the following key extension reforms: (1) Facilitating convergence of farmer centric programmes in planning, execution and implementation; (2) Ensuring an integrated, broad-based extension delivery mechanism consistent with farming system approach with a focus on bottom up planning process; (3) Encouraging multi-agency extension strategies involving Public/Private Extension Service Providers; (4) Adopting group approach to extension in line with the identified needs and requirements of the farmers in the form of CIGs &

FIGs and consolidate them as Farmers Producer Organizations; (5) Addressing gender concerns by mobilising farm women into groups and providing training to them.

ATMA seeks to reach the farmer through well planned institutional mechanisms at state, district, block, and village levels. The Second Green Revolution has sought to improve rice production, and help farmers move away from the low yielding subsistence cropping practices. The Horticulture Mission has also introduced plantations in different districts through the National Rural Employment Guarantee Act (NREGA), enabling *Adivasi* farmers to develop permanent plantations as an alternative to shifting cultivation.

Odisha Tribal Empowerment and Livelihoods Program (OTELP)

Several special programs were devised to address the needs of India's indigenous population in particular, like the Odisha Tribal Empowerment and Livelihood Programme (OTELP) have also been taken up for the *Adivasi* regions. The OTELP was taken up by a coalition of development partners including the British Department for International Development (DFID), the International Fund for Agricultural Development (IFAD), the World Food Programme (WFP) as well as the Government of India and Government of Odisha who expressed a common concern for the welfare and economic development of indigenous communities in India.

The strategy for this project worth around 80 million EUR focused on empowering the indigenous communities to enhance food security, increase incomes and improve the quality of their lives through efficient natural resource management, effective watershed management and improved agricultural practices. The programme was to adopt a 'watershed plus' approach using the watershed as the basic vehicle for natural resource management but with the scope to address broader livelihood issues of sustainability including savings and credit, access to resources, off-farm/non-farm income generation, issues related to non-timber forest products and the improvement of community infrastructure. The programme was also expected to work in partnership with the Government of Odisha to address policy issues relating to land and natural resource management. The WFP food assistance was designed to assist food insecure households to participate in and benefit from development initiatives.

But what has been the impact of all these measures like ATMA, OTELP and other development programs like the National Horticulture Missions and the Integrated Watershed Development Programme on *Adivasi* livelihoods? To what extent has poverty and distress amongst indigenous people been addressed?

FALLING AGRICULTURAL PRODUCTIVITY

In the district of Nabrangpur, many farmers like Domburu have switched to hybrid maize cultivation. In some villages they have discontinued it, while in others they wait for the new seeds promised by the agent. However, this maize does not form a part of their diet in any way. Most farmers have retained a small portion of their backyard to grow traditional maize and other local crop varieties. The rest of the land is used for commercial maize cultivation.

When asked who bought the maize, an answer was: 'The trader comes to our village and only buys the crop they told us to grow. This crop gives us income, so why should we not cultivate it?' That is a legitimate question, but Nageshwar Rao, a local farmer asked a different one: 'Why can't the traditional millets of the indigenous people be cultivated with the same amount of inputs? Then they would also give the same high yield.' This is a pertinent question, too. In getting people to cultivate commercial crops for the market, is it the food security of the Adivasi communities or the interests of the seed producing companies that is being promoted? If the commercial crops have led to better income, there is little sign of it in the villages in Nabrangpur: The children are as undernourished as ever and there is as much distress migration in these villages as we have seen anywhere else. The highly fluctuating yields of maize might provide the farmer with an income boost in some years, but there is little contribution to long term food security.

The conditions are similar in Gunupur and Rayagada blocks of Rayagada district, where farmers have completely switched from millets and pulses to cotton after they got reliable irrigation. However, the cultivation of cotton is a complete gamble. And even if the yield is good, farmers complain that the prices on the market will go down and, consequently, the revenue is again low. Even though an larger area has been brought under cotton over the last decade, the lack of market infrastructure disturbs proper pricing. In the absence of government encouragement for cultivation and sale, the traders of Andhra Pradesh and Tamil Nadu exploit the Adivasi farmers to procure cotton at very low prices by helping them with advance payments at the time of plantation and harvest. The farmers in Gunupur, however, are in a slightly better position than their counterparts elsewhere as the process of setting up government procurement centres in the area has begun. In Rayagada, however, though people have switched to cotton because of the increased income, women express much grief, as locally produced foods are no longer available and everything has to be purchased.

The situation in Titijhola village, in Lakhimpur block, Koraput district is particularly revealing. Lakhimpur is a region of stark contrasts. Towering hills lead to exquisite valleys where Adivasi communities have carved out paddy lands on the stream beds. These fertile fields shape the hopes and the dreams that define the contours of indigenous living. In Titijhola village, the abundance of water helps the farmers to cultivate twice or even thrice a year. But most of the traditional crops have been given up for commercial varieties, and people are now bound by the patterns of the market economy. Though the vegetables they produce are taken in truck loads to the urban markets of the state, the farmers themselves hardly make any profits. 'It is only because we do not count the value of our own labour, that we get any kind of profits,' the farmers say. 'In bad years, even that thin margin of profit is lost, and we have to depend on wage labour, for which we migrate to the nearby townships of Kakriguma and Koraput.'

The misfortune of poor markets for agricultural produce, coupled with the increasing uncertainty of the weather continues to dog indigenous farmers across the region. In Nuapada, the farmers brought their insect-affected stocks of paddy and dumped it in the middle of the meeting place. 'You tell us what to do with this!', they said. Between 40 to 60 per cent of their paddy crop has been affected by pest attacks, which not only drastically cut their production but also brought down the value of the crop in the market. None of the usual pesticides worked. This pest attack is because of excessive rains at the wrong time, the farmers explained. 'We will suffer a heavy loss, and will not even have enough to eat.' For many, the only option is migration to find work elsewhere.

The Odisha Government is the recipient of many National Awards for Agriculture Development. However, even the consumer needs are not internally met, and there are heavy imports of foods including fruits, vegetables, fish, eggs, pulses and edible oil from neighbouring states, as well from other countries. For example, the lentils and oil required for the Integrated Child Nutrition Scheme (ICDS) and mid-day meal are now imported from western Gujarat or other states. Edible oil is brought in even though traditional *sal* and *mohua* seeds grow in Odisha's forests and huge quantities of oilseeds, including groundnut, mustard, linseed and sesame are cultivated in the state. The lack of local processing capacities results in most agricultural produce going out of the state in the raw form. When imported back in packaged form, the goods are out of reach for the poor in terms of availability as well as price.

However, such items can be easily produced and marketed locally, provided there is adequate infrastructure for production, processing, storage and marketing. This is perhaps, more than anything else, the major flaw in the government's programmes and policies, and indicative for the state of agriculture in the whole state of Odisha.

Despite the effects of global climate change in India, the Adivasi areas of Odisha still have climatic conditions conducive to a wide range of agricultural and horticultural production. The traditional crops of the indigenous people are suited to these conditions, and can not only provide food and nutrition security but also livelihood security. However, the government has neglected these areas, despite the persistence of extreme forms of hunger, distress and deprivation. Even as the regions are known for starvation deaths and large scale migration, the Adivasi also have a strong sense of contentment with their land. 'We don't need anything from outside except salt and kerosene', is a saying that prevails in the lands of the *Kondh* community.

SMALL FARMERS NEED TO BE SAVED!

As far as Adivasis and *Dalits* are concerned, government programmes to support nutrition and health had little impact, even if they include special provisions for small children, adolescent girls or pregnant women. The prevalence of low body weight remains the highest amongst those communities, although it must be noted that the problem is worse among Dalit children.

A survey done by *Agragamee* in 1,000 villages across ten districts and 20 blocks revealed that under the NREGA scheme, out of 954 villages, 265 received no work, and 63 villages received no payment for work.[8] Thus, 328 villages or 34 per cent of villages surveyed received no benefit from NREGA. Almost 50 per cent of the villages surveyed report incomplete work. One-third of the villages surveyed have received less than two weeks work. When it comes to the Integrated Child Nutrition Scheme (ICDS), only 83 per cent of the villages have *Anganwadi* or Outreach Centres available at a distance of less than one kilometre. Nine percent of the villages surveyed have no centres at all. Each of the programmes mentioned has institutionalized mechanisms for people's participation and involvement. Yet, people know little about these programmes.

The plethora of issues outlined above is not unique to the Adivasis of Odisha. This is rather the situation of indigenous farmers in many parts of the country as well as small and indigenous farmers all over the world. Climate change, modern day technologies, the pressures of the market, and a failed global economy that disregards the work of the food producers have destroyed farming systems and impoverished communities to the point of starvation. All over the world, people realize the urgency to protect local communities of farmers because of the immensely rich biodiversity of their crops, their highly evolved knowledge systems and their low carbon foot print which provide an example for others to follow.

Agragamee has been working with indigenous farmers for more than a decade now, and we helped them rebuild their production systems in innovative ways to meet the need for increased cash income, while also improving the production of indigenous crops. *Agragamee's* programme with Adivasi women helped them to reclaim their commons and rebuild family farms on rain-fed uplands. Together with the indigenous women's group *Ama Sangathan*, we helped indigenous communities in 100 villages rejuvenate degraded wastelands and reclaim them for plantations. This could pave the way for autonomous eco-villages, which could recreate Mahatma Gandhi's dream of village self-governance, or *Gram Swaraj*.

The programme for watershed development in 150 villages helped indigenous communities to take up soil and water conservation measures. Much more importantly, people also learnt the basics of soil and water conservation which contributed to impeding the destruction of more than 5,000 hectares of uplands. More recently, *Agragamee* has taken up work with small farmers to help them create family farms that can provide livelihood security through integrated crop systems by combining subsistence and cash cropping. These technologies don't need much external input and strengthen autonomy and sustainability of the farms. These activities provided *Agragamee* with broad experiences in the field of alternative modes of agriculture and this knowledge can be put into practice to help farmers design their own sustainable and viable land use systems.

We need a landscape approach which recognizes the interconnections of the Adivasi people and their environment. This would identify the different ecosystem services that a community requires and helps them to plan for an integrated solution. The pivotal role of women as keepers of the ecosystem would be emphasized and their perceptions, needs and priorities would be factored in. At the same time, the community as a whole would be promoted through trainings, exposures, and dialogues to improve the governance of their natural resources, with focus on equity and sustainability. At the policy level, we need more focus on retaining and promoting local seed varieties, prioritizing farmers' needs and respecting their knowledge. This should go hand in hand with local capacity building so that the development of improved seed varieties and the invention of appropriate agronomic practices for long term crop sustainability are conveyed to the farmer.

Realizing the importance of indigenous cultivation practices, different civil society organizations are joining together to boost traditional crops like millets and pulses in the Adivasi regions. There is a collective effort for the 'comprehensive revival of millets', wherein the promotion of this valuable crop will be taken up at all levels, from production over value-addition to marketing. The focus will be the increased inclusion of these crops under the National Food Security Act.

Conclusion

Agricultural development and food security are of prime importance for the Adivasi communities today. However, these challenges need to be taken up with sensitivity and understanding, as indigenous eco-systems have been severely undermined by the onslaught of commercial and exploitative forces over the last several decades. Without the necessary understanding, development interventions only lead to further destruction of the fragile eco-systems and will not result in any improvement in the quality of life. However, sensitive interventions are essential considering the extent of poverty and underdevelopment in the Indian hinterlands, especially in states like Odisha, Chhattisgarh and Jharkhand. Thus, development planning and intervention must necessarily take a holistic approach, keeping the people's needs and the balance of the eco-system as the central foci.

There is an urgent need to rethink the current paradigm for Adivasi regions, and reinvest for the benefit and rejuvenation of the indigenous communities and the eco-systems. Based on the experience in the field, *Agragamee* identified different issues as central for improvement in food security of Adivasi households. First of all, ecological and nutrition-sensitive agriculture must be developed locally. Practices of land, water and forest resource management must take into account the community's needs as well as local bio-diversity. In Adivasi areas, no land should be treated as waste land as it has the potential to produce the maximum crops provided there is due care for the soil and moisture. Traditional methods of terracing and water harvesting practised by the indigenous people are more effective compared to most contemporary industrialized methods. The principle of 'catch rain water where it falls' must be adopted.

Second, forest protection is crucial as it provides the best food and nutrition security for Adivasi communities. Third, people's participation in local governance processes must be ensured and their criticism and complains about government schemes like NREGA or NFSA must be taken seriously. This is even more important for the participation of women. Fourth, women's pivotal role in agriculture must be acknowledged and their priorities and perceptions must be included in rural development plans. For example, the establishment of community grain banks managed by women proved to be very effective in improving food sovereignty. Finally, all such measures need to be embedded in pro-poor policy advocacy on all state levels.

A change of policies is needed on all levels to improve food security, assure sustainable livelihoods and provide ecological securities to Adivasis and other vulnerable communities. First, a proper analysis of all relevant legislations, programmes and practices, like the ones suggested above, is essential. We need to scrutinize the national orientation of food production programmes and review all agriculture technologies applicable to Adivasi areas. To what extend do they fit the local requirements and actually contribute to sustainable solutions? Agriculture needs to be nutrition-sensitive and especially women's priorities need to be taken into account during planning, formulation and implementation processes. There is a need for people-centred planning, taking into account the knowledge systems and the rich genetic resources of the local communities. These are resources which have been built up over centuries, handed down from generation to generation, and have led to the rich and diverse eco-systems of the Adivasi regions

One example for the development of such innovative, but sensitive agricultural solutions are the eco-villages. They will be based primarily on sustainable, ecological family farms and on the management of commons, especially taking into account the priorities of women, to meet the livelihood needs of the community. In particular, eco-villages must be developed on the basis of traditional, indigenous cultures and in accordance with nature. First and foremost, this means the organic, local production and processing of food. Moreover, it includes permaculture, energy from renewable sources, construction using ecologic materials, sustainable waste management and the recycling of bio-mass. The whole concept needs to be embedded in a governance system of Adivasi self-rule, participative conflict resolution and access to education for all.

In contrast, market forces dancing to the tune of profits imposed upon people can very easily destroy local knowledge, which have already been rendered fragile through the processes of commercial felling, and displacements for industries and power projects. Multi-lateral and World Bank projects with large funds but little understanding are more of a threat to tribal livelihoods and knowledge systems. The paradigm shift towards people centred, eco-sensitive planning and development is now more urgent than ever before. Only in this way can the mistakes of the Green Revolution be rectified and a new, Evergreen Revolution become possible.

NOTES

1. Education for All. (2007). *Education for All Global Monitoring Report 2007*, Strong Foundations. Paris: UNESCO Publishing.
2. United Nations Development Programme. (2016). *Human Development Report 2016, Human Development for Everyone*. New York: UNDP.
3. Skillshare International India. (2014). *State of the Adivasis in Odisha 2014: A Human Development Analysis*. New Delhi: SAGE Publications.
4. Naandi Foundation. (2011). *HUNGaMA Survey Report*. Hyderabad: Naandi Foundation.
5. The Orissa Government Land Settlement Act, 1962. Available at https://www.igrodisha.gov.in/pdf/OGLS_Act.pdf
6. The Orissa Prevention of Land Encroachment Act, 1972. Available at http://www.lawsofindia.org/downloadfile.php?

lawid=2525&file=orissa/1972/1972OR6.pdf&pageurl=%2Fsingle%2Falpha%2F20.html

7. State Agriculture Policy 2013, Agriculture Department Odisha. Available at https://agriodisha.nic.in/content/pdf/State_Agriculture_Policy_2013_e.pdf
8. Agragamee. (2014). *Agragamee Basline Survey*. Available at http://agragamee.org/wp-content/uploads/2017/02/compressed_ar-2014-15.pdf

Report on Hunger and Malnutrition in Assam

Amarjyoti Borah

Amarjyoti Borah mostly focuses his research and reporting activities on the Northeast of India, especially Assam. Taking all kinds of issues related to climate change into account his work covers topics such as nutrition, land use, reforestation, working conditions in agriculture etc. He has a deep understanding of the living conditions and challenges of people in Assam and experience in making their struggles understandable for people living in different environments.

Introduction

In India's north-eastern state of Assam, malnutrition is a widespread problem among children. Despite recent government support programmes targeting low-income families, the situation hardly improved in rural areas. This study provides examples from different villages in Assam's Morigaon district. The region has been selected because it has been exposed to different environmental changes over the last few years: Floods of the Brahmaputra River became more intense, soil erosion more severe and rain patterns increasingly erratic. These all are major threats to local farmers, as most of them don't have access to irrigation facilities or agricultural machines. As a consequence, agricultural income dwindles and especially pregnant women, young mothers and children suffer.

After a short description of the study location, eight examples from four different villages illustrate what challenges families are facing and how they are trying to adapt to the changing circumstances. In their reports it becomes obvious that the state support programmes often do not match their realities and various obstacles prevent them from accessing the entitled benefits. In the following section, the farmers' reports on the changing weather patterns in Morigaon district show how global climate change has devastating effects at the local level. Subsequently, the people's assessment of the support programmes will be summarized, followed by an overview of the most important social policies. The article concludes with a demand for better inclusion of farmers' demands into policy making and a determined reform of the health and welfare departments in charge.

ABOUT THE STUDY LOCATION

Assam is one of Indian's seven north-eastern states, which are only connected with the rest of the country by a narrow strip of land between Nepal and Bangladesh. Assam covers an area of 78,438 square km and shares international borders with Bangladesh and Bhutan. According to the last census of 2011, the state's population 32.2 million, of whom approximately 13 per cent fall under the official category of 'Scheduled Tribes', as some indigenous communities are termed in India. Since the early 1950s, the state has repeatedly been the site of violent conflicts between different ethnic groups, the causes of which did not only lie in religion and ethno-nationalism, but were also grounded in economic disparities. The state's literacy rate is around 73 per cent and hence slightly below the national average. The gender difference in literacy accounts for more than ten percentage points: While almost 79 per cent of men have at least basic literacy skills, the female literacy rate amounts to 67 per cent. The urbanization rate of 13 per cent is clearly below the national average, and accounts for around one-third of the total population. Accordingly, agriculture is the largest sector in Assam's economy and it supports more than 75 per cent of the state's population directly or indirectly. Despite tea being Assam's major export good, more than 85 per cent of the farmers are involved in small or medium scale subsistence farming.

This study was conducted in Morigaon district, located in central Assam. The district lies along the southern bank of the Brahmaputra River, and is traversed by its two important tributaries Kollong and Kopili. Morigaon district consists of 632 villages organized into 85 *gaon Panchayats*. The total area encompasses 155,100 ha out of which approximately one-tenth is covered by forest and almost 60 per cent are used for agriculture. According to the 2011 census, the district's total population is 957,853, of which more than one-fourth is directly working in agriculture. The number of people depending on agriculture is, of course, much higher and agriculture is the economic mainstay of Morigaon's population. Despite the district's very poor irrigation infrastructure, the farmers had successfully practiced rain-fed cultivation for generations. While some farmers irrigate their land with shallow tube wells and pump sets supported by schemes of the Assam state government, the majority of small scale farmers still fetch water manually from nearby bodies of water like ponds, rivers and wetlands. According to the Assam agriculture department, the soil of the district is ideal for production of all seasonal rice paddy and other crops like pulses, oil seeds, spices and various types of vegetables.

Despite this agricultural richness, Morigaon is among the most malnutrition-affected districts in the state. Regular floods and continuous soil erosion pose a constant threat to the farmers. However, according to Assam's health officials, the most important reasons for malnutrition in the district are the poor paternal and maternal health status as well as the general lack of hygiene. As a consequence, worm infections which aggravate malnutrition are widespread. Although the health-personnel carries out de-worming in the state continuously, the problem has not been solved yet.

One reason is that many people still don't have access to proper toilets and don't observe proper hygiene. Moreover, health officials state that, despite their efforts, dietary guidelines are not followed and especially children don't get the nutritious food directed by the health personnel. Although the introduction of Nutrition Counselling and Management Centres (NCMC) in 2013 led to some improvement, the outcome could be better. Several parents don't bring their children to the NCMC and in some cases don't even bring them to the hospital when they are sick. That is because travelling to the next town would mean losing a day's wage, which the families are highly dependent upon.

However, Morigaon district still fares comparatively better in terms of human development compared to other parts of Assam.

According to the fourth National Family Health Survey (NFHS) covering the years 2015–2016, Morigaon has fewer underweight children than the state average and also the share of births at official health institutions is a little higher in comparison.[1] The same is true for young mothers who consume the important iron folic acid for at least 100 days after delivery and the share of children under the age of three who were regularly breastfed. On the other hand, the share of anaemic children and those who are too small for their ages is again worse than the state's average. As one can see, the problems and difficulties presented in this study are by no means restricted to Marigaon district but common to many places in Assam, if not the whole of India.

VILLAGE LEVEL CASE STUDIES

For the study, selected families were interviewed in the villages of Bhurbandha, Jurgaon, Mikirgaon and Nautaka in late August 2016. To put the findings in a larger context, focus group discussions were conducted on agriculture and malnutrition with farmers, pregnant women, activists and mothers of malnourished children in the same villages. Besides this, government officials, researchers and activists were interviewed as well.

Bhurbandha Village

Bhurbandha is a remote village of around 450 houses close to the Brahmaputra River. It is mainly populated by the indigenous Tiwa people and of the more than 2,000 people living in the village, around one-third belong to the official category of 'Scheduled Tribes'. According to the 2011 census, 73 persons belong to the category of 'Scheduled Castes'. The literacy rate is 81 per cent, significantly above the state average, while there is a large gap of more 10 percentage points between men and women. Most inhabitants are dependent on agriculture and work as main or marginal farmers. Some are employed as daily wage labourers as well and in the last few years, repeated bad crops made some youths migrate to nearby cities or even to other Indian states in search of a more reliable source of income.

As there are no irrigation facilities available in Bhurbandha, the farmers have always been dependent on the rain and on water from nearby ponds and rivers for irrigation. The elder farmers of the village reported that they never had any problems with this kind of agriculture and they had been able to produce enough for their families. However, this got increasingly difficult as the rain became more erratic and nearby bodies of water began to dry up. Many blamed climate change for this development. The impact on agriculture has affected several families, most severely the small scale farmers of the village. To provide adequate care for the already malnourished children became even more difficult under such circumstances and their health has been affected severely.

Erosion of Arable Land

Umeshwari Bodoloi is the 30-years-old mother of a one-year-old malnourished boy. The ASHA (Accredited Social Health Activist) workers, whose responsibility it is to take care of the women's health in the village, said that despite their efforts to improve the child's health, there has been no improvement at all. The main problem, as Umeshwari and her husband Babulal report, is the steep fall in production from their agricultural land over the past five years. The declining crops forced Umeshwari to start working despite her pregnancy to supplement the family's income.

The family said that two problems are responsible for the crop shortfall: First, they have always been fully dependent on the rain for their cultivation as they lack access to irrigation facilities. Therefore, the recent change in rainfall patterns severely affected them. Second, their agricultural land on the banks of the Brahmaputra was more and more frequently hit by unpredictable, powerful flood waves. This not only destroyed seeds and crops, but also eroded the fertile soil and deposited barren sand. In earlier days, the family earned around 20,000 to 30,000 INR per season from Babulal's work on their three *bighas* of land, an area roughly equivalent to one acre. But now their income has decreased and they are not able to earn more than 10,000 INR per season.

Moreover, Umeshwari and Babulal report, that the government schemes to support farmers during crisis situations such as drought periods are mostly availed by richer farmers. For example one programme has been launched to lease out water pumps to groups of farmers. However, they have to arrange for the fuel necessary for running the pump themselves, which is very difficult for small-scale farmers. Buying diesel worth 300–500 INR per day is only possible if they borrow money. But, if by any chance the crops fail or they are not able to produce as expected, they can get into major trouble.

Umeshwari, in an attempt to supplement the family income, started to work as an informal daily wage labourer on other farmers' land, for which she earns a wage of 100-120 INR per day. However, she works for eight hours, five to six days per week. This is not only a sacrifice at the cost of her own health, but also at the cost of the health of her child. Umeshwari had to work six months into her pregnancy and started working again less than five months after the delivery. Since she works as an informal daily wage labourer, there is no fixed time to go home and feed the child. On a few occasions she tried to take the child with her to work, but the boy fell ill soon. Consequently, Umeshwari never tried to take him to work with her. Now she leaves her child with his grandmother, who is very old and not able to cook anymore. Therefore, an early improvement of the child's health seems very unlikely.

The diet of the child has not been healthy all through, and though the ASHA workers have tried to convince Umeshwari and her family to improve the food quality, there has been no change. Under the Integrated Child Development Services (ICDS), which is the nutrition and health schemes initiated by the government, the local Anganwadi workers regularly deliver nutritious food to small children and their mothers. But the ASHA and Anganwadi workers in Bhurbandha pointed out that the family doesn't follow their advice and guidelines. 'We are doing all we can—giving advice and giving the prescribed nutritious food. It is not possible for us to cook the food and force-feed the mother and the children,' said Promila Bordoloi, an ASHA worker of the village.

Loss of Water Sources

There are many such farmer families who face a bleak future. Gayatri Malang is a 26-years-old mother with a two-years-old malnourished child. The child weighs only 10 kg. Together with her husband, Jayant Malang (age: 35 years), she owns three bighas of land. They face a severe financial crisis as the production from their land has sharply come down due to impacts of climate change. Apart from the paddy cultivation in the Kharif season, Jayant used to cultivate *Boro* rice and earned comparatively well. While he earned around 25,000 INR from the former, the *Boro* rice harvest again brought the family between 30,000 to 35,000 INR of income. Jayant said that with this money, he was easily be able to sustain his family and save something as well.

Around eight years ago, the production from the field declined and the family's earnings dropped. Just like thousands of other farmers, Jayant said that he has always been dependent on the rain. But now with the rain becoming erratic, his production has started to come down. His paddy cultivation in the Kharif season declined by more than 50 per cent. That is mostly due to the delayed and erratic rainfalls, he explained. However, the biggest setback has been his failure to take up any *Boro* rice cultivation in the past three years at all. Earlier, he said, he was able to cultivate *Boro* rice despite not having any irrigation facilities, as there were several ponds nearby, and he could fetch water from those. But now, they have all become dependent on the river after the ponds were eroded, and several smaller bodies of water have been encroached upon. To buy a water pump on loan would be the family's last option, but Malang considers it too expensive and risky. Instead, they invested all their remaining money and started a road side eatery this year. So far, the business is yet to pick up.

As a result of the depletion in their income, their malnourished child has been severely affected. Gayatri and Jayant said that the ASHA workers and the support staff from the Anganwadi centres visit them every month. Apart from giving some nutritious food for the child and carrying out some health tests, the social workers asked the parents to take the child to the NRC for treatment. Jayant said that this is not a feasible option as they both have to work at the eatery every day to be able to earn money and feed the family. Gayatri said that now they will hopefully earn sufficient money from the eatery to start the necessary treatment for their child.

Jurgaon Village

Jurgaon is a medium size village in Morigaon district. Out of the 324 inhabitants, almost all belong to the category of 'Scheduled Tribes' and women constitute the slight majority of the population. Approximately half of the inhabitants are working somewhere outside their home, most of them as small scale farmers on their own land. Similar to Bhurbandha village, none of them has access to irrigation facilities. A small portion of the populace earns a daily wage as informal labourers. Some people have also migrated to bigger cities like Guwahati, Dimapur, Kolkata, Chennai, Bangalore, Trivandrum and New Delhi in search of work.

Lack of Awareness about Support Programmes

Sona Prabha Bordoloi is 20 years old and the mother of a three-years-old malnourished male child. Her husband Jintimoni Bordoloi, who is ten years older to her, is a small scale farmer who owns four bighas of land. Until five years back, they were well off and the family used to earn 15,000 to 20,000 INR per season from their land. Now, things have become difficult after erratic rainfall led to a series of bad harvests at Bordoloi's land. The yield dropped by half and this is too little to retain any money in hand. The family hasn't conducted any farming activities in the last three years.

Since then, Jintimoni started working as a daily wage labour in the hope of earning better than from agriculture. Now, he earns a wage of 200–250 INR per day, but this is not enough to sustain the family. Therefore, Sona also started working as a daily wage labour on bigger farmers' lands and sometimes in other people's houses. As the wage gap between the genders is very high, she only earns 100–150 INR per day. Sona started working less than six months after the birth of her child, which contributed to the boy's poor health and malnourishment. Currently, the child weighs only 14 kgs and the family members are clueless what to do. Asked about government support schemes or child care in the hospitals, both parents replied that they are not aware of such assistance.

Insufficiency of Government Support Programmes

Gagan Deori's family, another farmer in the same village, has also been affected in a similar way. Gagan is a 34-years-old farmer who owns three bighas of cultivable land. His wife Promita Deori is 20 years old and they have a two-years-old daughter. She, too, is malnourished and weighs only 13 kg. For a long time, Gagan used to grow two crops a year and was able to keep a portion of the harvest for the family, while selling the rest to earn enough money to survive throughout the year. For the past three to four years, Gagan's cultivation has been severely disturbed, and production from both the *Kharif* (autumn-monsoon) and *Rabi* (winter) season declined. Like many other small scale farmers, he is fully dependent on the rain for his cultivation and over the years, the revenue from his plot of land has halved. For the last three years, Gagan was not able to grow anything during the Rabi season, as the nearby ponds on which he used to depend for water, have been encroached upon by floods and made unusable. With their current meagre income, he reports, his family finds it difficult to survive.

Gagan explains that though the local Anaganwadi workers give them some nutritious food for the child every month, this is too little by far. After regular counselling sessions with both parents, the ASHA workers handed out lists of nutritious foods to be given to the child. Gagan, however, says that this is not possible for them as the expenses go beyond the family budget. Instead, he said, they raise the child just like they would have if it was not malnourished. Gagan added that he also spoke to the doctors at a temporal medical camp held near their village in July this year. They also asked him to improve the quality of the child's food, but he will be able to ensure better nutrition and medical treatment for the child only if the production from his field improves, Gagan explained.

Mikirgaon Village

The village of Mikirgaon is home to 545 families and quite large compared to the other villages visited for this study. Nevertheless, the patterns of employment are similar and almost 3,000 people work in agriculture. Mikirgaon is among the most severely flooded and erosion-affected villages of the district, and both residential property and agricultural land of several people have gotten eroded.

Loss of Housing

Purna Hazarika, a 45-years-old farmer is among the victims of flood and erosion in Mikirgaon. Four out of his five bighas of cultivable land has got eroded in the past six years, and two years back his house broke down, too. Since then, Hazarika and his wife Prarthana have been living at a makeshift camp on the bank of the river. Prarthana gave birth to a child last year, but the one-year-old girl is malnourished and weighs less than 8 kg.

Hazarika explained that he gave up cultivation as very little arable land remained. The family spent the last savings to set up a shelter in the make-shift camp and buy at least the most essential items. They are now experiencing difficulties in managing even one decent meal a day. Earlier, Hazarika remembers, he harvested two times per year and was able to earn between 20,000 to 25,000 INR per season. The family even managed to save around 4,000 INR annually. Now, he has been without any income for the past year. Both parents say that their new-born daughter has been worst affected as they don't have a proper house to live in. 'Our house collapsed around the time when our daughter was born, and from a decent house we had to move to a provisional camp on the embankment close to the Brahmaputra river', Hazarika said. 'Earlier, we were well off and never faced any crisis, but for the past year, I don't have any work and we have been homeless.' He plans to start working as a daily wage labourer soon, but fears that the earning won't be sufficient to make a living for him and his family.

ASHA workers visited the family on a regular basis and asked them to provide a healthier diet for the child. Sometimes, Anganwadi workers delivered some nutritious food to the family for the girl, but Prarthana complained that it was simply not enough to improve the child's health. She added that the ASHA workers asked her to take the child to the next hospital and the Nutritional Rehabilitation Centre (NRC) at the district headquarter. This, however, is difficult for the family. 'It is unsafe to leave our home with all the belongings here and stay in the hospital at the town for one to two weeks. Our home is ramshackle and thatched. It is unsafe,' said Hazarika. Moreover, he added, it would be near to impossible to ensure that the child will stay healthy after returning from the NRC, as they will not be able to ensure nutritious food afterwards.

Precarious Work

Other victims of erosion have similar stories. Tridip Das is a small-scale farmer with just one *bigha* of land. Initially, he had inherited four bighas of cultivable land but lost three of them to erosion.

This has impacted his earning severely. Earlier, he used to harvest two times per year and easily earned from 20,000 to 25,000 INR per season. With just one *bigha* of land left for him to cultivate, life has become very difficult. Together with his wife Joba, he has three children aged one, six and nine years. The youngest son is malnourished and weighs only 7 kg. Das said that he is not even able to earn 7,000 INR from his land reliably, which is far too little to feed the entire family. Being asked if any other factors have impacted the production as well, Das said that water has never been a problem. Even in case of erratic rainfalls, the nearby river always provides enough water. As a result of the loss of land, Joba started working as a daily wage labourer in other people's house to supplement the family's income. She works in two to three houses on a part-time basis and in one month, she earns 4,000 to 5,000 INR.

The loss of income directly affected the health of their children. Though both Das and Joba are aware of the ill-effects of malnutrition and about the importance of health care, they said that they are not able to do anything for the child. With the money which they earn, both emphasize, it has become difficult for the family to survive. At least the education of the both elder children has not been affected, as they attend government schools, where education is almost free. However, both expressed worries over their youngest and its nutrition. Though ASHA and Anganwadi workers visit them regularly and have asked them to take the child to the NRC at the civil hospital, both parents deem this impossible. If his wife stays at the hospital for about two weeks, Das explained, her job will be occupied by others and she will not be able to get it back. As both parents are just earning enough to sustain thc family, being absent from work could make the family face hunger in the future. Moreover, Das added that it is important for Joba to earn and get used to work, as he might even lose his remaining bit of agricultural land to erosion soon.

Nautaka Village

Naukata is a medium size village of 191 families. According to the latest census, the population is 890 and men make up a slight majority. Approximately one-fifth officially belong to the 'Scheduled Tribe' category. Most people in Naukata are engaged in agriculture, but a small proportion is associated with daily wage earning as well. Most people are small-scale farmers with no irrigation facilities, and were always dependent on the rain-fed irrigation. Therefore, they are directly affected by the increasingly unpredictable weather conditions.

Children and Wage Work

One of Naukata's small-scale farmers is 42-years-old Umaron Bora, who owns two bighas of land and used to have a comfortable life with his family. However, since the past three to four years the yield from his land has declined due to the erratic rainfall. While many of his fellow farmers without irrigation facilities got water pumps on rent, he was not able to afford this. As his income was shrinking from more than 13,000 INR to less than 8,000 INR per season, Umaron was forced to borrow money to sustain his family. To supplement the family's income, he sold half a *bigha* of his land for 30,000 INR and opened a small grocery shop for his wife Malama Bora.

Less than a year before they opened the shop, Malama had given birth to a son. As the delivery had taken place at a hospital, the social workers briefed the parents very early about the dietary needs of the new-born. ASHA and Anganwadi workers said that they have been providing nutritious food for the child since then. However, Malama has to work full time at the shop and there are no close relatives around who could take care of the boy during the day. From opening to closing, she has a lot of work to do at the shop and they don't earn enough to hire an assistant. As a result, she is not able to take care of her child properly and feed him the necessary nutritious food.

Now, the child is eighteen months old, weighs only 10 kg and is malnourished. In August 2016, Malama stayed with the child at the NRC for two weeks and received nutrition supplements. But she explained that, after getting discharged, it was not possible for her to follow all the advice given by the doctors and the nutritionists. Both parents are aware of their son's suffering, but they don't see any alternative and are hopeless. So far, the shop does not return much profit and Umaron was not able to repay his debt. He assumes that it will take almost a year to establish the shop properly, and until then he will have to continue working at his field to be able to feed his family and himself.

Loans and Debt

Another affected farmer in Nautaka is the 38-years-old Bhava Hazarika. He and his 24-years-old wife Dalimi Hazarika have a 15-months-old malnourished child, who weighs less than 9 kg. Just like most other farmers in the region, his three bighas of arable land are not irrigated and he mostly depends on rainfall for his cultivation. Earlier, he focused on the Kharif season and harvested enough rice once a year to earn more than 20,000 INR. On top of that, he used to take up small jobs in nearby Morigaon town after the harvest, where he earned around 10,000 INR per month. As a result of the erratic rainfall, his production became less than half over the years. Due to the lack of water, Bhava is not able to grow crops during the Rabi season.

Three years back, Bhava mortgaged two bighas of his land for 45,000 INR in the hope of starting a business of his own. With the money he started a small road side eatery, run by him and his wife. From his farm work during the Kharif season, he only earns about 10,000 INR, but manages to keep enough rice to feed his family for the rest of the year. After the harvest, he works with his wife at the eatery. Although the eatery is yet to give good returns, the family is hopeful that it will be a stable income source soon.

With the 3,000 to 5,000 INR they make from the eatery every month, Bhava is able to pay back his loan gradually.

However, the health of their child has suffered as the parents are not able to follow the repeated suggestions by officials of the health department. As the medical guidelines are mainly about feeding and resting at regular intervals, Bhava Hazarika said, this would only be possible if Dalimi gave up her work at the eatery. As this would make it impossible to pay back their loan and they might eventually lose their remaining land, this is not an option for the family. Hazarika emphasizes how concerned they both are about the child.

IMPACTS OF FLOOD AND CLIMATE CHANGE ON FARMERS

These individual reports are mirrored by many farmers in Morigaon district and there are plenty of stories about how the impacts of climate change damages their crops and diminishes their income. Several elder villagers said that the small-scale farmers never suffered from weather changes like they do now, and blamed climate change for this. The rise in temperature and the increased frequency and intensity of floods especially threaten their lone source of livelihood. In times of sufficient rain, they had to apply very little fertilizer and the yield was satisfactory nevertheless. Nowadays, it sometimes rains very little or very excessively.

An analysis by Rajib Lochan Deka from the Assam Agriculture University confirms these observations by the villagers:

> Since 1981, there has been a significant change in rainfall and temperature patterns of the state. Especially due to the declining monsoon rainfall, the total annual amount of water has been decreasing continuously. The last decade under investigation since 2001 has even been the driest for more than 100 years. The analysis also shows how the annual mean temperature in the Brahmaputra valley increased significantly due to the rise of both maximum and minimum temperature during the 60 years under investigation

(1951–2010). The warming trend in the valley has been strongest since 1981 and was 1.6 times higher than the Indian average.

Such changes in natural phenomena leave the farmers helpless. On being asked how much they have suffered financially, the majority of the farmers said that the decline in production ranges from 30 to 50 per cent. They explain how they were easily able to produce 450 kg to 600 kg of rice from one *bigha* of land in the Kharif season earlier. Every farmer used to keep a portion of the production for the family's consumption and sell the rest, which brought enough money. Similarly in the Rabi season, the farmers were able to earn more than 15,000 INR from one *bigha* of land. Many farmers of the district used to cultivate *Boro* rice. But since this rice breed needs a lot of water and is cultivated in the dry winter season, many farmers had to give it up. Of course, some luck in selecting the right crops has always been there, the farmers said. But small-scale farmers face more difficulties when growing the most profitable Rabi crops, as bigger farmers can afford to use water pumps. The small farmers, in contrast, had to fetch water from nearby water bodies manually. Nowadays, many of the water sources on which they used to depend heavily have ceased to exist because of various natural and man-made factors like climate change, encroachment, erosion and filling up of those bodies for developmental projects such as roads and buildings.

Consequently, the lives of many of these small-scale farmers have been jeopardized. The women especially reported how the male members of their families gave up farming after a few consecutive bad crop seasons and have gone to take up work in towns and cities outside of Assam. Oftentimes, many women said, this worsened the respective family's situation, especially if there were pregnant women or young children below five years of age. Sosi Nanda Bordoloi, a social worker in the district, said that people moving to other states in search of work leave with high hopes regarding income opportunities. However, they are disappointed in most cases and end up doing inadequate jobs where they are not able to earn enough money to send back home anything. As a consequence, the wife who stayed at home is forced to take up work to be able to supplement the family's income. Most of the married women are basically homemakers without much education, and therefore it is difficult for them to find a good job. Mostly, working as a daily wage labourer is the only option, which creates a lot of problems for their own health as well as the health of their young children. Taking care of the child full time, managing the house and earning outside is a huge, but common challenge, as many women explained.

Many of the elderly farmers also said that in earlier days, a flood used to be a blessing as they used flood water on the fields for one or two days which brought fertility to their field. Nowadays, it became different as the intensity of the floods is much higher and it often devastates their land. Moreover, the accompanying erosion destroys cultivable land and other property permanently. According to the Assam government, close to four lakh hectares (400,000 ha) of land has been eroded because of floods. In March 2015, the provincial government framed the 'Chief Minister's Special Scheme for rehabilitation of erosion affected families in Assam' (No. RGR.785/2014/6) to support people who have lost their livelihood due to erosion.[2]

Inequalities and Structural Gaps

During the course of the study, it became obvious that the government neglected several important issues at the village level. One of the biggest problems faced by the farmers is the lack of irrigation facilities, and farmers said that although every government promised irrigation for all the farmers, nothing ever happened. According to reports of the Central Ground Water Board, the irrigation potential in Morigaon district created by the government's current flow irrigation scheme is only 3,100 ha, and

2,945 ha by lift irrigation. As a result, only a very small portion of the farmers in the district are able to reap benefits from irrigation. The state agriculture department has attempted to provide support to farmers through pump sets. It has launched an initiative under which only 21 farmers are given a pump set at 50 per cent of the price, while they have to pay themselves for the other part and the oil necessary to run it. The outreach of this programme is, of course, minuscule.

The farmers also complained that the government designs policies which treat farmers as a homogenous whole, while it is necessary to look differently at small scale and marginal level farmers. They explained how the marginal level farmers live from hand to mouth, and usually don't have much by way of savings. Furthermore, they added how they would greatly benefit if the state government starts the process of a minimum support price for the farmers. For paddy, they demanded a minimum support price of at least 2,000 INR per quintal. Many farmers don't have savings or corpus money, and though they had opened bank accounts about two years ago under the government's *Jan Dhan Yojana* scheme, they have not been able to save and deposit any money.

Many of the women complained about the inappropriate health and nutrition schemes of the government for women and children. Although they have been widely publicized and the local ASHA workers also campaign for them, it is often difficult to be able to convince the elders in the family about these schemes' benefit, as they often deem them unnecessary. The women also argued for a special scheme, through which needy mothers with malnourished children are provided with a minimum monthly wage until the child reaches five years of age. Moreover, they complained about the wrong incentives for the ASHA workers. While they only get 150 INR for taking care of a malnutrition case, the incentive for deliveries is twice as much. Therefore, they focus more on pregnancy and delivery cases, and much less on cases related to malnutrition.

GOVERNMENT SCHEMES TO TACKLE MALNUTRITION

The Assam government has launched several initiatives to enhance the population's health, especially focusing on issues related to women and children like malnutrition and anaemia. In the following, some examples of the most important schemes are given:

Nutrition Counselling cum Management Centres (NCMC): The Assam government established these centres at the district level to supplement the Nutritional Rehabilitation Centres (NRC), which have been set up by the Government of India to tackle malnutrition. The NCMCs are outpatient centres, and the counsellors at the centre measure the height and weight of pregnant women, calculate the body mass index and provide counselling on nutrition and health needs. Besides this, the counsellors also attend young mothers in the post natal period, and provide guidance regarding breastfeeding practices, and about the nutritional needs of children until they reach five years of age.

Meanwhile, the counsellors conduct screening camps and take anthropometric measures of the children below the age of five. The nutritional status of these children is regularly monitored to identify cases of malnutrition. Cases of severe and acute malnutrition (SAM) are referred to the next NRC for treatment. In critical cases, both mother and child are admitted at the NRC to be kept under the supervision of a nurse, a nutritionist, and a doctor from the hospital. To ensure that working mothers from poor families do not lose their income, the women are provided 150 INR per day. They are usually kept at the centre for one week, but if the child's condition does not improve, the period is extended to 15 days.

Mission *Tejaswee:* Keeping in mind that Assam has a large number of anaemic patients, the state government launched the health mission *Tejaswee* in 2015 to treat and tackle anaemia across Assam. The activities included the administration of iron and folic acid (IFA) syrup to children between the age of six to 59 months, the distribution of IFA tablets to pregnant and lactating women, and awareness campaigns on anaemia's causes and its treatments.

Mamata: The Assam government initiated the *Mamata* programme to address the high maternal-mortality rate by encouraging deliveries in health institutions, which reduces their own as well as their child's vulnerability to health problems in the future. This scheme incentivizes mothers to remain at the health facility for 48 hours after the delivery in order to receive medical care. According to the health department, this scheme has two major positive impacts. It provides direct healthcare to the new-born, and also ensures that the mother receives the necessary postpartum care. After the delivery, mothers are handed a baby kit, which contains essential items for the child like baby clothes, powder and a mosquito net.

Mamoni: Under this scheme, a cash assistance of 1,000 INR for nutritional support is given to pregnant women in two instalments. Its aim is to encourage pregnant women to undergo at least three ante-natal check-ups to identify possible health problems during pregnancy. Every pregnant woman receives a booklet containing tips on safe motherhood and new-born care at the time of registration. At each of the two subsequent health check-ups, the pregnant women receive 500 INR to be spent on nutritious food. Every government health institution in the state provides these schemes.

Morom: With this scheme, the Assam health department provides financial support to patients admitted at government health institutions as compensation for wage loss during hospitalization and to buy supplementary nutrition as well as other post-hospital expenses. The scheme is for poor patients only, and at the medical colleges the family receives 75 INR per day for a maximum of seven days. People admitted to district hospitals receive 50 INR per day for a maximum of five days.

Majoni: This special scheme under the *Assam Bikash Yojana* is especially designed for young girls. After a female baby is born in a government hospital, a fixed deposit of 5,000 INR is made in her name for a period of 18 years, and the girl will be able to receive it only after her 18th birthday. However, the deposit is forfeited if she gets married before this age. This scheme is provided only to families with two children or less.

Sneha Shivir and Crèche Service under the Integrated Child Development Services (ICDS): The three districts of Nagaon, Golaghat and Karimganj are mostly affected by malnutrition and had therefore been selected for the pilot phase of this special programme. Selected Anganwadi Centres (AWCs) provide day care support to malnourished children and a crèche service for mothers working in the informal sector. The social welfare department plans to extend these special facilities. Both the health department and the social welfare department promote and support Infant and Young Child Feeding (IYCF) to malnourished children and children of working mothers. The social welfare department intends to establish at least one of these centres in each district of Assam.

Breastfeeding Support Group: These support groups are organized by lactating mothers with children below the age of five years who voluntarily work to motivate others to adopt breastfeeding practices. They provide support on the family and community level to continue breastfeeding and optimal IYCF practices by providing solutions to commonly experienced problems such as lack of milk or breast engorgement. ASHA workers assist the group members. According to officials of the health department, such groups have been formed in different parts of the state and have been received positively.

Mother Support Groups (MSGs): In 2012, the social welfare department constituted Mother Support Groups in 62,153 operational AWCs in all the ICDS projects in Assam. These MSGs have been formed with the objective to support the beneficiaries in applying for government services through counselling and awareness-building. At the same time, these groups should monitor the effective operation of the programmes and schemes under ICDS. Such groups comprise of seven mothers with children below the age of two, and are registered at the local AWC. They are elected for one financial year by all the beneficiaries registered at AWC and notified by the concerned Child Development Project Officer (CDPO). The MSG provides support through home visits and by spreading awareness among pregnant women and mothers of children below the age of two. They also provide targeted counselling on nutrition, health, malnutrition and anaemia to women in need. Moreover, MSGs prepare recipes of nutritious food using locally available ingredients.

Supplementary Nutrition Programme (SNP): Under this programme, which is part of ICDS, the government aims at enhancing the nutritional and health status of children below six years of age, pregnant as well as lactating women and mothers of late-adolescent girls. The financial standards were last revised in 2008, and according to the current norms, children between six and 72 months are allotted 6 INR per day, severely malnourished children of the same age group are allotted 9 INR per day, and pregnant women as well as nursing mothers are allotted 7 INR per day. Every month, officials from the AWCs deliver nutritious food on the basis of calorific calculations worth the amount to the beneficiary. Children between the age of six and 72 months are given food worth 300 calories and 8 to 10g protein per day. Children suffering from severe and acute malnutrition are provided with food having double the calorific value and protein. Pregnant women, lactating mothers and adolescent girls are given food worth 500 calories and 20g of protein per day.

SUMMARY

Although the overall malnutrition scenario in Assam has improved on some parameters, the state government needs to devise new strategies to be able to deal with the problem in the rural areas. This study showed how the rural populace in the state basically depends on the agriculture sector and how the children of these farmers face the threat of malnourishment. Many farmers reported that there is a direct relation between the ongoing agrarian crisis and the malnutrition amongst the children, especially those of small-scale farmers. As these farmers mostly live from hand to mouth and have neither savings nor alternative sources of income, they are especially vulnerable to changes in the environment.

This becomes particularly visible at Morigaon district, where floods and erosion are especially severe. Those farmers who have agricultural land near the river are among the most affected as the flood water damages their cultivation and they lose their land to erosion over the years. Till date, the Assam government has not been able to compensate such farmers by providing land in other areas. Moreover, small water bodies on which many small scale farmers largely depend for their cultivation, have started to dry out or were encroached upon in many areas. Adverse impacts of climate change like erratic and unpredictable rainfall have worsened the situation for small scale farmers even further. Those without irrigation facilities have been affected worse, as they are fully dependent on rainfall. The farmers reported how over the past decade, the rainfall has become erratic and unpredictable and how their production and income dwindles.

This loss of income severely affected families with malnourished children and pregnant women. Oftentimes, even pregnant women and mothers of young, malnourished children have to work to be able to contribute to the family's income. Even the best efforts of the local health and welfare officials failed, as the women cannot give up work without endangering the family's survival. The health and family welfare department implemented schemes to tackle malnutrition which delivered good results in urban areas. However, the farmers in the rural areas are often not aware of these support programmes.

As these are specific problems of a certain population in rural areas, they are mostly unnoticed—or ignored—by the policy makers. In the future, the government must take issues like land erosion, decreasing agricultural income and children's malnutrition more seriously when designing support schemes. Furthermore, it is important for the state government to combine the programmes on malnutrition by the health and family welfare department and the social welfare department under one roof of one office. Currently, many people are just aware of the schemes of one department, but don't know about the others. The government also needs to devise a concrete, long-term action plan including all key and related departments, which include health and family welfare, social welfare, finance, agriculture, irrigation, water resources, Panchayat and rural development.

NOTES

1. Ministry of Health and Family Welfare. (2016). *National Family Health Survey 2015–16*. New Delhi: Government of India.
2. Government of Assam, Revenue and Disaster Managmenet Department. (2015). *CM's Special Scheme for Rehabilitation of Erosion Affected Families of Assam*. Dispur: Government of Assam.

Hunger and Malnutrition amongst Adivasi Communities in Raigad District of Maharashtra

RAJEEV KHEDKAR

Rajeev Khedkar formerly coordinated an action-research programme on Social Analysis Systems in Raigad District as well as some of his work on medicinal plants focused on this particular area. At present he facilitates a network of NGOs to collectively address the problems faced by tribal communities in that region.

INTRODUCTION

Maharashtra is India's third-largest state by area and second-largest by population. Moreover, it is considered to be one of the wealthiest and most developed states of the union, contributing 25 per cent of the country's industrial output and 23.2 per cent of its GDP (Census of India, 2011).[1] However, there are wide disparities in the indicators of development and well-being within the state in terms of regions as well as social groups. For instance, the regions of Marathwada, Khandesh (Dhule-Nandurbar) and some districts in Vidarbha are considered less developed or even 'backward'. Similarly, in terms of social groups, indigenous *Adivasi* (so-called 'Scheduled Tribes'), Dalits (so-called 'Scheduled Castes'), nomadic and denotified communities and the urban and rural poor amongst Muslims form the most deprived section of the population in Maharashtra. The poor amongst these groups constitute anywhere between 15 to 20 per cent of the population of the state.

Adivasi are the single most marginalized social group in Maharashtra. The state is home to 10.5 million Adivasi people who represent about 9.4 per cent of the state's population. Surprisingly, the state has the second highest population of Adivasi people in the country after Madhya Pradesh. Overall, 47 distinct Adivasi communities live in different parts of Maharashtra, with three Adivasi communities (*Katkari, Madia Gond* and *Kolam*) notified as Particularly Vulnerable Tribal Groups (PVTGs) by the Government. Nearly 60 per cent of Adivasi people live below the poverty line and especially the poor nutritional situation of Adivasi children in Maharashtra has been grabbing public attention for a long time. There are reports of malnutrition related deaths of Adivasi children from Thane, Palghar, Amravati, Dhule,

Nandurbar, Nashik and Bhandara districts every year during the months of monsoon. The precarious nutrition situation of these children in Maharashtra has been confirmed by India's National Family Health Survey which indicates that between 50 and 60 per cent of Adivasi children aged below five years have stunted growth due to chronic malnutrition.

Stunting and wasting in early childhood is life-threatening and for those who survive, it causes lasting damage, including a lower attention span, poor memory, mental retardation, behavioural issues, poor performance at school, reduced lean body mass, short adult stature and—when accompanied by excessive weight gain later in childhood—a higher risk of chronic diseases. It is a shame that India occupies a prominent spot in the global map of childhood stunting, as out of the globally 165 million stunted children below five years of age, 61 million (37 per cent) are from India. With around 47 per cent, the country has the highest percentage of malnourished children under the age of five in the world. Within India, stunting is highest among children of *Adivasi* people, where 54 per cent are affected.

Unfortunately, there are serious gaps in tracking and monitoring the efficacy of efforts aimed at reducing malnutrition in India. The collection of nutrition data in India suffers from a total lack of standardization, with the result that most datasets are not comparable. This leads to several data gaps, and experts cannot say for sure whether a particular policy was responsible for the improvement or not. For instance, since 1992 several major nutrition surveys have been conducted in India. There were three National Family Health Surveys (NFHS) in 1992–93, 1998–99 and 2005–06, four District Level Household and Facility Surveys (DLHS) in 1998–99, 2002–04, 2007–08 and 2012–13 as well as three Annual Health Surveys (AHS) in 2011, 2012 and 2013. Moreover, different one-time surveys were conducted like the Rapid Survey on Children (RSOC) by UNICEF in 2015 and the

Hunger and Malnutrition Survey (HUNGaMA) by the Naandi Foundation in 2011.

A comparison of these surveys shows wide variations across their geographical coverage, frequency of data collection, parameters, criteria, etc. Researchers claim that there is little actionable intelligence on which to base policy prescription. Similarly, the shifting reference points for child anthropometry (which includes collecting data on stunting and wasting) ruin any chances of clear deduction in the scale of improvement. Hence, official claims about reduction in malnutrition have to be taken with a pinch of salt.

A number of studies have been done by researchers, academicians, administrators, policy makers and NGOs to understand the causes of malnutrition amongst Adivasi children and to suggest remedial measures. Some of these studies were even supported by the government. The measures taken up to address malnutrition following the recommendations from such studies, however, generally follow a symptomatic treatment approach. Thus, despite the myriad of programmes and schemes with impressive titles and intent by both central and state Governments, the scourge of malnutrition continues to haunt the Adivasi population. For instance, more than 600 malnutrition related deaths of Adivasi children were reported from Palghar and Thane districts of Maharashtra during the monsoon of 2016 alone.[2] When questioned about this stark reality, the Maharashtra Tribal Development Ministry refused to acknowledge the situation completely.

The same story is reported from Adivasi areas across other states. An important reason for the persistence of malnutrition in Adivasi areas is our inability to address the root causes of the problem. The fact that the central government has decided to spend only 1.23 per cent of the GDP on health, could further aggravate the crisis. What portion of this amount is really spent on addressing the health needs of Adivasis is a moot question. So-called Particularly Vulnerable Tribal Groups (PVTG) bear the brunt of the political neglect given the fact that they are socio-economically marginalized and live in smaller populations.

Given these realities, it was necessary to conduct a study that would aid to develop a better understanding of issues related to malnutrition amongst the Katkari community, a PVTG, in Raigad district of Maharashtra. Findings of the study may be useful in devising meaningful strategies and also in conducting similar studies in different Adivasi areas of India.

ABOUT THE STUDY AREA

Raigad district is strategically located between the important areas of Mumbai, Thane, Pune, Satara and Ratnagiri. On the eastern side, it is endowed with rich forests in the mountain range of the Western Ghats and the long coastline of the Arabian Sea on the western side. The Jawaharlal Nehru Port, which is a key channel for the transit of goods flowing in and out of the country, is located at the city of Uran in Raigad district. While Mumbai is known as the financial capital of the country, Raigad is one of the most industrialized districts in Maharashtra. With the growing congestion and crumbling infrastructure in Mumbai, the government of Maharashtra initiated the process of expanding Mumbai city by relocating many businesses and offices from the city to the adjoining Raigad district. This expansion was named Navi Mumbai.

After the apparent success of Navi Mumbai, the government plans to set up a new international airport near Kharghar in Raigad district along with further expansions of Mumbai city in the Karjat and Khalapur blocks of Raigad district. A report prepared by the Ministry of Micro, Small and Medium Enterprises declares,

> India is growing in economic power and Mumbai is known as the commercial capital of India. Raigad District is positioned as

an alternate proposition to Mumbai. Raigad District will have unique distinction of being India's well planned district in terms of infrastructure, construction, development and transport.[3]

Raigad thus gains strategic importance in the current growth narrative of India. However, just like the state of Maharashtra, there are stark disparities within social groups in Raigad considering the fact that nearly 12 per cent of the district's population comprises of Adivasi communities, namely *Thakur*, Katkari and *Mahadeo Koli*.

ABOUT THE PEOPLE

This study was conducted amongst Katkari and Thakur Adivasi families in Raigad district. The name Katkari (also: *Kathkari* or *Kathodi*) derives from the former vocation of the community of making kath or catechu from *Khair* trees (*Acacia catechu*). The community is one of the so-called 'Particularly Vulnerable Tribal Groups' (PVTG), which are—according to the Ministry of Tribal Affairs—considered to be economically backward, with low levels of literacy, a declining or stagnant population, and a pre-agricultural level of technology. The Katkari mostly live in the districts of Raigad and Thane and, as per the 2011 census, the population is 285,334 persons. Experts consider two endogamous groups of the community namely *Dhor-Katkari* and *Son-Katkari*. However, some people tend to consider *Dhor-Kathodi* and *Son-Kathodi* as additional endogamous groups. The rate of literacy amongst Katkari is very low. Over 90 per cent of Katkari families are landless and are dependent on wage labour for their livelihood. A large number of Katkari hamlets are located on private land, rendering Katkari families vulnerable to arbitrary eviction by the landlords. This insecure status of villages translates into poor civic amenities in Katkari hamlets. Hunger and malnutrition are also major problems of the Katkari community.

Katkari are socially and economically on the lowest rungs of the development ladder. Many families seasonally migrate to work as bonded labourers on brick kilns or charcoal units in faraway places. A large number of these families are caught up in a vicious cycle of poverty, indebtedness, bonded labour, and alcoholism. To make matters worse, the Katkari community was notified as a so-called criminal tribe during British rule. This legal status allowed the colonial government to resort to collective punishment and other draconian measures vis-à-vis such communities. The stamp of criminality in the eyes of the mainstream society continues to be a major handicap for the Katkari community even today.

The Thakur or *Thakar Adivasi* community is scattered in different parts of Maharashtra. As per the 2001 census, the population of Thakur in Maharashtra was 487,696 persons.[4] There are two endogamous divisions within the Thakur community—*Ka Thakur* and *Ma Thakur*. Members of this community are found mainly in Raigad, Thane, Nashik, Ahmednagar, Pune and Dhule districts of Maharashtra. In Raigad district, the Thakur community has stayed close to forest areas and has adopted a settled lifestyle by practising agriculture as their main source of livelihood. As a result, Thakur families have more secure land holding as compared to the Katkari and are also much better off in terms of other socio-economic indicators.

The study shows higher rates of malnutrition amongst Katkari as compared to children from the Thakur community. Among the former, the severity of malnourishment is also much graver: While around 30 per cent of the malnourished Katkari children can be categorised as Grade I, 54 per cent fall into Grade II. And 16 per cent are in Grade III, also known as severely acute malnutrition (SAM). In comparison, 'only' seven per cent of the malnourished Thakur children fall into this Grade III/SAM category. Almost 50 per cent of them fall under Grade II and 45 per cent under Grade I. Malnutrition not only has long term effects on the children's health and results in high costs for medical treatment, it also leads to concentration disorders, poor educational performances and a higher likelihood of drop outs from schools.

METHODOLOGY

For this study, focus group discussions and community-based surveys were carried out in 16 Thakur and 14 Katkari hamlets in Karjat and Khalapur blocks of Raigad district. Topics of the study included family composition, land ownership and agriculture, livelihoods, forest foods, knowledge about and access to government schemes, health, alcoholism and more. The study covered around 100 Katkari and 50 Thakur families over a period of 26 days during October and November 2016. The villages were purposefully selected based on their locations closer to roads, forests, rivers/dams, non-*Adivasi* villages or even cities along with villages that are remote or located on hillocks. The variations were built in intentionally to understand the possibility of how a particular location influences the probability of hunger. The survey was supplemented by tools of participatory social analysis which cannot be fully elaborated here due to the scope of the study. However, the results of these analyses were included into the following sections to better understand the prevalence of malnutrition amongst children.

SURVEY FINDINGS

Housing, Land Ownership and Basic Amenities

Among the Adivasi communities in the studied region, nuclear families are the norm. Sons generally build their own houses after marriage and live separately. However, in the Thakur community some families let their old parents stay with them. Another common feature in Adivasi communities is two or sometimes even three families (generally brothers) stay in the same house due to a lack of alternatives. These cannot be considered joint families though since each family maintains a separate kitchen and they live as separate families in the same house.

Ownership of agricultural land is extremely important for the livelihoods of Adivasi families in the region. There are three types of land in the Adivasi area: low-lying paddy land; sloping uplands or *Mal Varkas*; and forest land. Millets, vegetables and other crops are grown on *Mal Varkas* land. In the case of the Thakur community, 54 per cent of the families own land, while 20 per cent have insecure tenure and 26 per cent of families are landless. Out of these 13 landless families, seven take land on lease from other farmers. Over 75 per cent of Thakur families cultivate food crops. Agriculture is thus a core livelihood for the community and most families have food security at the household level.

Legally speaking, a village should have ownership of the land on which it is located. However, a number of Katkari villages do not have their own land and are located either on private land or on land owned by the forest department. In the case of private land, the landowners do not allow the Adivasi families to set up backyard gardens or to keep livestock. Moreover, the Katkari families living in such insecure villages always face the risk of evictions if the land is sold to an outsider. Villages with insecure land generally do not have proper civic amenities. While all 16 Thakur villages have their own land, only three out of 14 Katkari villages do so. This precarious situation is reflected on the individual level, as 94 out of 100 Katkari families are landless. Of the six families who own land, only two families are cultivating land by growing crops. Only 11 families take land on lease from other farmers to cultivate vegetables. Thus nearly 90 per cent of Katkari families do not have food security at the household level and depend on the public distribution system (PDS) or the market for their needs.

Three-fourth of the Thakur families have set up their own small patches of gardens in the backyard of their house, where they grow vegetables such as gourds, egg-plant, okra or field beans during the months of monsoon. Some families also continue to grow a handful of vegetables even during the dry period. Moreover, many of these families grow useful trees around their homes, from where they can harvest fruits such as guava, drumstick, jackfruit, mango or lemons. Such trees are a source of necessary vegetables and fruits.

In contrast, only 15 per cent of the Katkari families have set up backyard gardens to grow vegetables. And even if they grow something, the diversity of crops is quite low. The small quantities of vegetables are consumed at home or given to neighbours and relatives. There is no surplus for sale in the market from such gardens. Overall, the contribution of backyard gardens to the food and nutritional security of Katkari families is thus extremely limited. Similarly, the contribution of useful trees is very limited in the case of Katkari families. Only eight families have grown one or two trees close to their houses. Therefore, there is a scope to intensify the cultivation of trees and of vegetables in backyard gardens in the case of Katkari families.

In general, most of the Thakur villages have decent civil amenities like electric lighting, proper roads, schools, health care facilities, community centres or provision stores. Most houses are permanent brick houses which offer proper protection from the elements besides providing better physical security. Moreover, most of the families have adequate facilities in their homes. For cooking, aluminium and steel utensils are used on mud stoves fuelled by wood. However, access to safe drinking water is a problem for more than 70 per cent of families and 80 per cent of families do not have toilets.

Out of the Katkari villages under survey, around one-third had basic amenities of average quality while two-thirds had amenities of poor quality. Safe drinking water is a problem in many villages as 58 per cent of families do not have access and the distance to the closest water source ranges from 0.3 to nearly 1 km. More than 80 per cent of the Katkari families only have *kuchha* houses made from wood which have to be rebuilt every three to four years. Hardly any family has a toilet in the house and most practice open defecation. Over 70 per cent of families do not have bathing facilities in the household. However, all the families have a basic kitchen facility with a simple fuel wood cook stove. Sometimes, these stoves are just made by stacking some bricks. While wood is the only fuel used for cooking, aluminium utensils are used predominantly for cooking and storing food or water. Most villages have electric lighting, but over 80 per cent of the Katkari families do not have legal meters since they are unable to afford the electricity bills charged by the public electricity provider MSEB. Some families who got legal connection reported excessive bills and harassment by MSEB officials over non-payment of bills.

Livelihood

The livelihoods of Adivasi are generally insecure. To strengthen their resilience, Adivasi families usually adopt a strategy of multiple livelihoods based on different resources like agriculture, wage work, forest resources and livestock. People usually find wage work in places like brick kilns, charcoal units, large farms or sand mines to do simple, but exhausting tasks. Agriculture consists of growing food crops for their own household food security or vegetable cultivation on a commercial basis. Forests are a source of uncultivated foods such as vegetables, tubers, fruits, flowers, seeds, honey, mushrooms, fish, crabs, birds and small animals along with various non-timber forest produce (NTFP) that can be sold in the market or exchanged with food grains in barter. Forests also provide fuel wood, timber for house construction, timber for furniture etc.

Agriculture, wage work and commercial vegetable cultivation are the main livelihoods for the Thakur community and they provide cash income as well as direct food security for the household itself. However, there are limitations to these livelihoods. The main constraints in agriculture are low land holdings, land alienation, poor soil fertility and difficulties in transporting the vegetables to the market. Wage work outside of agriculture is often not available, with the result that individual families get work opportunities for only two or three days a week.

In the Thakur community, over 75 per cent of families are engaged in agriculture, wage labour and vegetable cultivation as their main livelihoods. Livelihoods of Thakur families thus favour food security over cash income. Thakur families also pursue other supporting livelihoods such as poultry, bamboo craft, NTFPs or forest foods. The average annual income for a family from different livelihoods adds up to 62,133 INR. Though there is still poverty amongst Thakur families, the situation is not so desperate given the fact that most families have their annual food security arrangements in place.

In stark contrast to the Thakur families, almost all Katkari families are engaged in wage work of one kind or another and usually both men and women work. Around one-third of the families migrate for long periods to distant brick kilns, mines or charcoal units. Most of the time, work there is associated with exploitation, makeshift housing, hazardous working conditions and no regulation of working hours. Many Katkari people travel to distant places in the states of Gujarat and Karnataka which makes it even harder to provide nutritious food to children or to send them to school regularly. The fact that 90 per cent of the community are landless, combined with their historical dependency on agriculture as a source of income is the major reason for this dependency on wage labour. Only one family in the survey is involved in agriculture and livestock as their main sources of livelihood. Katkari livelihoods are thus based mostly on wage labour and their average annual income from this source is 31,557 INR per family. Many supplement this income through sale of goods like forest fruits, uncultivated vegetables, tubers, fish, crabs or fuel wood. All sources of income taken together, a family's annual income is 50,420 INR on average. Considering the fact that Katkari do not have much food grain from own fields, a lot of cash income is spent to purchase food from the market. Consequently, over 80 per cent of the families face considerable poverty while the rest still struggles with medium poverty. Overall, the income security is extremely low in Katkari villages and people there don't have any option but to adopt a multiple livelihood strategy depending on different sources. All this translates into precarious food security.

Diets, Food Storage and Children's Nutrition

Thakur families eat breakfast, lunch and dinner. Lunch consists of rice *roti* with vegetables, dal and rice while on some days, dry or fresh fresh fish is cooked as well. Similarly, dinner consists of beans, rice, chicken curry or fish curry. Thakur families regularly consume pulses, vegetables and beans. However, the consumption of green leafy vegetables is low and bakery products as well as other fast foods are on the rise amongst children. In the Katkari community, over 80 per cent of the families do not eat a proper breakfast. For them breakfast consists of a cup of tea with bakery products like toast and butter. Some eat the previous night's leftover as breakfast. Lunch consists of rice or *roti* with a hot, spicy dry fish curry, sometimes with a small quantity of vegetables. Dinner consists of rice with a spicy chicken curry. The consumption of pulses, vegetables, green leafy vegetables or fruits is extremely low in the case of Katkari families. Nearly 30 per cent of the families do not even prepare proper dinner since both parents are too drunk by the evening to cook any food, alcoholism being a major problem in the community (Please see section on *Alcoholism and Health)*.

Most Thakur families store adequate quantities of rice, paddy, finger millet, black gram, and various other sorts of spices, vegetables and other food products in their homes. They dry and store various vegetables, fish and meat for use for five months and more. For instance, surplus fresh fish caught in the rivers during June and July is boiled in salt water and dried over the smoke of the *Chullah*. This dried fish is stored and used when fresh fish is not available. Similarly, raw fruits of *Mahua* are dried and stored for more than five months. Thakur families also make mango pickles to be eaten with rice, dal and vegetables. Moreover, many families purchase a broad range of vegetables, fresh fish and chicken from the market to supplement their nutrition.

The average weekly expenses on provisions by a Katkari family are significantly less and they spent especially little on vegetables. Katkari families purchase rice from the PDS shop each month along with daily provisions from the local store. Chilli powder, turmeric and salt are the most common spices generally available in Katkari kitchens. Hardly any food stuff is stored in the homes of Katkari families and they usually do not preserve and store food at home. Even if there is a surplus catch of fish from the river on a particular day, the Katkari family will eat as much as possible and try to sell the rest in the market for cash. A lot of cash obtained in this way is spent on alcohol and gambling. The lack of food preservation deprives Katkari families of food security during times of food scarcity.

Food preferences of small children have undergone a drastic change over the past ten to fifteen years. From nothing but home cooked meals and forest food, children are now mostly eating poor quality bakery products, biscuits, samosas, noodles, *vada-pav*, snacks, wafers and other packaged fast foods from local shops. In the Thakur community, small children eat bakery products or noodles for breakfast with tea. For lunch and dinner, the meals are more balanced and children get vegetables, dal, beans, pulses, dried fish, fresh fish and sometimes chicken. However, it is sometimes difficult for the parents to convince the children to eat it, as especially small children prefer eating bakery products and other packaged foods from the market.

In Katkari families, children have toast, butter, *khari* or biscuits with a cup of tea for breakfast. For lunch, parents prepare a mixed curry of dry fish and vegetables with rice and chicken curry for dinner. Katkari children love to eat broiler chicken and most Katkari now even refer to broiler chicken as 'vegetable'. Between meals, children keep eating fast food and snacks and buy packaged products such as chips, wafers or noodles from local shops. Older children routinely eat 'Chinese Food' sold on carts in many villages. Such food contains high quantities of Ajinomoto or monosodium glutamate (MSG), a substance that is known to have adverse health impacts especially on children.

Adivasi communities have been relying on a wide range of forest products like vegetables, fruits, flowers, seeds, tubers, honey, mushrooms, fish, crabs, birds and small animals. It is estimated that more than 100 different plant-based foods, 20-odd different fish species, six types of crabs, 65 different birds and more than 20 small animals are consumed as food by Adivasi communities in Raigad district. It is important to note that the availability of forest foods is best when other sources of food dry out during the months from May to August. Then, hunger and malnutrition are at their peak and forest foods are a welcomed relief. Forest foods thus play an extremely crucial role in meeting the food and nutritional security needs of Adivasi people during periods of food scarcity. However, consumption of forest foods has declined considerably over the past ten to fifteen years.

Thakur families consume many different forest vegetables, fruits, tubers, mushrooms, fish, crabs, birds and even animals throughout the year. Although their consumption of forest foods has declined, Thakur families still consume much more than the Katkari families. Many women collect and sell forest vegetables and fruits in urban markets. Forest foods are thus an extremely important supplementary livelihood for Thakur families.

While Katkari people still eat quite a lot of fish and crabs from the forest, the consumption of forest vegetables has declined significantly. On average, they now consume barely six to eight types of vegetables compared to more than 40 types that they used to consume before. Similarly, the consumption of birds and small forest animals declined drastically due to shrinking game availability as well as inability of the Katkari to find time for hunting given the pressure to earn daily wages.

Katkari are considered different from other Adivasi communities in Maharashtra due to their practice of hunting and eating rodents. However, even the consumption of rodents has declined considerably in the younger generation due to social taboos and imitation of other communities. A lot of fish and crabs are consumed by Katkari families from June to November. Katkari families also sell surplus fish and crabs during this season in local markets and manage to earn an additional income of around 8,000 INR per year. On the positive side, some Katkari families also discovered the economic benefits of selling forest vegetables and fruits at urban markets. Katkari families from more than ten villages close to the Mumbai-Pune-Highway are now involved in the collection and sale of forest foods to urban consumers. Migration to brick kilns and wage work have declined in these villages and forest-based livelihoods seem to be making a comeback.

In livestock, Adivasi families mostly keep cows, bullocks, buffaloes, goats and poultry in their households. While larger space is required for cattle and goats, poultry can even be reared in small houses. The bigger part of the work in managing livestock is usually done by women. In Thakur communities, over 70 per cent of the families maintain household poultry, usually between 15 to 20 birds at a time. Most of the birds are sold in the market while a few are eaten at home. A bird brings from 400 to 500 INR at the market and, on average, poultry birds contribute 4,300 INR to a household's income. Some families even manage to earn as much as 15,000 INR from household poultry. The money earned is usually the women's income and they spent it on family needs. Approximately one-third of all Thakur families keep cows and bullocks. Cattle provides power for ploughing and transportation, cow dung and urine for agriculture and some milk during the months of monsoon. The average annual income from cattle is 3,700 INR. At around 15 per cent, significantly few families keep goats. On average, they earn an additional income of around 3,500 INR per year. Overall, Thakur families thus depend a great deal on livestock for supplementing their livelihood.

In Katkari communities, far fewer families keep livestock on their own. Only one third of all families keep household poultry and the number of birds per family is very low. In most cases, it's just five to six birds. Discussion with families who kept poultry revealed that all the birds were sold in the market and none were eaten at home. The average annual income from poultry is 1,320 INR. This money was spent mostly on alcohol and purchase of broiler chicken over three to four days. Only two families kept goats and cows while the others mentioned lack of space, time and family labour as chief constraints in pursuing livestock-based livelihoods. Families who migrate to brick kilns or charcoal units for six to seven months cannot keep any livestock at home. Overall, livestock-based livelihoods are extremely weak in Katkari families.

Government Schemes and Programs

Different government departments, agencies and branches like the Integrated Tribal Development Project (ITDP), *Zilla Parishad, Panchayat Samiti* or *Gram Panchayat* are active in *Adivasi* villages to implement various government programmes and schemes. In general, Thakur families have more awareness about such schemes and better legal documentation at hand. Consequently, they enjoy government support much more often than Katkari families. The latter find it difficult to access the support programmes either due to the unavailability of various legal documents or because they don't even know of their existence. In addition, one must keep in mind that the implementation by the officials is also extremely poor.

Out of the Thakur families, 85 per cent have ration cards. However, every second family reports problems like cards being issued with wrong names or missing the names of spouses and children. As a result, those families get less than their legally ensured share. Almost all ration card holder are under the official poverty line, but none is notified under the *Antyodaya Anna Yojana* scheme to support the poorest families. In contrast, all Katkari families with ration cards are also notified under this additional scheme. Therefore, each family is entitled to receive 25 kg rice and

10 kg wheat at a highly subsidised rate. However, most families only get 20 kg of rice per month, as the shop owners sell the wheat on the black market. To even get to the PDS shop, the families have to travel as far as five kilometres.

In Thakur communities, more than 85 per cent of the families have access to *Anganwadi* centres and in most cases children get nutritious food from there. However, the quality of food leaves a lot to be desired. Only two-thirds of the Katkari families had an *Anganwadi* centre in their village and almost every second Katkari child received no food from *Anganwadi* centres.

Alcoholism and Health

Alcoholism is at moderate and manageable levels in the Thakur community. Their average annual expense on alcohol is 1,950 INR, ranging between 2,500 and 9,000 INR per year and family. Alcoholism does not have a direct negative impact on the food and nutritional security of children in the case of the Thakur community. In contrast, the consumption of alcohol is very high in the Katkari community. Here, in 86 per cent of the families someone drinks alcohol and in one-third of the cases both parents do. The average annual expense on alcohol is as high as 17,973 INR, ranging between 3,000 and 60,000 INR per year. In families where both parents drink, dinner is often not cooked in the house. Parents give some money to the children and ask them to buy something from shops. Hence, alcoholism has an adverse impact on the food provision of small children. It is also likely that women drink alcohol during pregnancy and there is an urgent need to further explore the incidence of Foetal Alcohol Spectrum Disorder amongst Katkari children.

Among the health issues of Thakur children besides malnutrition, the most common ailments are diarrhoea, dysentery, fever, cough, cold, stomach ache, worm infestations and skin diseases. Exclusive breastfeeding for the first six months was done in only 12 per cent of the cases and in all other cases, the infants received outside milk and food within the first six months. Such diets don't meet the nutrition requirements of infants and are a major contributing factor for malnutrition. In cases of sickness, over 85 per cent of the Thakur families consult private doctors and less than ten per cent consult doctors at government health centres. But even then, they too go to the private doctors subsequently. Around one-third of the families have to travel three kilometres to the nearest government health facility; almost 28 per cent have to travel between four and six kilometres and 40 per cent between seven and nine kilometres. In these areas, government health centres do not function well. Poor infrastructure, lack of hygiene, absence of doctors, corruption, lack of medicines, indifferent staff, and a lack of effective monitoring are some of the main concerns. Therefore, most families prefer private doctors although they have to spend a lot of money for their treatment.

Besides malnutrition, the most common ailments of Katkari children are diarrhoea, dysentery, fever, cough, cold, stomach ache, worm infestations and skin diseases and therefore quite similar to Thakur families. Exclusive breastfeeding for the first six months was done in only seven per cent of the cases. More than two-thirds consult private doctors first, while most of the others turn to traditional herbalists and healers like *Vaidus* or *Bhagats* instead. Only a small minority of people turn to the government health centres as first option. Subsequently, they too go to private or traditional doctors. Approximately one-third of the people have a government health facility within a distance of less than three kilometres, another at the distance between four to seven kilometres and the rest between eight and twelve kilometres.

Gender Differences

Thakur women have to handle a very heavy workload at all stages of their lives. They do the housework, take the clothes for washing in the river, fetch water over a long distance, look after the children, cook food for the family, wash utensils, clean the cow shed, manage the livestock, periodically plaster the floor with cow dung, help on the fields, manage backyard gardens, sell agricultural and forest produce in nearby markets, collect NTFPs, go fishing; fetch fuel wood from the forest and much more. Katkari women, too, have to handle a heavy workload. However, they do not have much work related to agriculture, backyard gardens or livestock. Instead they go for wage work at distant work sites with their husbands.

Nutrition, health and education for girls is generally neglected in both communities. At lunch and dinner, boys and men are served first and they are given the best portions of meat, fish and vegetables. Women eat at the end and have to put up with the leftovers. Girls are married at a very young age, often between fifteen and sixteen years of age. Immediately after the marriage, there is pressure on girls from their family-in-law to produce an offspring within a year. Otherwise, they are threatened that the boy will leave them and marry another girl. Young married girls have to do all the heavy work at home and in the field throughout their pregnancy, often almost until the day of delivery. Pregnant women are generally given small portions of 'light' and 'easily digestible' food which, unfortunately, has very little nutritious value. Dishes like finger millet, chicken, mutton, crabs, papaya, jackfruit, drumstick and even wheat are often prohibited for pregnant women. Often, they don't get any breakfast on the assumption that too much food is not good during pregnancy.

IDENTIFICATION OF PROBLEMS

During the discussions in villages, a range of reasons for malnutrition came up repeatedly. To make them more tangible, competing goals exercises were conducted with the people of the villages of Malegaon Thakurwadi and Varose Katkarwadi. Some reasons for malnutrition were mentioned both by Thakur and Katkari people. The lack of hygiene in the village, the unavailability of health facilities, shortages of nutritious food at home, poor employment opportunities and marriages/pregnancies at a young age were repeatedly mentioned by members of both communities. However, there were some differences as well. Landlessness, indebtedness, the lack of safe drinking water, the burden of illnesses as well as the lack of information about government schemes and legal entitlements were all very important to the Thakur community, but almost absent among the Katkari people. In contrast, they complain about mismanagement in the Nutritious Food Programme by the Integrated Child Development Service (ICDS), the spread of alcoholism, increasing migration out of the region and the lack of education in combination with the persistence of superstition.

Following the general discussions, separate interviews with groups of men and women from both communities were held to understand how gender affects the perspective on malnutrition. The comparisons within the communities are summarized in Tables 1 and 2. Subsequently, an attempt was made to compare the priorities of Thakur men with Katkari men and Thakur women with Katkari women on factors that were common to both the communities. The results of this exercise are summarized in Tables 3 and 4.

In the case of Thakur community, there is a wide disparity between men and women regarding the evaluation of early marriages and pregnancies. While women cited them as most important reasons for malnutrition, men ranked it last. For them, unemployment is the most important reasons, which women only rank in the middle. The evaluation of landlessness is almost mirrored and women mention it as second most important reason for malnutrition. Other factors where men and women differ considerably in their priorities are the lack of hygiene, indebtedness and unsafe drinking water. While safe drinking water is considered quite important for good nutrition by women, men don't see it as very crucial. In contrast, they rank the lack of hygiene in the village and indebtedness much higher compared to the women. Overall, the level of disagreement between the genders is quite high. To tackle malnutrition effectively, there is a need for the Thakur community to reach some sort of consensus regarding the most important driving forces contributing to malnutrition.

Table 1: Level of Disagreement – Thakur Community (Malegaon Thakurwadi)

S. No.	*Factors*	*Men*	*Women*	*Difference*
1	Landlessness	4	2	2
2	Lack of awareness	9	10	1
3	Lack of hygiene	3	8	5
4	Early marriage	10	1	9
5	Lack of nutritious food	6	5	1
6	Lack of employment	1	4	3
7	Indebtedness (Debt)	2	7	5
8	Burden of illnesses	7	9	2
9	Unsafe drinking water	8	3	5
10	Lack of health facilities	5	6	1
	Total Difference			34
	Level of Disagreement			68%

Table 2: Level of Disagreement – Katkari Community (Varose Katkarwadi)

S. No.	*Factors*	*Men*	*Women*	*Difference*
1	ICDS negligence	3	6	3
2	Poor health facilities	4	4	0
3	Alcoholism	8	5	3
4	Early marriages	7	1	6
5	Migration	2	8	6
6	Poor hygiene	9	9	0
7	Unhealthy food	6	7	1
8	Lack of employment	1	3	2
9	Superstition	10	10	0
10	Lack of education	5	2	3
	Total Difference			24
	Level of Disagreement			48%

Table 3: Ranking of Common Factors by Men

S. No.	*Factor*	*Men (Katkari)*	*Men (Thakur)*	*Difference*
1	Poor health facilities	4	5	1
2	Early marriages	7	10	3
3	Poor hygiene	9	3	6
4	Unhealthy food	6	6	0
5	Lack of employment	1	1	0
	Total Difference			10
	Level of Disagreement			56%

Table 4: Ranking of Common Factors by Women

S. No.	*Factor*	*Women (Katkari)*	*Women (Thakur)*	*Difference*
1	Poor health facilities	4	6	2
2	Early marriages	1	1	0
3	Poor hygiene	9	8	1
4	Unhealthy food	7	5	2
5	Lack of employment	3	4	1
	Total Difference			6
	Level of Disagreement			33%

In the case of Katkari community, once again there is wide disparity regarding the evaluation of early marriages as an important factor contributing to malnutrition. Like Thakur women, Katkari women too have given it top priority. Katkari men have ranked it higher than their Thakur counterparts, but it remains among the less important issues nevertheless. A similar gap between the genders exists regarding their views on migration. While men mention it as the second most important reason for unsafe nutrition, women rank it very low. Other interesting, however smaller, differences came up in the answers regarding education, food provision through ICDS and alcoholism. Nevertheless, there is a much larger consensus on most of the other factors amongst Katkari men and women.

The comparison of the most important, common factors for malnutrition for men from Thakur and Katkari communities shows that unemployment is considered as the most important factor by both groups. They also concur on ranks for unhealthy food and poor health facilities, which rank in the middle in both groups. However, there is a difference of opinion with relation to early marriages and poor hygiene. Katkari men have ranked poor hygiene very low, while Thakur mention it as third most important factor. For both Thakur and Katkari women, early marriages and pregnancies emerge as the most important factor for malnutrition. This is quite understandable given the fact that young mothers bear the brunt of the situation. The low priority of men for this factor in the case of both the communities does not augur well for concerted action against malnutrition. Also with regard to the other factors, women from both communities show much larger commonalities, especially in their view on poor hygiene and unemployment.

CONCLUSION

The study shows higher malnutrition amongst children of Katkari community as compared to children of Thakur community. The causal factors behind it are diverse. Amongst the former community, economic reasons like poverty, landlessness, and insecure livelihoods have a direct, adverse effect on the nutrition situation of children. However, they are reinforced by social factors like early marriages and pregnancies, seasonal labour migration or the increasing consumption of junk food. Moreover, high alcoholism amongst adults and a general lack of hygiene in the village amplifies these factors. On top of it all, the government nutrition schemes are not properly implemented and proper medical care often not available.

Amongst Thakur children, the challenges to proper nutrition are not very different. Where malnutrition prevails, poverty, bad hygiene, increasing consumption of junk food, and poor medical assistance are mostly the reasons. However, a number of factors strengthened the Thakur community's resilience. Kitchen gardens, cultivation of mixed crops, consumption of forest foods, collection of NTFPs and the production of bamboo craft can provide protection against income insecurity and unemployment. Major factors for the Thakur community are the continuing practice of early marriages and pregnancies as well as the poor health care for young mothers. Especially the reports of women showed the existing awareness of this problem. However, there is a need to bring about further changes in the mindset of people, especially men, so that they follow the legal limits for age of marriage and take better care of their new-born children through proper nutrition.

Moreover, strategies for addressing malnutrition of children in Adivasi areas should give consideration to the following factors to address the issue on multiple levels. First of all, there needs to be more awareness about the long-term negative impacts of malnutrition. Especially when children are affected at a young age, the effects are often likely to continue throughout their lifetime. The same goes for pregnant or lactating women. Second, the problem of alcoholism needs to be addressed, especially amongst the Katkari people. Third, land and forest rights of Adivasi people need to be strengthened to secure their traditional livelihoods from these sources. Finally, people need to organize and mobilize to advocate for proper implementation of government programmes in Adivasi villages.

The onus for bringing about a positive change is as much on the people as it is on the government. Especially enforcing the minimum legal age of marriage and good health provisions for mothers will perhaps do much more for addressing malnutrition than any other actions. Enabling people to grow food crops on cultivable land would make the issue of unemployment possible to address to some extent. When the Katkari people are able to obtain sufficient nutritious food from their surroundings, they will become independent from the 'nutritious food' supplied by the *Anganwadi* Centres or PDS shops for the nourishment of their children. They will be able to exercise their own agency in addressing the problem of malnutrition and ensure a healthy and happy future for their children.

NOTES

1. Ministry of Home Affairs. (2011). *Census of India 2011.* Available at http://censusindia.gov.in/2011-Common/CensusData2011.html. New Delhi: Government of India.
2. United Nations Development Programme. (2016). *Empowering Local Youth to Improve Socio-economic Status of Katkari Tribe.* Available at http://www.in.undp.org/content/dam/india/docs/UNV/Strengthening_NYKS_and_NSS_Best_Practices/NYKS_NSS_Empowering_Local_Youth_to_Improve_Socio-economic_Palghar_District.pdf. New Delhi: Ministry of Youth Affairs and Sports.
3. Ministry of Micro, Small and Medium Enterprises. (n.d.). *Brief Industrial Profile of Raigad District.* Available at http://dcmsme.gov.in/dips/raigad_final.pdf. Mumbai: MSME-Development Institute.
4. Ministry of Home Affairs. (2001). *Census of India 2011.* Available at http://www.censusindia.gov.in/2011-common/census_data_2001.html. New Delhi: Government of India.

Advancing Food Security in India

The National Food Security Law and Its Aftermath

Harsh Mander[1]

Harsh Mander is a writer, human rights and peace worker, and researcher. He works with people living with hunger, homelessness, and victims of hate violence. He is the Director of the Centre for Equity Studies, Delhi. Email: manderharsh@gmail.com

Over many years my many colleagues and I have tried to comprehend (to the extent that it is possible for a person to do who has never known involuntary hunger) the consequences of subsisting with prolonged deprivation of food and recurring uncertainty about food availability as an unalterable element of life. What does it mean to live with the reality that you cannot feed yourself, your loved ones, those dependent on you—your children or parents? This results in enormous and varied forms of suffering and coping, including teaching oneself to crave less and less food, self-denial of meals; filling one's stomach with often harmful grasses and tubers that are freely available; sacrifice of other survival needs like medicine; the loss of dignity in trying to secure nutrition through foraging and begging; and desperate choices like debt bondage, migrating thousands of kilometres for any low-end, highly underpaid work; and sending a young child to work, sometimes into bondage.(2)

It is estimated that over 805 million children, women and men live with hunger and malnourishment on the planet.(3) This results in intense and—what is important always to remember—preventable human suffering. It takes a grave toll on children, thwarting their minds and bodies from growing to their full potential, and making them far more vulnerable to illness and death; placing special burdens of hunger on women, older persons, persons with disability, gravely ill, poor and destitute persons; and ironically also on many producers of food. In both scholarship and human rights initiatives to advance the right to food around the right to food, it is important to be continuously mindful of the intense human suffering that is associated with hunger. Living with hunger is 'an unremitting way of life: insidious, furtive and unforgiving' that 'lurks not just in the teeming countryside but also in the shadows of glittering cities'.(4)

It is imperative also to understand that there is mounting global evidence that today hunger and malnourishment are *preventable*. This brings centre-stage the role of a democratic state to reduce and prevent hunger through appropriate policies, laws and programmes locally and nationally; and indeed globally. Our focus in this article is on the role that a democratic but neo-liberal state like India, can and should play to reduce and ultimately end hunger and malnourishment.

There have developed around the world a very large body of scholarship and policy conversations that focus on the broad area of what is called 'food security'. FAO identified in the literature more than 200 different definitions of food security.[(5)] Several (but not all) scholars, policy makers and activists today agree that global or national food security is not enough; people need a legal right to food security at local, and household levels, and even individual levels given intra-family inequalities of gender and age (and also vulnerable single-member households). The UN Special Rapporteur said in 2012 that legislation on the right to food should go beyond just ensuring access to adequate food.

> The right to food is an inclusive right. It is not simply a right to a minimum ration of calories, proteins and other specific nutrients. It is a right to all nutritional elements that a person needs to live a healthy and active life, and to the means to access them.[(6)]

This view runs counter to a more widely held global belief about the appropriateness of economic strategies that prioritize rapid economic growth led by global private businesses, with a reduced role for the state. According to this counter-view, the state should not be intervening in the economic functioning of the country. There are variations in the way these business-friendly and minimalist state economic strategies have played out in different countries. Scholars have given various accounts and theories of the developments of the last 30 years during which these ideas have been the dominant influence on public policy in the majority of states of the world: for the purposes of this paper we will refer to this process as neoliberal capitalism.[7]

The emergence of growing global advocacy for legislating social and economic rights have facilitated the resurfacing of debates about state's responsibility vis-à-vis provisioning of public goods, especially in developing countries such as India. The short history of the evolution, and eventual formulation into law, of the National Food Security Act, 2013 is reflective of the pressures the changed scenario has engendered and is an account of how hunger and malnourishment were sought to be addressed (however incompletely) by state action.

Like in India, several countries across the world are dealing with the contention between the demands of neoliberal orthodoxy, which dictates that the state should not intervene in an active manner, and the consensus about combating the worst forms of human suffering such as hunger and starvation. Different countries are choosing varying pathways to ensure adequate food and nutrition for their people, and thus have a great deal to learn from each other. The FAO believes that,

> ...the protection of human rights through constitutions is the strongest form of legal protection as constitutions are considered the fundamental or supreme law of the land...every law in a country must conform to the constitutional provisions and, in cases of conflict, the constitutional norm will always prevail. [8]

A study by Knuth and Vidar found that 56 countries throughout the world have recognized the right to food in their Constitutions. 23 countries explicitly recognize the right to food in various forms: as an independent right, the rights of a specific segment of the population (i.e. children), or part of other human rights such as the right to development. South Africa, Bolivia, Guyana, Haiti have made explicit reference to the right to food for all persons. Brazil, Colombia, Cuba mention the right to food for specific categories such as children; and South Africa for prisoners and detainees.[(9)] In India,[10] Nigeria and Bangladesh, constitutions do not recognize the right to food as a fundamental right enforceable in courts of law, but as Directive Principles which represent the values to which the society aspires.[(11)]

The experience of countries like South Africa demonstrate that the inclusion of the right to food as a fundamental right in the progressive constitution does not in itself guarantee that people who live with hunger can exercise that right. The Indian experience shows that the realization of the right requires governments to ensure institutional arrangements, enforcement and grievance redress mechanisms. A number of countries have legislated, or are in the process of drafting legislations, for the right to food; these include Argentina, Brazil, Bolivia, Equador, Guatemala, Honduras, Indonesia, Malawi, Mali, Mexico, Mozambique, Nicaragua, Peru, South Africa, Uganda and Venezuela.[(12)] The Indian Parliament passed the National Food Security Act in September 2013,[(13)] at a time where many other countries were considering the drafting of such legislations. Brazil, meanwhile, has in place a comprehensive programme called Fome Zero (Zero Hunger) that consists of 31 programmes with local-level grievance redressal officers to take up individual violations of the right to food. Ecuador passed a framework law in 2009 that includes provisions for small-scale farmers such as the promotion of access to capital, resources and inputs required to produce food.

The focus of this review paper is to attempt to trace and analyze the four-and-a-half-year long, sometimes choppy voyage of India's historic National Food Security Act, 2013 (NFSA) from its initiation to its final passage, and the status of its implementation four years after its passage.

The design of India's legal and policy framework for the right to food (mainly through state provisioning of food) would be instructive in the context of other countries for many reasons. It is a rich and well-documented debate that unfolded for more than a dozen years in the public domain, in which government actors, political parties, law-makers, activists, scholars and other citizens joined. India shares common ground with many countries with large food provisioning programmes, and those with the right to food contained in their constitutions and statutes. The experience of its implementation in the first four years can help illuminate how effective socio-economic rights legislation is in guiding executive action.

This review paper will begin with tracing the journey of the law through its many official versions over four-and-a-half years between 2009 and 2013. The second part will describe in detail the debates that went into the various provisions of the NFSA, 2013, and the choices and decisions that were made at various stages of the evolution of the law. It will, in the third part of the paper, trace the process of implementation by the central and state governments of the law in the first two-and-a-half years after the passage of the law. The last part will conclude with an overall evaluation of the law and its implementation to secure the ambitious social and economic rights that were guaranteed to food insecure populations of India by its Parliament.

BRIEF JOURNEY OF THE NFSA

It is possible to trace the beginnings of the journey of the NSFA to the centuries of famines that devastated India through the long years of colonial rule. The sombre shadows of the Great Bengal Famine of 1943 fell long over the deliberations of India's Constituent Assembly after India won freedom in 1947, nearly as much as the cataclysmic death of 10 million people in religious riots during the Partition. Speaking to the Constituent Assembly on 22nd January 1947, Jawaharlal Nehru dwelling on 'the agony and hopes of the nation coming at last to fruition' declared:

> The atmosphere is surcharged with these quarrels and feuds which are called communal disturbances.... But at present the greatest and most important question in India is how to solve the problem

> of the poor and the starving. Wherever we turn, we are confronted with this problem. If we cannot solve this problem soon, all our paper constitutions will become useless and purposeless.

Ending hunger and communal strife, along with caste and gender discrimination, illiteracy and poor health, and centuries of de-industrialization, were the major preoccupations of the Constituent Assembly as it laid out the blueprint of new India. The Directive Principles enjoined the state to raise levels of nutrition and public health and ensure maternity benefits.

State provisioning of food in India began in the mid-1960s which were years marked by successive crop failures, drought and very low agricultural productivity, and looming memories of colonial-era famines. Policy-makers universalized an existing public distribution system established in colonial India to ensure cheap food to select cities to mitigate poverty and food insecurity; this was restricted to persons identified to be poor in the 1990s. States piloted and expanded young child feeding centres since the 1970s, as well as school meals. Pensions for the aged began only in the mid-90s.

However, until the turn of this century, these programmes were modest in scale, uneven in coverage and uncertainly linked to budgetary availability. But this changed after the PUCL petition filed in the Supreme Court in 2001 in the context of overflowing official warehouses of rotting grain and large-scale hunger, even starvation, which demanded the legal right to food of all persons. The Supreme Court held that the fundamental right to life was also a positive human right assuring every person all that is required for a life *with dignity*. This includes importantly the right to food. India's highest court therefore converted the range of food provisioning and social protection programmes into legal entitlements, expanded and universalized these, and established an independent system of its Commissioners for the enforcement of these entitlements.

Therefore a more proximate milestone in the journey for the right to food in India is the landmark case Civil Writ Petition 196/2001 in the Supreme Court of India, PUCL vs. the Union of India, popularly known as the right to food case. I have traced the history and significance of this case (a mandamus that continues 15 years later even up to the point of writing this paper) in my essay, Food from the Courts,[14] and will not repeat this here. But in this and other matters related to socio-economic rights, the Supreme Court expanded the interpretation of Article 21 of the Constitution for the Fundamental Right to Life to include not just the negative right to protection from encroachment of a person's life or liberty by the state except by due process of the law, but also to include all that is necessary for a life with dignity to become possible. And this of course includes the right to food. In its order in the PUCL case on 2nd May, 2003, the Supreme Court observed as follows:

> This Court in various orders passed in the last two years has expressed its deep concern and it has been observed, in one of the orders, that what is of utmost importance is to see that food is provided to the aged, infirm, disabled, destitute women, destitute men who are in danger of starvation, pregnant and lactating women and destitute children, especially in cases where they or members of their family do not have sufficient funds to provide food for them. In case of famine, there may be shortage of food, but here the situation is that amongst plenty there is scarcity. Plenty of food is available, but distribution of the same amongst the very poor and the destitute is scarce and non-existent leading to malnutrition, starvation and other related problems. The anxiety of the Court is to see that the poor and destitute and the weaker sections of the society do not suffer from hunger and starvation. The prevention of the same is one of the prime responsibilities of the Government—whether Central or the State. Mere schemes without any implementation are of no use. What is important is that the food must reach the hungry.

> Article 21 of the Constitution of India protects for every citizen a right to live with human dignity. Would the very existence of life of those families which are below poverty line not come under danger for want of appropriate schemes and implementation thereof, to provide requisite aid to such families? Reference can also be made to Article 47 which, inter alia, provides that the State shall regard the raising of the level of nutrition and the standard of living of its people and the improvement of public health as among its primary duties.

By its series of interim orders in this ground-breaking case, the Supreme Court converted many major food, nutrition and social protection schemes—such as school meals, old-age pensions, subsidized cereals under the TPDS,(15) supplementary infant feeding and health monitoring and services under the ICDS,(16) and others—into legal entitlements, expanded and universalized these entitlements, and established an independent mechanism of Supreme Court Commissioners to monitor on behalf of the Supreme Court, the implementation of these schemes.(17) The central government contested many of these orders in the Supreme Court, but eventually the orders led to an unprecedented many-fold expansion of budgetary allocations and coverage of these food and nutrition schemes.(18)

This culminated eventually in the passage of the food security law in the Autumn of 2013, which became a moment of intense national debate both inside and outside Parliament, about whether indeed the state should provision food at all as a component of its duties for social protection. Public opinion in India still remains deeply divided about the merits of this law which legally mandates public food provisioning.

The Indian National Congress Party when it fought the polls in the general elections of 2009 for the first time formally promised in its manifesto to pass a national food security law. It pledged to,

> ...enact a Right to Food law that guarantees access to sufficient food for all people, particularly the most vulnerable sections of society. The Indian National Congress pledges that every family living below the poverty line either in rural or urban areas will be entitled, by law, to 25 kgs of rice or wheat per month at Rs 3 per kg. Subsidised community kitchens will be set up in all cities for homeless people and migrants with the support of the Central government.[19]

A more cynical view could be that the Congress Manifesto promised this possibly because it was anyway forced to implement many measures related to state food provisioning and social protection as part of its obligations to the Supreme Court in the case 196/2001 in the Supreme Court of India, PUCL vs. the Union of India. However, it must also be admitted that it had already laid out during the first term of the United Progressive Alliance government, an impressive record of rights-based laws, including the Right to Information Act, 2005, the Mahatma Gandhi National Rural Employment Guarantee Act, 2006, The Scheduled Tribes and Other Traditional Forest Dwellers (Recognition of Forest Rights) Act, 2006, and the Right to Free and Compulsory Education Act, 2009, and the NFSA was a continuation of the same trajectory and social and political philosophy.

The UPA government first entrusted the task of drafting the proposed Bill to an Empowered Group of Ministers, who resorted to a very minimalist interpretation of the idea of national food security, and reduced the government's resolve to end hunger to merely the distribution of 25 kg of foodgrains (wheat and rice) a month to the 37.2 per cent of the country's population considered Below Poverty Line (BPL) according to the Planning Commission estimates.[20] Faced by severe opposition to this highly truncated understanding of food security, the government then passed on the task of drafting a National Food Security Bill to the National Advisory Council (NAC).

After re-election, the Prime Minister reconstituted the National Advisory Council (NAC) chaired by Congress President Sonia Gandhi, a body mandated to advise the union government about all aspects of social policy and law, especially for disadvantaged groups. This began functioning from June 2010, and in its first meeting, it laid highest priority to the drafting of the National Food Security Bill for consideration of the union government. A working group for the drafting of the NAC draft was constituted among the Members of the NAC.(21)

The NAC draft involved a year-long extensive series of consultations between Members, with senior officials of the union government and Planning Commission, and experts and members of the right to food campaign, among others. The final NAC draft was submitted in July 2011 to the Prime Minister by the Chairperson Sonia Gandhi.

Prime Minister Manmohan Singh consulted widely about the draft, including with his Economic Council and constituted a Group of Ministers to finalise the Government of India draft. The National Food Security Bill, 2011 was introduced in the Lok Sabha on 22nd December, 2011 (henceforward referred to as the 2011 Bill), and was subsequently referred by the Speaker to the Standing Committee of Parliament.

The Parliamentary Standing Committee received about 150,000 representations, many of these reflecting enormous expectations from those who were disappointed with the highly reduced entitlements of the 2011 government draft of the Bill. Over a period of one year, the Committee sought views of several state governments, ministries, members of the Parliament and representatives of organizations and researchers working on various aspects of food security, and finally submitted its report on 11th January 2013.

The NAC draft of the Bill, negotiated for over a year, was criticized by the Left parties and the Right to Food Campaign for failing to universalize the entitlement of subsidized food rations under the Public Distribution System (PDS). The strengths of the draft were its guarantees for food and nutrition security of food vulnerable groups such as children, women and people in conditions of starvation, the homeless, migrants and people affected by emergencies or disaster, and the independent institutions and mechanisms that it contained for enforcement of this rights-based law.

It was hoped by many that the Parliamentary Standing Committee would expand and remedy the gaps and slashes of the 2011 Bill—regarding the amounts and coverage of subsidized grain entitlements, and the many guarantees for women, children and vulnerable groups, and independent enforcement mechanisms, that had been excised from the NAC draft. But the hopes pinned on the Standing Committee were substantially belied. With the notable exception of recommending uniform entitlements for everyone covered under the PDS, extending the school midday meals to children up to 16 years of age, and proposing nutrition support also to adolescent girls, the Standing Committee recommendations further eroded the guarantees of the Bill.

The Union Government first passed the law in the form of an ordinance on 5th July 2013, and finally after debating the Bill in both houses of Parliament, it became a law on 10th September, 2013. Parliament's food security law mandates firstly that up to 75 per cent of rural and 50 per cent of urban residents receive 5 kilograms of highly subsidized grain each month. For poorest of poor households, titled Antyodaya, the entitlement is 35 kilograms a month. It further mandates universal maternity benefits and a free daily meal for pregnant and lactating mothers, school meals for all children from 6 to 14 years in government and aided schools, feeding of children below 6 years of age in ICDS centres and an additional meal for malnourished children.

The law itself had prescribed a full roll-out of the identification of persons eligible for subsidized grain by state governments under the provisions of the law within 365 days of its passage, but as we shall note later in this paper, it took much longer to roll out even the PDS component of the law. Universal maternity benefits have still not been implemented four years later, until the writing of this paper.

Major Debates and Choices in NFSA

In the second part of this essay, I will attempt to trace the evolution of major debates which transpired during the development and passage of the NFSA, in the four-and-a-half years of the official writing and consideration of the food law. These debates cover several questions about the nature and extent of the state's duties and possible strategies for food provisioning as part of a larger framework of social protection. They unfolded in the NAC, union government, Parliamentary Steering Committee and Parliament, and of course outside Parliament and government, in civil society, the press and academia.

The Food and Agriculture Organisation of the United Nations published in 2015, my account titled 'State Food Provisioning as Social Protection: Debating India's National Food Security Law',[22] that I wrote to summarize various sides of these debates, including during the years from the filing of the PUCL petition in the Supreme Court until the passage of the NFSA in 2013. The purpose was to assist policy makers and civil society activists in other countries who are considering a food security or rights law or policy, and not to trace how the debates actually evolved in various official forums in India. In this short book for FAO, I listed the choices finally contained in the NFSA with regard to each of these debates, but not how these choices varied and evolved in successive official versions of the draft law.

This potentially historic—but continuously contested—piece of social legislation carried within it the imagination of reducing endemic widespread hunger and malnourishment in India. The statute created legally binding obligations for the state to provision food—as subsidized grain, infant feeds, free cooked meals and social security cash transfers—to every child, woman and man who is deemed by states to lack assured access to sufficient food for an active and healthy life. In a country which—despite galloping economic growth—was home to every third malnourished child in the world,[23] and had the largest numbers of chronically hungry people (approximately 213.8 million people[24]) on the planet, it would have been reasonable to expect substantial national consensus for the proposed bill.

But many in the country's senior leadership, law-makers across all parties (barring the Left), as well as many planners, economists, industry representatives and the influential middle class were sometimes ambivalent, sometimes openly hostile to the idea of a food rights law. Some were convinced that it was populist, profligate and administratively not implementable. No wonder that the proposed law was continuously trimmed at every stage of its four and a half year consideration, and its implementation has been marked by delays, inadequate budgeting, and some dilutions.

The early draft law prepared by India's National Advisory Council (NAC),[25] sent to the Prime Minister in July 2011 contained many robust protections for children, women, destitute groups, malnourished children and people in starvation.[26] It was however criticized by the Left parties and right to food campaign for failing to universally cover all households with subsidized food grains, and for not containing protections for farmers. The union cabinet further curtailed many of the NAC recommendations in the Bill it introduced in Parliament in December 2011, and thereafter the Speaker referred the Bill to the Standing Committee of Parliament. The Standing Committee proposals were to cover all households with uniform entitlements of subsidized grain except those which were excluded by transparent criteria, and to extend school meals to children up to the age of 16 years, up from the current 14 years. But it otherwise diluted the already truncated official draft, with many disappointing and (in the opinion of this writer) indefensible deletions. The expectation that the Parliamentary Standing Committee would restore the body and soul of a strong food law, as it had done for the Right to Information statute, was not realized.

The Parliament finally in the autumn of 2013 debated and decided the contours of this law. Although the final law that emerged from Parliament curtailed many of the entitlements that were originally envisaged in earlier official versions of the draft law, and even more the demands from right to food campaigners and Left parties, it was still in the sheer scale of coverage of the legal entitlements it guaranteed larger than any social protection programme backed by law in the world. Its guarantees to 75 per cent rural and 50 per cent urban populations amounts to roughly 813 million persons,[(27)] 25 kilograms a month for a household of five persons' extremely cheap rice, wheat or millets; universal maternity benefits; universal school meals for all children in government and government-aided elementary schools (estimated to be around 174 million children[(28)]); supplementary meals for all children below six years (around 165 million children[(29)]) and pregnant and lactating women (around 5.1 million women[30]); and an additional daily meal for malnourished children and stunted (around 48 million children[(31)]) children. The Act also mandates that the state promotes exclusive breastfeeding for children below 6 months of age among all pregnant and nursing mothers in the country.

The debates that went into the drafting of this law can be analyzed in many ways. In this essay I use a kind of cognitive funnel, moving from the widest questions to others that are progressively more specific. These start with the broadest questions of whether the state should have the duty to provision food to its populations, or whether individual and household food access should be left to markets; and if so should this be simply by programmes or the binding mandate of law? At a second level, the debates examine what should be the scope of such a law, including who should be covered, if the law should be universal or targeted, and conditional or unconditional. And at a third level, the debates are concerned with questions of inclusion of most vulnerable groups—of starvation, of gender justice, of concerns about children, about especially vulnerable groups like homeless persons, and aged, infirm and disabled persons. At the final level, the debates concern the enforcement mechanisms, to what forums and through what processes would persons who are denied access to food find redress and be able to realize their rights. Below I analyze 10 major debates.

Debate 1: Should the state have the duty to provision food to its populations?

The opposition to the idea that the state should provision food to its food-insecure populations was firstly to its costs, the use of large public resources to feed the poor. Its opponents asked if it made economic sense for the state to subsidize food rather than stimulate economic growth; and if the additional spending was affordable. The critics of the food security law were of the opinion that if large public resources are expended on food subsidies, it will impact investment and growth, and damage the pace of economic development, the creation of jobs and people's capacity to earn enough to buy (or grow) their own food. They felt that the law forced the state to transfer unproductive subsidies to the poor.[32] A related cluster of criticisms of the food law was that it was not implementable and the investment therefore was wasteful, because state administrations demonstrably lacked the capacity to actually deliver the promises of the law, evidenced by even official studies which confirm enormous leakages of subsidized grains into the black market. They feared it would create dependencies, and would dis-incentivize work.[33]

This view was reflected in widespread middle-class opposition to, even rage against the law, reflected in television studio debates, articles in newspapers and so on. Food subsidies were described as freebies, doles, hand-outs and populist (Rahul Bajaj[34], Sadanand Dhume, Gurcharan Das). Yashwant Sinha, Finance Minister in the former NDA government, dubbed it 'senseless welfarism.'[35] The basic premise of these often visceral critiques was that a morally and intellectually bankrupt government was trying desperately to use tax-payers' money to bribe impoverished voters by offering them freebies. Critics like Bhagwati (who launched a very visible and excessively personalized public spat with Amartya Sen for his advocacy of the food law)[36] believe that the answer to hunger is not for the state to feed people, but to stimulate economic growth.

Between 2011 and 2013, when the Parliamentary Standing Committee was considering the bill, there was not a great deal of enthusiasm to make the bill stronger or more comprehensive. In fact the Standing Committee further diluted a bill which the union cabinet had already made a much weaker version of the draft formulated by the National Advisory Council. It removed most provisions dealing with vulnerable populations, such as community kitchens for the destitute and homeless, and all the provisions related to starvation and state responsibility. But once the national public arc-lights came to rest on this measure, opposition parties across the spectrum from Left to Right introduced 237 amendments to further strengthen the entitlements of the bill; however, none were eventually accepted. Nevertheless, the bill was passed in Parliament. It is significant that not a single political party —from the Right to the Left—opposed the principle that the state should provision food to those who are food-deprived or food-insecure.

On the other hand, supporters of the bill pointed to weighing the costs of the law to the costs of not implementing it, given existing rates of poverty and malnutrition. Dismayed at the Opposition's stalling of India's Parliament which led to the delay of consideration of the NSFB, Nobel-winning economist Amartya Sen spoke in a press conference of how every day's delay was resulting in the avoidable deaths of hungry and malnourished children.[37] It has also been observed that much of economic growth has not generated employment as expected,[38] and senior policy-makers in India do not assure the end of even minimally defined poverty for many decades.

They point to the fact that it is misleading to suggest that India is spending too much on subsidizing the poor. Oxford economist Sabina Alkire in an article offers a telling global comparison. She points out that India,

> …has a higher proportion of stunted children than nearly any other country on earth, yet spends half the proportion of GDP that lower, middle-income Asian countries spend on social protection and less than one-fifth of what high-income countries in Asia spend.[39]

In lower, middle-income countries, these expenses are 3.4 per cent of GDP. India's is a mere half of that at 1.7 per cent and even this low level is reached largely because of the rural jobs guarantee programme that ensures 100 days of paid work to all poor households in villages. The average for upper, middle-income countries is 4 per cent of GDP and 10.2 per cent for high-income countries. Japan spends 19.2 per cent and China, 5.4 per cent. Even Singapore spends more than twice as much as India, at 3.5 per cent of GDP. Proponents of the law also argued that it is not right to assume that the pot of public revenues is fixed and given. If India spends more on food, it does not mean pulling back on other important expenditures or increase deficits. The option exists to raise more taxes, and in the light of India's low tax to GDP ratio, scholars suggest that there is considerable scope for higher tax efforts.[40]

They also point out that it is disingenuous to oppose state spending for the poor, while supporting this for the better-off segments of society, and most of all for big business. Economist Pranab Bardhan protests the talk of the 'politics of dole' to describe public money spent on anti-poverty programmes.

> Most of the subsidies of the Indian government are actually to the business class and middle and upper classes, but that is not regarded as dole. Giving help to the poor for education, health, food or employment is called dole... (which) serves to distract from the huge amount of subsidies and hand-outs of the government to better-off people in the form of petroleum subsidies, diesel, fertiliser, LPG and several other subsidies. There are estimates that suggest that the amount of subsidies for better-off people is about three to four times more than the money the government spends on anti-poverty programmes.(41)

Costs for the food bill are estimated to lie between 1.25 trillion and 3 trillion rupees—supporters argue that real additional costs would amount to only 250 billion. This could be mitigated by increasing taxation on the rich and cutting down on corporate tax holidays that amount to 5 trillion rupees and more annually. Tax exemptions in 2012–13 totalled over five trillion INR, or 5.7 per cent of the GDP.(42) On the other hand, an Asian Development Bank report estimated that India spent only 1.7 per cent of GDP on social protection schemes for the poor, in 2009. Such a comparison shows that the 'lack of resources' defence runs thin, and points to the order of priorities that the Indian state has been espousing, which has disproportionately benefitted the better off. It must be borne in mind that the priorities of a state are always an outcome of political choices and are not naturally given.

Some supporters often also make a moral case for the food bill. Supporters argue that it is morally untenable for a government to let a situation persist where one child in two is still malnourished at that time,(43) and an estimated 230 million(44) persons sleep hungry every night. It was not their claim that the answer to mass hunger is for the state to feed people deprived of adequate food in perpetuity. Far from it, they recognized that what is needed is a range of measures to tackle the causes of poverty and hunger. These include stimulating economic growth, accelerating sustainable agricultural growth, sanitation, clean water, health care, social and gender equity, and decent and assured employment, among much else. But while all of this unfolds, they argued that it is economically (and morally) unacceptable for people to have to live with preventable hunger and its consequences, and this is why the state must provision food as long as it remains necessary.

> In a country which for too long is scarred by its absence of outrage about and suffering with desperate inequality, the greatest imperative for a right to food law is to breach our collective indifference. There is a great gaping hole in our collective souls, which we must mend. The people of this ancient land must push into history the enormous silent hopeless agony of generations, over centuries, of the inability to feed one's loved ones and oneself.[45]

Debate 2: Should the state's duties to provision of food as social protection be embodied in law?

As we observed, debates outside Parliament continued to contest the idea of a law which legally mandates public spending for food provisioning. But at no point was the *idea* of the law officially contested by the union government or any political party. In terms of declared policy at least, India's political consensus seems to support a law to ensure food security. But outside Parliament, this remained highly contested.

The two sides to this debate are well-known. Even among those who accept that the state should provision food as a part of social protection, there are some who still oppose a statutory provision to that effect in the law, because they are convinced that the law should not encroach on the jurisdiction of the executive. According to this view, the executive should have the freedom, untrammelled by courts and the law, to decide the amount of tax that should be imposed, on whom these burdens should fall and how these resources are to be invested. These should legitimately be political decisions of the executive, domains where the law and courts should take care not to tread.

This debate has long played out globally, around the suggested opposition of 'positive' and 'negative' human rights. These resulted in two separate covenants emerging from the United Nations Declaration of Human Rights in 1948, one elaborating civil and political rights and the other economic, social and cultural rights.[(46)] These were respectively the International Covenant on Civil and Political Rights, and the International Covenant on Economic, Social and Cultural Rights. The latter prescribed a large range of social and economic rights, including those related to the right to food. The recognition of these rights required states to do certain things, and not simply to restrain them in ways that civil and political rights did. The ICESCR itself suggested the middle path of 'progressive realization': to 'take steps…to the maximum of its available resources, with a view to achieving progressively the full realization of the rights…' But the Food and Agriculture Organisation of the United Nations in 2004 was much more categorical in recommending the pathway of legislation.[(47)]

Courts and constitutions also long tended until recently to accept the argument that social and economic rights laws would encroach on legitimate executive discretion. Although they sometimes advanced these rights, it was mostly with the careful caveat that rights involving substantial state expenditure such as for food and housing should be progressively realized only to the extent and at the pace that it was considered fiscally feasible by the elected government of the day. When the Indian Constitution was written in the late 1940s, it accepted the prevailing side of this debate, that civil and political freedoms alone, like protections against illegal detention and freedoms of expression and association, should be enforced through courts. These were listed in a chapter on Fundamental Rights. It reserved another chapter for social and economic rights, which it called Directive Principles of State Policy, which were morally rather than legally binding.

India's Supreme Court changed this with a series of rulings in the past two decades, which vastly expanded the frontiers of

Fundamental Rights. Article 21 of the constitution guarantees that 'No person shall be deprived of his life or personal liberty except according to procedure established by law'.[48] This was long perceived to be a negative right restraining the state from taking the life and liberty of a person without due process of law. The Supreme Court now held that this right is not just a negative right, but also a positive right to all that is required to enable a life with dignity, recognized as enforceable rights several socio-economic rights, including the right to food, right to housing, and right to work. The Court's decisions in People's Union for Civil Liberties v. Union of India, Writ Petition (Civil) No. 196 of 2001,[49] and many other cases,[50] had a lasting impact on expanding the scope of Article 21's right to life to cover the state's duty to protect a person's right to live *with human dignity*—a long distance from the original conception of the right to life as the state's duty to not interfere with a person's liberty. The Court's expansive interpretation of Article 21's right to live with human dignity places positive duties on the state to assure people the means to do so.[51] In this way, the right to food was recognized by implication as a core fundamental right derived from the fundamental right to life.

Debate 3: What should be the scope of the food security law?

There are two main sides of this contestation. One side believes that a food security law should address all causes of food (and nutritional) insecurity. The other side feels it should be restricted only to the duties of the state to provision food to food-insecure populations.

Supporters of the idea of a broad-scoped law argue that receiving food transfers from the state is only one of the ways a household's food rights can be secured. Other ways include growing one's food needs, or buying food. Therefore they argue that the food law should include also duties to enhance capacities of households to grow and buy food, and indeed their labour rights, and not just the duties of the state to provision food.

There is a strong body of civic and political opinion on the left in India that a food security law is incomplete if it does not contain guarantees for farmers to sustainably grow food. Nutrition and health experts and activists are also convinced that a law on food security should also contain guarantees for ensuring the absorption of this food, which in turn requires inter alia clean water, sanitation and health care. The view that prevailed finally in the NAC was to restrict the operational part of the law to state food provisioning obligations, and to list the other aspects as non-enforceable 'enabling provisions'. There was thereafter little debate to question the decision in government and Parliament to this compromise of limiting the operational scope of the Act to some aspects of food provisioning.

The right to food campaign and Left parties, and some Members of the NAC, argued strongly that a food security law is incomplete without farmers' protections. Since the 1991 economic reforms, farmers have experienced declines in farm income, consumption, employment, and credit availability.(52) Farmers suffer from unemployment or declining wages in agriculture in comparison to other sectors of the economy. They suffer displacement, landlessness, and chronic hunger. Most of India's 194.6 million hungry people live in rural areas and depend on some form of agricultural work to survive.(53) Additionally, unabated farmers' suicides and the below subsistence food expenditures of farm households reflect the depth of crisis in agriculture.(54) India's crisis in agriculture is linked to its crisis of hunger, which has resulted in the view that the revival of the agrarian sector is key to economic growth as well as food security.(55) Scholars argue that food security requires that farmers are assured equitable access to land, water, and affordable inputs required to meet India's food requirement.(56) Their reality is far distant from this goal, as farmers continue to suffer from unemployment or declining wages in agriculture in comparison to other sectors of the economy, displacement, landlessness,[(57)] and chronic hunger; each of these problems have increased since the post-reform era as a result, in part, of decreased public investment in agriculture and corporate incursion into all aspects of the food supply chain.[(58)] Government reduced public spending at the same time it adopted fiscal policies that benefited the corporate sector; economic reforms not only resulted in trade imbalances in agricultural goods but have also affected the conditions and patterns of cultivation for the small farmer(Ghosh, 2005).[(59)]

Therefore they argue that legislating food provisioning without protecting sustainable food production is like wiping the floor while leaving the tap running. For food security, farmers require land reforms for equitable access to land, and affordable inputs, a minimum support price guarantee for farmers, farmers' income protection, access to cheap credit, crop insurance and technical assistance, raising productivity of small farms and dry-land farms, preventing diversion of land and water from food production, enhancing public investments in agriculture, research and development, extension, micro and minor irrigation and rural power supply. Food producers also require protection of forest, water, grazing and fishing rights. Many commentators also regard as crucial protections for food sovereignty, such as farmers' control over inputs like seeds, and promoting decentralized food production, procurement and distribution systems.[(60)]

As far as including non-food measures for nutritional security in the law, proponents argue that addressing hunger is a public health concern which requires more attention to the biological relationship between starvation and under-nutrition. Scholars, including John Butterly and Vandana Prasad among others,[(61)] argue not just insufficient food but also unsanitary conditions, including unclean water, can lead to a state of malnutrition because the body is doubly vulnerable. The lack of nutritious food harms the body from the inadequate intake of protein, energy, and micronutrients, and the exposure to unsanitary conditions makes it easier for viral or bacterial infections to occur. Therefore a deeper understanding of both the biological basis of starvation and the economic conditions in which the poor live is required to understand how policies should be implemented to secure rights to live free of hunger and malnutrition, and that therefore the law should also contain guarantees for clean water supply, public sanitation and also health-care.

The various drafts of the law, from the NAC right up to the draft approved by Parliament, stayed with the limited scope to only food provisioning. Most opposition to this expanded scope of the law were practical, rather than principled. A law with such wide scope would carry the danger that adding several more entitlements would make it very difficult to implement, and it would collapse under its own weight. The complexity would grow further if the law tried to address also the second mode of household food security, namely defending the capacities to buy food. The latter required above all employment guarantees and labour protections, which are and must remain the subject of distinct laws.

The disagreements to including elements necessary for nutritional security were pragmatic rather than on principle. One was again the worry of burdening one law with too many diverse and distinct (even if complementary) rights. As germane were worries about how a law can best guarantee the food security of infants and young children, since research confirms that malnutrition sets in most irreversibly in the first 1000 days from conception (UNICEF, 2009).[62] For the first six months, a child's nutrition is best secured with exclusive breast-feeding. An impoverished woman worker in the informal sector mostly has no option soon after childbirth except to return to work, and leave her child in the care usually of an older sibling. The infant child then suffers a double nutritional whammy, being deprived of breast-milk and becoming vulnerable to repeated infections through insanitary oral intakes.

Therefore, to support the nutrition of the new-born child, the mother requires maternity benefits to enable her to rest and stay at home as well as crèches near her workplace which would allow her to regularly breastfeed her child. Many experts and activists wished to write both these into the food security law as well.

The final law (again from the NAC draft until the final NFSA) contains provisions of near-universal maternity benefits for the first time in the country, leaving out only women who work in government, the public sector or the private sector, which already provide these entitlements.(63) But the second requirement for infant and young child nutrition, of regular breast-feeding, required work-place crèches was not incorporated. However, its exclusion was not based on principle, but the accountant's logic of budgetary calculations.

Debate 4: Should state social protection be in the form of food or cash transfers?

An on-going debate at every stage, in both the drafting and implementation of the NFSA relates to whether it is more beneficial to transfer social protection as food or cash. Cash transfers in lieu of the PDS(64) would involve the transfer of money directly into bank accounts of identified poor households. The amount of cash transferred then would be the difference between the market and subsidized price of the grain. Recipients would withdraw this money to buy food of their choice from the market instead of going to their local ration shop to purchase subsidized grains.

The NAC draft did not include any provision for substituting food with cash. However, the 2011 Bill left the window open for 'introducing schemes such as, cash transfer, food coupons, or other schemes, to the targeted beneficiaries in lieu of their foodgrain entitlements'. The Standing Committee was more cautious, stating:

> Introduction of cash transfer at this juncture may not be desirable. Government should ensure that banking infrastructure and

accessibility to banking facility are made available in all parts of the country including remote, rural and hilly tribal areas before introducing cash transfer in lieu of food subsidy.

However, the final NFSA retains the enabling provision for cash transfers as worded in the 2011 government bill.

The arguments supporting replacing food with cash include the conviction that providing subsidies in the form of cash directly to the poor would enable them to access goods currently denied due to a defunct PDS beset by corruption.[(65)] Further, it would enable people to buy food of their choice from the open market, and not be restricted to items sold in the PDS, which are often inferior in quality and very limited in range. People could buy food which is of better quality, as the food in the open market is sold at market price and subject to competition.[(66)]

Providing subsidy directly to the poor would both bypass brokers as well as reduce holding costs of grains in government silos, which accrue wastefully due to lack of local storage and transportation facilities. The amount of grain actually required for India's buffer stock needs for price stabilization could be held in better quality warehouses, eliminating wastage and rotting. Cash transfers would help reduce the fiscal deficit by curbing the amount of expenditures earmarked for the PDS that are siphoned off through corruption, as well as the substantially higher costs of transferring food rather than cash.

Most opponents of cash transfer clarify that what they oppose is not the principle of transferring cash to people, but the substitution of food transfers with cash. After all, many forms of important social protection involve cash transfers, including maternity benefits, which is included in the NFSA, and old age pensions, which are not. They are unconvinced that cash transfers would bring about drastic reductions in leakages in welfare programmes, as there is nothing intrinsic to cash transfers which renders them less vulnerable to leakages. Indeed, empirically, irregularities are found to be high also in existing cash transfer programmes such as pensions and maternity entitlements. There are also practical concerns that India's banking system will take a long time to be genuinely inclusive of people in remote rural regions. When the nearest bank or post-office branch is far from a village, each cash withdrawal entails additional cost and time burdens. Therefore accessing cash from distant banks may burden people even more than current modes of food transfers.

Cash transfers also make it possible to spend the money on non-food items, which would decrease the amount of household money left for buying food. Research confirms that decisions relating to cash in households tend to be made by men, who may or may not spend it on food. Decisions relating to food are culturally made by women, and these are more likely therefore to end up as food in the child's stomach. Further the PDS provides rations at a constant price, irrespective of the fluctuations in the market prices of these rations. This therefore provides a shield against inflation, a benefit that cash transfers cannot match.

The PDS requires the government to procure food from farmers. It is feared replacing this with cash transfers would dismantle this obligation of the government, with adverse impact on agriculture and farmer protection. Indeed, the guarantee of Minimum Support Price (MSP) purchase by the government for wheat and rice is the most important instrument for protection of farmers' income in India. This would become infeasible if the government could not offload a lot of this grain back through the PDS.

Given the high levels of poverty, illiteracy and inequality in gender relations and insufficient banking infrastructure in the country, India is currently ill suited for the replacement of services with cash transfers. Dismantling the PDS will rob farmers—ironically among the most food insecure segments of the population—of guaranteed procurement at minimum support prices, and deepen the agrarian crisis. Since the government has failed to increase the amounts of current cash assistance such as pensions and maternity benefits commensurately with inflation, there is little reason to believe that cash transfers for food will also increase adequately with rise in food prices. Finally, given the fungible nature of cash, there is always the risk of money for food getting spent on other items.

Debate 5: Coverage with subsidized PDS grain

Who in the population resident in the country should fittingly be provided subsidized grain guaranteed by the food law? The question has two parts. One relates to whether food provisioning should be restricted only to citizens or provided to all residents, regardless of citizenship; and the second whether these rights should be universal or targeted to the officially identified vulnerable populations. We shall take each of these in turn.

Coverage: Citizens or Residents?

If we analyze the debates in the NAC, union cabinet, Planning Commission, Economic Council and other official bodies and Parliament, we find that no serious case was officially made at any stage to restrict this right only to citizens. The language of the law refers to 'people', 'children', and 'women' without the caveat anywhere of the requirement of citizenship, thereby implicitly accepting its application also to non-citizens and unregistered migrants. But the union government by notification requires proof of identity from beneficiaries of PDS, which automatically restricts entitlements to citizens.

The question may be asked if socio-economic rights (which involve budgetary implications) should be restricted to legal citizens. The constitutional position in India is debatable. Some legal scholars suggest that fundamental right to life under the Constitution extends to all residents. As we have seen earlier, the right to life has been interpreted by the Indian Supreme Court to include the right to food (and other rights essential for a life with dignity). If this is accepted, then the right to food also would extend to non-citizen residents because it is part of the fundamental right to life. The ICESCR also speaks of ensuring the right to food of 'everyone' within or under jurisdiction of the state, and explicitly bars discrimination on the basis of nationality, among other grounds.(67)

International covenants and declarations explicitly advocate the formulation of a legal framework by states to protect vulnerable populations of non-citizens from discrimination. The right to food and freedom from hunger is recognized as an integral part of ending discrimination and should extend to all individuals, based on their personhood, irrespective of national identity. Most states that provision food, with or without a rights-based framework, limit entitlements to its citizens (except South Africa). India is home to millions of immigrants with varied legal status, at any point in time, but does not have a legal framework to address the status of non-citizens with respect to public services. Although by notification, the condition of providing identity proof for the public distribution system restricts these to citizens, but feeding programmes for women and children do not contain any such requirement, therefore by implication and at least in principle these can potentially be extended to non-citizens.

Besides, on the ground, problems of exclusion of people of contested citizenship remain for some immigrants, homeless populations, forest dwellers and those residing in remote areas. These vulnerable populations often lack any kind of citizen documentation, often sought by officials.

Coverage: Universal or Targeted

The other part of the issue of coverage—of whether the entitlements should be universal or targeted—was much more contested. For the Left parties, the right to food campaign and some NAC Members, it was an article of faith that the entitlements under the NFSA must be universal. Supporters of a universal PDS argue that the state has a moral duty to provide basic public goods to all citizens, or residents within a jurisdiction; therefore considerations of fiscal discipline and efficiency are of secondary importance in this framework. Building on the idea that each person has a fundamental human right to life with dignity, they argued that a constitutional democracy must guarantee a set of basic rights—or what are sometimes described as basic public goods—to all persons under the constitutional and statutory scaffolding of universal socio-economic human rights, including the rights to food, health-care, education and social security, and given that of these are part of the Fundamental Right to Life, they cannot rightly be restricted to some, excluding others. Some leading economists like Prabhat Patnaik estimate that a full contingent of these universal rights would cost an additional 10 per cent of GDP.[(68)] One has to consider the case for increasing the tax to GDP ratio to provide for the finances required to ensure these fundamental rights. India's tax to GDP ratio remains low at 10.3 per cent; even if it is enhanced to 24 per cent, it will still be less than that of the US.[(69)]

This ethical argument for universal entitlements is bolstered by the dismal empirical experience of targeting in India, which has been found to exclude delivery to those most in need. Official studies themselves admit that if you are poor, chances are high that you will not be included in official BPL lists.[(70)(71)(72)] The criteria for poverty identification are often defective and opaque, leaving great scope for official discretion at the lowest levels, and high rent-seeking. Poorest households also are unable to understand and negotiate the official processes to identify the poor, all of which lead to grave exclusion errors, skewing targeting with a non-poor bias. Due to the various benefits of the poverty reduction programmes, many non-poor try to get selected as officially poor by manipulation or deceit (such as a wealthy farmer who manipulates land records to prove that his adult sons are landless).

In its practical operation as well, it has been found that a universal PDS performs better than the targeted PDS. States with a universal PDS show the best performance, followed by states with near-universalization, in turn followed by states with an expanded PDS. The performance of the states with targeted PDS is the worst (Khera, 2011).[73]

Further, targeting also does not consider the dynamic nature of poverty, instead assuming that a fixed pool of disadvantaged people exist at any given point in time, thereby, leading to the false belief that disadvantaged people can be identified accurately and affordably (Krishna, 2007).[71] This is one of the main arguments against targeting, especially in the most vulnerable countries: those exposed to frequent shocks and with very limited capacities. Proponents of universal schemes also argue that 'self-selection', where people from higher socio-economic strata would choose not to avail of food security schemes because of the lower quality of foodstuff available, would reduce actual off-take and expenditure on such schemes. But at the same time it can open the door to other diversions and leakages, like 'ghost' beneficiaries, and diversions to feed livestock.

There were strenuous arguments also against universal entitlements, in the NAC, union government and Parliament, which ultimately won the day. Experts argued that budgets and grain are both finite, and if they are provided to all, to the wealthy and well-fed as much as the impoverished and hungry, it will result in high wastage of both public money and food, and the spreading of these will be much thinner, so in the end the poor will get a much smaller share of public resources and subsidized food. This is especially relevant when other rights or needs are considered, i.e. access to clean and safe water, health and nutrition, education and social security. Examples of countries from North Africa, which have experimented with universal approaches, were also advanced to argue that this increases the cost of the programmes, reducing resources available for other needs.[74]A more powerful argument was also made on grounds of equity. Universal social security programmes have been criticized for lacking an element of affirmative action. Food denials and vulnerability between household vary hugely and many have asked if universal also means uniform entitlements. They question the justification of giving a rich landlord or wealthy businessperson subsidized grains in the same quantity and price as a destitute landless widow or homeless disabled beggar. But universal rights need not be uniform rights, and may recognize that whereas everyone has a right, the needs as well as the barriers to that right may vary for different segments of the population, and therefore may well entail different programmes for diverse groups within the framework of a universal right.

India went in finally for a greatly expanded albeit not a universal system; but also it had grades, with greater entitlements for those considered most vulnerable. It therefore tried to incorporate affirmative action for the poorest within a greatly expanded but not universal set of entitlements. But it left the crucial questions of how to identify those to be covered and excluded by both the expanded and 'poorest of the poor' entitlements to the states.

It is important to note that the debate of targeting addressed only the context of the PDS. There were no serious debates to target other entitlements like pre-school and pregnant mother feeding and school meals. They are virtually universal for public schools and child centres, for all those who seek it. In other countries, universal programmes have worked in practice as regressive targeting, with remote rural areas being left out. In India, too, there is in practice low coverage of these universal programmes in rural settlements of disadvantaged caste and tribal communities, and also urban slums. Also other problems of de facto targeting remain, such as of the out-of-school child who cannot access school meals. This last example will be discussed in a later section. The case of maternity benefits is also distinct and we shall consider this presently.

Debate 6: What should the law guarantee for food and nutrition security of children?

All versions leading up to the NFSA reflect, although to varying degrees, a recognition that children are especially vulnerable in accessing their right to food, being physiologically and psychologically dependent on adult protection and care, for food as well as a range of other survival needs and rights. Small children are unable to grow or procure food, and infants are also unable to communicate their needs. Children also have special food requirements. Inadequate consumption of nutritious food, especially in the first 1000 days of their life from conception, can have devastating life-long consequences on their health and future development.[(75)] The role of the state for child nutrition is therefore critical, especially for children whose families are challenged or unable to secure their full nutritional needs.

The NAC draft contained extensive provisions for food and nutrition security for children, and while these were gradually curtailed in some ways through successive drafts, the duty of the state to provision supplementary feeding to children is retained in the final NFSA.

For infants below six months, the NAC mandated support for practicing exclusive breastfeeding for six months through assistance at birth, skilled breastfeeding counselling, and related assistance.[(76)] The final NFSA more tersely mandate that 'exclusive breastfeeding shall be promoted' without elaborating what this will entail. For children from six months to 14 years, all versions mandated the provision of age-appropriate nutritious meals, free of charge, provided through *anganwadis* and schools. The final law also dropped the NAC provision for the state to ensure 'services including but not limited to supplementary nutrition, immunization, health check-ups, referral services, growth monitoring and promotion and pre-school education as may be prescribed, to all children in the age group of 0–6 years'. But the 2011 Bill and final NFSA limit the duties of the state to only provide extra meals to malnourished children.

There are also variations between various drafts and the NFSA of what constitutes 'meals' for children: Are these locally cooked hot fresh meals or can these also be packaged food? The NAC draft limits meals to the former. NFSA however takes an ambiguous position on this issue, by only prescribing 'meals' to children from six months to 14 years, and defining a 'meal' as 'hot-cooked or pre-cooked and heated before its service meal or take-home-rations…'.

It is also only the NAC draft which tries to protect the right of supplementary nutrition of children who are out-of-school, who are likely to be the most food and nutritionally vulnerable children in this category. It does so with the important clause:

> Any child below the age of 14, including those that are out-of-school, may approach any feeding facility such as anganwadi centres, school mid-day meals, destitute feeding centres etc., as defined under this Act, for a freshly cooked nutritious meal; no such institution may deny a freshly cooked nutritious meal to such a child on any grounds whatsoever.

There is also an important even if non-binding provision in the NAC draft for 'residential schools for all children in need of care and protection who are deprived of responsible adult protection'. This too was eliminated from the NFSA.

These exclusions effectively bar the food security of the most excluded child, such as the child without adult protection, street children and working children, the children of migrants and homeless parents. These children either don't have families, or their families are unable to provide their food needs, because the children are in exploitative and often unsafe work, or because they accompany impoverished parents into distress migration. The law as finally passed by Parliament is sadly silent and indifferent to the special needs and vulnerabilities of these children who are most at-risk of hunger, and debars them from accessing feeding programmes in schools.

Debate 7: Ensuring gender-just food entitlements

Probably more than in any other aspect of food security, some progressive measures for promoting gender-just food rights were retained through the various versions from the NAC draft right through to the NFSA. These are to designate adult women as heads of households for PDS ration cards; supplementary feeding; and universal maternity benefits for nursing and expectant mothers.

After children, women are the largest population group which suffer from food-deprivation and malnutrition, including due to intra-family inequities. These are therefore important measures to promote gender-just food entitlements. Women play a crucial role in guaranteeing their families' nutrition security. Those who are able to access livelihood opportunities are more likely to spend a greater part of their income on the family's nutrition than men.(77) However, because of the various forms of discrimination endured by women and girls, including those within the family—in owning land and other means of production and in accessing livelihood opportunities—a large proportion of women and girls are highly vulnerable to food insecurity; women and girls also face barriers in accessing education, healthcare, clean drinking water and sanitation, all of which are essential for nutritional security. On the other hand, recent evidence points to no significant food and nutritional differences between boys and girls, but women in families have higher anaemia than men(78) and tend to eat least and last.(79)

One important measure contained in the NAC draft—and supported across parties and groups without debate into the final NFSA—is to designate the eldest adult woman in every household as the household head for the purpose of issuing ration cards. Only in case a household does not have an adult female would the eldest adult male member of the household be considered the household head. If such households have girls less than 18 years of age, they would assume the status of household heads on becoming adults.

Other measures retained in NFSA include for every pregnant and lactating woman the entitlement to supplementary feeding during pregnancy and until six months after the child's birth and six months' maternity entitlements. Pregnant and lactating women have enhanced nutritional requirements to facilitate the growth and development of the foetus and the infant, as well as for maternal metabolism and tissue development specific to reproduction. Therefore, pregnant and lactating women are particularly vulnerable to malnutrition; nutritional deficiencies amongst pregnant women are a leading cause of maternal and child mortality, and can also have irreversible impairments on the development of the foetuses and infants.[(80)] The NAC draft provides for either take-home rations or freshly cooked meals for pregnant and nursing mothers, and this is retained in the final law.

Whereas this is very welcome—and indeed one of the most progressive elements of the NFSA, the provisions still raise many questions. The first relates to the amount of the maternity benefit. Critics argue that since maternity entitlements are provided as wage compensation to enable women to quit work and stay at home, they should be equivalent to the minimum wage and inflation indexed. Even if it is half the regular monthly minimum wage for unskilled workers, it should be at least around 4000 rupees a month in the city like Delhi.[(81)] Reproductive health experts also suggest that maternity benefits should be provided for not just six months, but for nine months, starting from three months before the expected date of delivery (Dand and Agarwal, 2014).[(82)] Second, there are worries whether given the low power of women within families, this cash amount will also just augment the family income, and not change the food and nutrition situation of women in any way? Small micro-studies indicate that indeed at least some of this money has led to better food and rest by women, but this undoubtedly needs greater study.[(83)]

The only dilution from the perspective of gender equity by the final NFSA over the NAC draft is the deletion of the provision of 14 kg a month to single person households. There are no special food entitlements for women who are not in the reproductive cycle, such as single and older women. In predominantly patriarchal societies, such as that of India's, women are viewed instrumentally as reproducers, caregivers, sexual outlets, and facilitators of a family's prosperity. Hence, single women are characterized by the absence of male 'protection' in their lives, which in most instances is actually an absence of male 'control'; this erodes the social status of women who are widows, divorced, separated, abandoned or never married (Singh, 2013). Women who leave their husband's families or are abandoned by their husbands are often not accepted back in their parents' houses, which leaves them with nowhere to go. Suggestions that the law should have automatically included single women headed households for coverage as separate households under the PDS even if the woman lives under the same roof with other people like her brother or parents, and pensions for single and aged women, were not accepted. There is a critique that the priority given only to the nutrition needs of women and girls who are mothers (or potential mothers) reflects a view that values women instrumentally only in their reproductive role.

Debate 8: Vulnerable groups and Starvation

It may be recalled that the 2009 Manifesto of the Congress Party pledged subsidized community kitchens to be set up in all cities for homeless people and migrants with the support of the Central government. This was in the NAC draft, and many other provisions in a special chapter for special groups, and another for the rights of persons living in starvation. However, both these chapters were completely deleted from the final NFSA.

The NAC draft mandated state governments to provide all destitute persons at least one nutritious and free freshly cooked meal every day close to their habitations, and affordable meals through Community Kitchens for homeless and other needy persons.[(84)] Subsidized meal programmes supported by public funding could become an important intervention to raise the nutrition status of urban homeless women, men and children. It would also free up a good portion of their daily incomes which they are forced to invest in relatively expensive street food which is low in nutrition and hygiene. It would be the last defence for survival with dignity of those who are forced to live at the edge. Debates in the NAC were first about whether this should be left to private charity, but evidence was mustered about how both religious and secular feeding charities have declined to negligible levels.[85] Questions arose also about how these should be organized, and suggestions ranged from extending the mandate of child feeding centres, to mandating religious and social charities with official support. There were discussions also about the desirability and feasibility of gate-keeping for these centres. Whereas it was considered feasible to prepare such lists in rural contexts, gatekeeping in the anonymous and highly mobile urban context even if desirable was not considered practicable. On the other hand, the opening of these centres to non-poor persons would enhance the dignity and quality of the services.

The NAC draft also gave migrants portable entitlements under the law at whatever location in the country that was their current place of residence. Migrants constitute a large proportion of destitute and homeless persons in cities across India.[86] These men, women and children often adopt circular patterns of migration, from the countryside to cities and back, and may usually be concentrated in certain vulnerable occupations and shelter-less environments. These individuals, in their struggle for survival, experience significant economic distress in cities, where they are exploited as cheap labour.[87] In such circumstances, they become vulnerable to multiple deprivations and face great difficulty in accessing social security programmes and basic facilities of food, health, housing and education. A major challenge is also the absence of portability of food rights, especially of PDS and pensions, but also admission into child feeding centres, even schools.

The NAC draft included provisions therefore for the state to recognize the portability of socio-economic rights for migrants who are seasonally on the move; they should be able to access their entitlements unconstrained by their physical location. This was retained in the 2011 Bill and not opposed by the Standing Committee. But this was finally dropped at the last mile of the NFSA, for reasons that were not stated, but perhaps because of unstated fears of larger movements of rural populations into cities.

For persons affected by emergencies and disasters, the NAC draft proposed to entitle them to two free meals a day for three months, and 200 days of wage employment or equivalent income for those incapable of working. All these entitlements for vulnerable groups were largely retained, even though with some caveats, in the 2011 Bill. However, surprisingly, it was the Parliamentary Standing Committee that opposed destitute feeding and community kitchens, in effect leaving those most vulnerable to food insecurity—the destitute and homeless—to fend for themselves. It proposed removal of the entitlements of affordable meals through community kitchens for groups such as the homeless people, on grounds of difficulty in identifying 'eligible beneficiaries', because the NAC had suggested that there should be no gate-keeping. It further justified the deletion by saying that such an entitlement risks 'breaking the social fabric as non-earning members of the family may be pushed out of homes to feed for themselves'(88)—a problematic claim with no empirical basis, and one that constructs poor families as those that would turn away their dependents only because of free meals. These objections unjustly stereotyped the poor as charity-seekers without basic dignity, and what is dismaying is that these arguments arose from law-makers.(89)

For decades now, the state governments of Tamil Nadu and Orissa have been implementing programmes which provide free meals to people in destitution. Evaluations of these programmes have revealed that they are administratively feasible, and without having any perceptible ill effects on society, prevent many vulnerable people from slipping into starvation.(90) The Standing Committee recommendations were accepted by the union government, and this entire chapter was deleted from the final NFSA.

Prominent among other highly food vulnerable groups are the aged.[91] Due to their diminished capacity to work, the aged are able to earn less than younger generations, which not only threatens to decrease their access to food, but also makes them more vulnerable to poverty, homelessness, untreated illness and violent abuse,[92] which in turn further undermines their right to food.[93]

Persons with disabilities[94] face huge educational, social and physical barriers and hence are at a significant disadvantage with regard to employment and therefore assured and dignified access to food. When disabled persons are also members of other highly disadvantaged social categories like tribal or Dalit people, their challenges to secure work and food are compounded. Single women who are widowed, divorced, unmarried, face various social restrictions and find it extremely difficult to secure gainful employment. Even when they are able to find jobs, they may be paid very low wages and forced to work for long hours. To sustain themselves and their children, single women often have to mortgage or sell their assets in distress, resort to undignified options such as sex work, begging and sending their children to work.

For all of these groups, early drafts of the NAC suggested inclusion of adequate unconditional monthly pensions in the food law. But these entitlements were finally eliminated from the NAC draft, not for any significant reason of principle, but for fiscal considerations based on negotiations with the union government.

The NAC believed that the first claim of a food law should be of people who live with starvation.[95] Amartya Sen (1982) demonstrated famously how democracy is the strongest defence against famines. But it seems powerless against endemic individual starvation. A right to food law was therefore seen to be meaningless if it neglected people living with—and dying of—starvation. Current Scarcity and Drought Codes, inherited and modified from colonial Famine Codes, contain no binding duties on states to prevent and address starvation.[4]

In this light, the Supreme Court Commissioners in the right to food case recommended adoption of a Starvation Code—a codified set of duties binding on public officials to respond to complaints of alleged starvation. The NAC draft accordingly provided comprehensive entitlements for persons suffering from starvation. It had a full detailed chapter on starvation that obliged state governments to establish mandatory protocols for identifying all persons and groups living in starvation or conditions akin to starvation, to take adequate measures to prevent starvation, provide effective and adequate relief in case of starvation, investigate starvation deaths, assign accountability and prevent non-recurrence. For persons identified to be living with starvation, it doubled their entitlements for freshly cooked meals, PDS grain allocations, maternity benefits and mandated 200 person-days of wage employment.

The 2011 Bill reduced these entitlements to the mandate for every State Government to 'prepare and notify guidelines for prevention, identification and relief to cases of starvation.' These heavily pruned entitlements in the government draft were simply removed from the Standing Committee recommendations. It also deleted from the 2011 Bill the safeguards for preventing hunger during emergency and disaster situations.

Accordingly, these entitlements were excluded from the purview of the NFSA law. No reasons were officially assigned for this deletion, but it can be speculated that probably this kind of accountability to prevent and address starvation was unacceptable for governments which typically deny the existence of widespread starvation.

Debate 9: Conditionality for food and social protection

Conditionality means that in order to become eligible for certain social security schemes, potential beneficiaries must fulfil some socially beneficial conditions.

It is significant that except for maternity benefits and implicitly for school meals, none of the drafts or discussions suggest conditionality for a person or household to become eligible for any food or social protection measures prescribed under the law. There has been no serious proposal for making PDS grain transfers conditional, before or during the discussions of the food law. Also not around the law's young child and pregnant mother feeding entitlements.

As stated earlier, all later versions struck down the clause in the NAC draft for out-of-school children. The argument was that whereas every effort should be made to enrol out-of-school children into school, they should not be barred on any ground if they arrive at a feeding centre and seek food. The deletion restricts mid-day meals only to children who study in schools (government and government-aided). Thus, implicitly, the law imposes the conditionality of school attendance for receiving mid-day meals, which deprives children who are unable to attend school from benefiting from nutritious, hot cooked meals. This penalises the most vulnerable children, who are excluded from both education and food.

The only other entitlement in which conditionality remains significantly contested is maternity benefits. In particular, there is a strong belief among many state officials that maternity benefits should be conditional on age of marriage, family size, ante- and post-natal check-ups, vaccinations, and institutional deliveries.(96) Many state officials as well as a section of reproductive health experts believe that these benefits should be subjected to the following conditions:

- the mother should be over 19 years old,
- she should receive benefits only for two live children,
- she should undergo ante-natal and post-natal health examinations, vaccinations and institutional deliveries.

The NAC draft did not include any conditionality for maternity benefits, and this was not tampered with even in the 2011 Bill. But the Parliamentary Standing Committee was the first to propose that 'Maternity benefit shall be admissible up to the birth of second child only in order to encourage stabilization of population'.

This restriction would be unjustly punitive for those who lack access to contraceptives and women without a say in crucial matters such as the number of children they are expected to bear. It is a gross violation of the rights of pregnant and lactating women to nutrition and rest, and of children of higher birth order to exclusive breastfeeding, who are anyway more susceptible to malnutrition. Past experience has demonstrated that such disincentives do not even contribute to their intended goals. India's fertility rate has been steadily declining and anyway approaching the level required for population stabilization.

In Parliament, most of the debates around NFSA concentrated on the PDS, and not the other major entitlements including maternity benefits. NFSA does not resolve these questions in a categorical way, as it guarantees near-universal maternity benefits to pregnant women based on the central government-prepared scheme. The language of the law does not clarify whether this scheme should or should not have conditions.

But these issues were contested keenly instead in the Supreme Court. Prior to passage of the NFSA, the central government ran a scheme for maternity benefits for poor pregnant women who fulfilled only two conditions—19 years of age and two births. But the central government subsumed this within a larger scheme subject to the entire range of conditions described above.[(97)]

The petitioners as well as the Supreme Court Commissioners, in what is popularly described as the Right to Food case, opposed these conditions in the Supreme Court. The court rulings broadly agreed with the views of the petitioners and Commissioners.[(98)] The central government argued strongly in support of the conditions, pointing to the need to incentivize higher age of marriage for the health of mothers (in a situation where the median age of marriage for girls hovers around 16.5 years); and to promote fewer births; and check-ups, inoculations and institutional deliveries.

There is evidence that indeed the imposition of these incentives was followed by improved maternal and neonatal health. Post-introduction, studies show an increase in rural institutional deliveries from 29.8 per cent in 2002–04, to 37.8 per cent in 2007–08 (IIPS, 2008);[(99)] and to a reduction of about four perinatal deaths (death of the foetus or neonate) and two neonatal deaths per 1000 live births (Dandona et al., 2010),[(100)] although attribution is contestable.

Moreover, the central government argued in the Court that if maternity benefits were not restricted to women who were 19 years and above, up to two live births, the scheme would discourage family planning and contravene the legal age for marriage.

In response, the argument by the Supreme Court Commissioners and petitioner was that these studies do not establish unarguably that these changes occurred directly because of the conditionality (Hanlon, Barrientos and Hulme, 2010).[(101)] Other arguments against conditions to access maternity benefits do not contest the benefits of higher age of marriage, fewer births, regular check-ups, inoculations and institutional deliveries. But, as the Commissioners argued, the purpose of maternity benefits is distinct from these objectives. It is to provide some form of social security to pregnant women and to enable them to access better nutrition during pregnancy. Making the cash entitlement contingent on the site of delivery would defeat its purpose.

Until the time of writing, the central government has not yet made any scheme for universal maternity benefits, it is not clear yet if the central government will in the end impose conditions of age of marriage, number of births, health check-ups and vaccinations, and institutional delivery, for pregnant women to become eligible for maternity benefits under this law. But the pilot scheme in 53 districts does contain many of these conditionalities.

Debate 10: Institutional enforcement mechanisms, fines and compensation

What distinguishes a rights-based law from a scheme or programme is that it creates obligations for the state, and the person who believes that her right is violated by the law has access to an independent and accessible authority who would hear her grievance, and in the event of violations, would have the power to impose penalties including inter alia fines and compensation.

This last section will try to map the provisions in various drafts of the law for establishing the following.

a) independent and accessible grievance redressal institutions and mechanisms, and
b) deterrent consequences for violations of the entitlements created by the law.

The NAC draft provided firstly for a National Food Commission that would be appointed by a Committee comprising, among others, the Prime Minister, Leader of the Opposition, and Chairpersons of various national statutory commissions. The Commission would have wide powers including to investigate, give advice, impose penalties including for the offence created by the proposed Act of dereliction of duties by public officials, direct payment of compensation and penalties for violations of the Act. A similar independently appointed commission with similar powers would also be appointed at the level of the state government. The 2011 Bill left it to the central government to notify the procedures for the appointment of the National Food Commission, and the state governments to notify the procedures for the appointment of the State Food Commission, which immediately rendered it less independent and credible. However, the law passed by Parliament did away completely with National Food Commission. The appointment of the State Food Commission was left entirely to the state governments, and its powers restricted to monitoring the implementation of the Act, investigating violations, and offering advice to the state government for effective implementation.

The NAC draft also laid great stress on the District Grievance Redressal Officer (DGRO), who would be appointed (on the lines of the All India Services) by the Central Government based on selection by the Union Public Services Commission,[(102)] and could be removed only based on a recommendation of the High Court. If effective and independent, this would be a proximate, accessible and low-cost institutional mechanism for persons to access their rights, and complain and receive remedies for any violations.[(103)] Their orders would be appealable to the State Commissions.

But the NFSA as it was passed by Parliament, again completely enfeebles this mechanism by simply requiring that the state government 'shall appoint or designate for every district, an officer' to be the DGRO. There is in this way no independent mechanism in place at the district or state levels, and none at all at the national level, to address grievances and ensure the implementation of the Act.

The NAC draft created an offence of dereliction of duty by public officials, for deliberate inaction, or 'colourable' action that results in violations of entitlements under the Act and/or starvation deaths, and for this the DGRO or State or National Commissions, as the case may be, can impose a fine up to 5000 rupees, with 100 rupees per day for further violations, and these can be charged to the salary of the offending officer. It also provides for compensation of up to three times the monetary value of the denied entitlement. The NFSA does away with compensation altogether, but retains the penalty of 5000 rupees. However, the chances of its fair and deterrent application are greatly reduced because both the DGRO and State Commission Members are appointed by the state government with no independent process of selection.

All effective rights legislations, like the Right to Information law, require strong independent grievance redress mechanisms, with penalties for violations by public officials. The 2011 Bill, the Standing Committee and the final NFSA diluted completely these enforcement systems, thereby critically weakening the law.

Overview of Debates: A Summary

This section has tried to summarize some of the most important debates that went into drafting India's National Food Security Act 2013. These debates 'unpack' diverse understandings of what constitutes the right to food, its scope, whether states should provision food, cash or neither as social protection, whether it should be legislated, its coverage, how it should be enforced, and a range of questions related to equity and the right to food, of gender access, children, vulnerable populations and starvation.

India's choices are not presented in this paper as a model for other countries to necessarily emulate, but it suggests that policy makers and scholars in various countries would benefit from a careful examination of its deliberations, contestations and the choices that need to be made. Although these debates occurred in India in the context of a national food security law, many of them would be equally relevant even if states assumed these duties, even without resorting to a binding and enforceable framework of law. It might help other countries which are considering ways to build a sturdier system of social protection and food security by diverse and expanded strategies and programmes for state food provisioning with or without legal frameworks, and those also considering new laws, or amendments to existing laws.

The discussion on these debates therefore can also inform understanding of how the conception of public goods is being shaped in a changed global politico-economic scenario. The preceding pages can be viewed as an account of how the contention between reigning neoliberal orthodoxy and a nascent consensus in academic and policy circles about ending the worst forms of human suffering such as hunger and starvation was sought to be addressed in India through the enactment of socio-economic rights-based laws like the NFSA. While it is only one example from one country, its relevance goes beyond its specific location.

We have seen that some believe that the facilitation of private markets is the best remedy to ensure that all households have the resources to secure adequate food. Others suggest that the state must also provision food to prevent hunger amidst the most food-insecure groups, as well as to ensure clean water, sanitation and health-care to prevent malnourishment. Some go further to suggest that states must advance protections of food producers, labour rights, and gender, caste and social equality. There are discussions about whether the state's duties should be in the form of a law or just programmes, also whether state provisioning should be conditional or unconditional, universal or targeted. There are also debates about what, if anything, must states do to ensure the access of vulnerable groups. And finally, if there is a law, what must be the mechanisms to secure legal rights.

In these ways the paper examines different views about what if anything can and should democratic states do to ensure equitable access with dignity of all persons to adequate food and nutrition. It does this by looking at the extensive, rich and well-documented debates that unfolded around India's National Food Security Act to draw larger lessons about contesting imaginations of the duties of the good state. The debates reflect also the on-going tensions between deeply entrenched historical inequalities dating back several millennia and the luminous pledges of India's constitution, as stated in its preamble, of justice, liberty, equality and fraternity.

IMPLEMENTATION OF NSFA: 2013–16

This section of the paper, based on evidence compiled from the winter of 2015 to the winter of 2017, examines the experience of implementing the NFSA in the four years that had elapsed since its passage. It will attempt to trace whether, and the ways in which, the executive—central and state governments—have complied with the mandatory duties as prescribed by the NFSA.

The law was passed under the leadership of the United Progressive Alliance central government in the dying months of its beleaguered second term, and the responsibility for leading its implementation fell on the shoulders of the BJP-led government that was swept to a majority in the midsummer general elections of 2014.

The law has been implemented by the new government and state governments, but with some delays and significant gaps. We will look at the gaps in its realization of four main kinds:

1. Weakened content of the entitlements
2. Inadequate resourcing
3. Problems in implementation
4. Problems in enforcement.

We shall look at each of these in turn in the sections that follow.

1. Weakened Content of Entitlements

There has been in some cases a gradual erosion of entitlements by resorting to definitions and criteria that have the effects of diluting entitlements or of enabling the exclusion of those who should have access to the entitlements under the law. This applies in particular to entitlements under the PDS and maternity benefits.

A major blow to PDS entitlements came with the PDS Control Order 2001.[(104)] This firstly restricted eligibility to receive entitlements under NFSA only to citizens and 'recognized refugees'. It is important to note that Article 21 of the Constitution guarantees the right to life to all *persons*, not restricted only to citizens. Therefore, the right to food, which derives from this fundamental right, also applies to all persons, and not just citizens. Accordingly, the language of the NFSA never lays down the qualification of citizenship. It speaks always of 'persons', 'women', 'children', never of citizens. This new requirement—contravening the position of both the Constitution and the law—would practically exclude the most vulnerable persons, among these are homeless persons, migrants, forest dwellers, nomads, de-notified tribes and separated women, who would find it nearly impossible to produce citizenship documents. (The states of Uttar Pradesh and Sikkim have formally notified the requirement of citizenship as mandatory to qualify for inclusion for subsidized food under NFSA).

The PDS order also freezes, until the next Census figures are available (effectively nearly ten years), any expansion in numbers of persons covered by the PDS. In practice, this would result in continuously reducing the percentage of population covered from levels prescribed in the law of 75 per cent for rural and 50 per cent for urban areas. New children born would be denied inclusion under NFSA for 10 years. As more children are born, households would get less and less grain per person. And there would be no scope to include new migrants, and new families which would slip into poverty.

The law left it to state governments to establish the criteria of who should be included and excluded for PDS entitlements. Although Section 38 of the NFSA empowers the central government to issue binding instructions to state governments for effective implementation of the Act, it has chosen not to issue any guidelines to states regarding the procedure and criteria for identifying eligible households. These criteria are not always in the public domain. But we tried to secure the relevant circulars from several state governments, and a careful study of these revealed that several of these had the effect of excluding the deserving households from these entitlements.

Of the 23 States and union territories for which we could collect information, only Odisha and Sikkim relied exclusively on exclusion criteria for identifying priority households. This in principle was the most inclusive method because state governments were required to identify not households which are poor but those which are rich, and exclude these from the PDS. All others would receive highly subsidized rice, wheat or millets. Many states like Himachal, Tripura, Madhya Pradesh, Rajasthan, Haryana and Punjab did not issue directions that current data (such as of the Socio-economic Caste Census or SECC of 2011) be used for identifying the households that should be included. Instead they used the Below Poverty Line (BPL) Census of 1998, data which is discredited and outdated. Bihar, Telangana and Assam on the other hand were good examples that relied on current data.

The natures of urban and rural poverty are very different, and required distinct criteria for eligible urban and rural households. But only UP, MP, Odisha, Bihar, Haryana and Rajasthan have different criteria for rural and urban households. For other states, there were common criteria applied for both rural and urban areas.

Income criteria for rural and urban poor households are rarely verifiable and objective, because most members of such households are engaged in informal work, much of this self-employed, intermittent and casual, for which actual earnings are impossible to assess transparently. Therefore for the selection criteria to be transparent and verifiable, it was necessary to abjure income levels for both inclusion and exclusion. The use of any income criterion only leads to unnecessary harassment, exclusion and corruption. Still the majority of states—including UP, MP, Rajasthan, Haryana, Tripura, Odisha, Bihar, Delhi, West Bengal and Chhattisgarh—used income as a criteria for exclusion and inclusion, despite advice that income for households in the informal sector cannot be reliably, objectively and transparently assessed. It was only Himachal among the states surveyed that did not use income, but only social and economic categories.

The law contains the highest entitlements for the Antayodaya (or poorest of the poor households). Since as we observed, income is not a sound basis to identify those who are the poorest, we believe that it should ensure inclusion of all members of clearly identifiable highly impoverished social groups, such as vulnerable tribal groups; households headed by single women even when they share a common hearth with other family members, old people, children and persons with disabilities; persons with stigmatized ailments like HIV and leprosy; casual daily wage workers; conflict-affected persons: i.e. persons that have been affected by communal and caste violence, including those who have had to leave their habitations in search for security as well as those who have not left their habitations, but have had their properties destroyed. However, we could not find states that have used such social criteria for universal inclusion.

There should be no requirement for any kind of identity proof in order to qualify for inclusion in the survey lists of priority or Antayodaya households. Any such requirement proves dysfunctional to the purposes of the NFSA and the Antayodaya programme, because the poorest persons—forest dwellers, circular landless migrants, single women, homeless persons and urban slum dwellers—tend to often have no documentation to prove their identity, residence or citizenship. In order to deal with anxieties that this will be vulnerable to misuse, the ration card could carry a clear disclaimer, that this is only prepared for entitlements under NFSA (and perhaps pensions) and is not the basis for any entitlements under other schemes, nor is it a de facto identity or citizenship card. However, no states have exempted the requirements of such documentation.

There has been even graver dilution of the maternity benefits created by the NFSA. (Incidentally, near-universal maternity benefits are in some ways the 'crowning glory' of the NFSA, because the ICDS and MDM[(105)] universal entitlements had already been created by the Supreme Court and were only being incorporated into the law, and PDS[(106)] was being expanded, but effectively universal maternity benefits were an almost new and substantial entitlement for nutritionally vulnerable women).

Universal maternity benefits were incorporated in the National Food Security Act not as a labour right of working women, but as an entitlement that was critical also for food and nutrition security, especially of children. For the first six months, a child's nutrition is best secured with exclusive breast-feeding. An impoverished woman worker in the informal sector mostly has no option, as we have seen, soon after childbirth except to return to work and leave her child in the care, usually, of an older sibling. The infant child then suffers a double nutritional whammy, of being deprived both of breast-food and becoming vulnerable to repeated infections through insanitary oral intakes. An underweight mother is likely to give birth to an underweight child, and the toll this takes is difficult to reverse later in the child's life.

Therefore, also to support the nutrition of the new-born child, the mother requires maternity benefits to enable her to rest, get better nutrition and stay at home; as well as crèches near her work-place which would allow her to regularly breast-feed her child in the months after she returns to work. This is why experts and activists wished to write both these benefits into the food security law. The final law contained provisions of near-universal maternity benefits for the first time in the country, but the second requirement of work-place crèches was not incorporated. NFSA creates a near-universal entitlement of a minimum of Rs. 6000 to all pregnant and lactating women, subject to such schemes as may be framed by the Central Government. It excludes only all pregnant women and lactating mothers in regular employment with the Central Government or State Governments or Public Sector Undertakings or those who are in receipt of similar benefits under any law for the time being in force. In a country in which more than 90 per cent women work in the informal sector,[107] with very high burdens of unpaid care work, the importance of this entitlement cannot be over-emphasized.[108][109] (Even many government employees, such as ICDS workers, do not receive maternity benefits).

It appears very likely from government announcements that the entitlement will not extend to all women in the informal sector. It has been restricted to mothers over 19 years, for only one birth[110] and for those who opt for ante-natal and post-natal health examinations, vaccinations and institutional deliveries. The purpose of maternity benefits is to provide some form of social security to pregnant women, to enable them to access better nutrition during pregnancy. It is not a reward for 'good behaviour'. Anaemia is prevalent among a higher percentage of women who have more than three children than among women who have fewer children, indicating they require more nutritional support. Malnutrition including anaemia contributes to a significant number of maternal deaths. Field evidence including a Centre for Equity Studies research suggests that cash transfers to pregnant women, if provided in time, were used in many cases towards food and health expenses during pregnancy, something that is otherwise not considered a high priority in household budgets. Excluding women who have two children or more would deprive 60 per cent poor pregnant women from the scheme. This would have been tantamount to putting their lives at risk and contributing further to the unconscionably high rate of maternal mortality. Furthermore, these conditions penalize the young, often adolescent and under-nourished mother, who is most often powerless in making decisions about her marriage and reproduction. There may also be constraints of available public infrastructure. Anaemia is prevalent among a higher percentage of women who have more than three children than among women who have fewer children, indicating they require more nutritional support. Malnutrition including anaemia contributes to a significant number of maternal deaths. Also, the amount of maternity benefits have been cut to 5000 rupees, from the 6000 rupees mandated by the law, which is usually illegal.

2. Low Resourcing and Coverage[111]

The timely and full implementation of the law has been stymied by inadequate budgetary allocations that would be required for fulfilment of the obligations under the NFSA, and also low coverage.

Let us consider firstly the question of the food subsidy. Under the NFSA, the entire costs of food grain mandated by the law (including procuring this grain from the farmers, its scientific storage and the subsidy to the consumer) has to be borne fully by the central government. The Union Budget in 2016–17 showed a decline by 45.84 billion rupees compared to the 2015–16 Revised Estimate of 1390 billion rupees.[(112)] However, this improved in the year 2017–18 when the Budget Estimate under NFSA was 1490 billion rupees, which is 121.65 billion rupees higher than the Revised Estimate of budgetary allocation under NFSA in the year 2016–17.

But the situation is much more complicated for other obligations under the NFSA, because the responsibility to ensure adequate finances for these vests with both the central and state governments. There is evidence that funding for many of these entitlements fails to cover the requirements if the law is to be complied with. For instance, the obligations for pre-school feeding are operationalized through its Integrated Child Development Scheme (ICDS). The official mission document of the Government of India for ICDS[(113)]calculated a total requirement of 300.25 billion rupees for the year 2017–18 to universalize this scheme as required under the law. The actual budgetary allocation in 2017–18 under ICDS was 167.45 billion rupees, representing a shortfall of 130 billion rupees against the amount calculated by the ICDS mission document itself.

Also, under NFSA all pregnant and lactating women were entitled to Rs. 6000 per child. In the financial year 2015–16 (actuals) the budgetary allocations under the Maternity Benefit scheme was actually reduced by 1.1 billion rupees, from 3.43 billion rupees in the financial year 2014–15 to 2.33 billion rupees in the year 2015–16 (actuals). Only 27 billion rupees were allocated under this scheme in the year 2017–18, which was only a third of what is required for universal coverage as per NFSA norms.[114] Further, as already noted, the rules issued by the Ministry of Women and Child Development (MWCD) restricted the benefits to Rs. 5000 and that too for just one child per adult woman. The inadequate allocation, reduction in the amount that women are entitled to and the one child restriction are evidence that the union government has in effect negated the right of women in India's large informal sector to maternity entitlements despite the obligations that are created by the NFSA.

The defence of the central government is that it has devolved much higher resources to the state governments, and with these larger financial resources in their treasuries, states will be able to allocate the necessary resources for fulfilling their commitments under the NFSA. But it is important to note that devolution has indeed meant greater flexibility to state governments in deciding how to deploy its financial resources, and not that significantly higher resources have been placed in the hands of the states.

The new financial architecture involves a higher devolution of untied resources to the states from 32 per cent of the divisible pool of central resources earlier, to 42 per cent.[115] It is erroneous to assume that this would necessarily result in a greater quantum of resources with states for possible allocation to the social sector. In fact, the situation is far more complicated because the central government also simultaneously cut back on transfers to states in the form of Central Assistance for State Plans and its outlay on many centrally sponsored schemes. The centre is also not substantially raising the quantum of its tax efforts. Therefore the overall accretion to states has risen only marginally, by a total of Rs. 450 billion.[116]

It is incorrect to assume that all states have either gained or lost the total amount of resources at their disposal compared with before these new financial arrangements. Manjur Ali of the Centre for Budget and Governance Accountability has carefully analyzed the impact of the new financial architecture on the net devolution of funds from the Union Government to the states. Among the states that have gained in absolute terms from devolution are Assam, Chhattisgarh, Madhya Pradesh, Tamil Nadu, West Bengal and Uttar Pradesh. But prominent among the states that have lost out are Bihar, Rajasthan, Andhra Pradesh, Telangana and Maharashtra.[(117)]

The Union Government allocations for ICDS saw a drastic 100 billion rupee fall in the 2015–16 Budget Estimates, compared with allocations in the 2014–15 Budget.[(118)]. However, only after the first and second supplementary budgets were these shortfalls met, and these came closer to the earlier year, at 154.89 billion rupees. The 2016–17 Budget Estimates show a reduction to 140 billion rupees.[(119)] Likewise, the Mid-Day Meal scheme (MDM) saw high budget cuts of 8.23 billion rupees in the 2016–17 budget (97 billion rupees) and 5.23 billion rupees in the 2017–18 budget (100 billion rupees) as compared to the actual expenditure in the FY 2014–15 (105.23 billion rupees),[(120)] and unlike for ICDS, these shortfalls were not made up in supplementary budgets.

Saumya Shrivastava of the CBGA has analyzed the budgets of four states to assess their spending on ICDS and the Mid-Day Meal scheme.[(121)] In Madhya Pradesh, for instance, she found a decline in allocations for ICDS in 2014–15 over the previous year's spending, and a marginal increase in the MDM. This despite the fact that Madhya Pradesh has a higher proportion of stunted and wasted children than the national average. Odisha also shows a substantial decline in ICDS allocations. She concludes that the budget cuts for nutrition related schemes in the 2015–16 Union budget, although reversed to some extent in supplementary grants, has adversely impacted investment in nutrition in some states. Whereas Maharashtra has been able to prioritize its state budget in favour of nutrition, this is not the picture that emerges from the other three states she studies—Madhya Pradesh, Odisha and Andhra Pradesh. All these states have witnessed a decline in allocations for nutrition-related schemes as a proportion of total budget expenditure. In Madhya Pradesh, the share of nutrition spending as a proportion of total budget expenditure fell from 12.4 per cent to 10 per cent.

All of this raises a larger question. Until the turn of this century, as noted earlier in the paper, the dominant prevailing conventional wisdom was that law, constitutions and the courts should not interfere with the primary authority of the executive to decide its budget allocations and priorities. This began to change with socio-economic rights-based court rulings, laws and constitutional provisions, in which India was a leader. Once Parliament passes a socio-economic rights-based law like the NFSA, the implication is that making adequate budgetary provisions to fulfil the duties of the state to provision certain public goods mandated now by law, is a binding legal obligation on the state. To this extent, the law places restrictions on the budgetary discretion of the executive. It must make the necessary allocations in its budgets as mandated by the law, or else it is free to go to back to Parliament to amend the law.

However, in India, we find that despite the passage of these socio-economic rights-based laws, it remains business-as-usual at Budget time for the executive. The union and state executive functions as though it is not in any way bound by the obligations laid down by these laws as it decides how much to tax, and how to spend these taxes (and its deficit financing). The most dramatic abdication—and we shall elaborate on this in a later section—is ignoring entirely the new entitlement of near-universal maternity benefits created by the NFSA. Four union budgets after the passage of the NFSA and we find no budgetary provisions for universal maternity benefits. The union and state Finance Ministers continue to tinker with budgetary allocations for food subsidy, ICDS and school meals, based on their political priorities, as they would have before the passage of the rights-based NFSA, as though the law does not create legally binding obligations for public expenditure.

Incidentally, we find the same ignoring—with impunity—the law and its obligations with regard to two other highly significant rights-based laws, the Mahatma Gandhi National Rural Employment Guarantee Act, 2006, and the Right to Free and Compulsory Education Act, 2009. The former is meant to be a demand-driven rights-based law, and should therefore receive as high allocations as there is demand for work on the ground. The latter is a constitutional right of all children, yet even six years after the passage of the law, less than 10 per cent public schools are compliant with this law,[122] and yet budget after budget of both union and state governments do not allot sufficient resources for achieving these legal (indeed constitutional) obligations.

Even four budgets after coming to power, financial resources have not been provisioned to implement a universal maternity benefit scheme. This despite Prime Minister Modi choosing to announce that such a programme will be introduced in his New Year eve address to the nation on 31 December, 2016. The government, in continuing violation of the Act, has failed to provide the required budget for its implementation. The figures just don't add up. India's birth rate is around 20 per 1,000.[123] The current population is around 1.3 billion.[124] So the number of births per year must be around 26 million. Thus as mandated by the law, at 6,000 rupees per birth, if universal maternity entitlements are to ensured which surely is the spirit of the NFSA, then (assuming, optimistically, that 10 per cent births are already covered under the formal sector) this would conservatively cost 140 billion rupees per year. However, in the plan presented in the official government press release,[125] the central government's contribution for the next three financial years from 2017–18 to 2019–20 is only 73.48 billion rupees, or 24.49 billion rupees per year. Ata 60:40 ratio for centre and state contributions, this means a total of barely 40 billion rupees per year, a little over a quarter of the budget (140 billion rupees) required.

Not just low budgetary allocations, other entitlements under the NFSA are also covering lower populations than what the law guarantees. Although the ICDS scheme should cover all children below six and all pregnant and lactating mothers who seek and need its supplementary nutrition, as per the Rapid Survey on Children RSOC (2013–14) data only 48 per cent lactating mothers of children aged 0–5 months and 46 per cent pregnant women reportedly received at least one service from ICDS centres. Further, among the children aged 6–35 months and 36–71 months, only 54 per cent and 48 per cent respectively received at least one service available from these centres.[(126)] Only 54.5 per cent of children below six and 70.3 per cent of pregnant mothers are covered by the services of ICDS. Since many ICDS centres are notorious for over-reporting, actual coverage is much lower. Therefore meal provision under the ICDS is far from universal as laid down in the Act and directed by the Supreme Court.

The situation is no better for free mid-day meals through schools. According to official data from 2017,[(127)] the scheme has failed to cover 25 per cent of the children (Primary and Upper Primary) enrolled in schools, resulting in deprivation of entitlement to as many as 32 million children out of total 129 million children enrolled. Among the states and UTs with large segments of children uncovered are around 54 per cent in Chandigarh, 45 per cent in Jammu and Kashmir, and Uttar Pradesh, 41 per cent in Jharkhand and Delhi, 40 per cent in Bihar and between 27 and 31 per cent in Rajasthan, Puducherry, Madhya Pradesh and Gujarat.

3. Problems of Implementation

The first implementation problem was the unlawful extension of time limits to roll out the entitlements of the Act. A time limit of 365 days from the commencement of the Act is laid down in Section 10 (b) of the NFSA for states to identify eligible households for subsidized food grains. Section 1(3) declares that the Act came into force from 5 July, 2013. However, when the 365 day limit was breached by most states and union territories (UTs), instead of coming to Parliament and seeking an amendment of the

Act, explaining reasons for the delay, the union government simply resorted to a series of extensions by administrative orders.

The first such order was dated 30 June, 2014, stating that only 10 states and one UT had begun implementation.[128] Another extension was ordered on 14 October, 2014. A third extension was ordered from 24 March, 2015, because the 25 remaining states or union territories had still not completed the required identification. These multiple extensions by administrative orders actually violate the law, and were challenged in another writ petition to the Supreme Court by the People's Union for Civil Liberties. In its petition, PUCL pointed out that as many as 459 million persons who were entitled under the NFSA to subsidized grains at Rs. 3, Rs. 2 and Rs. 1 for rice, wheat and millets respectively, from 4 July, 2014 were not receiving grains at the specified prices due to the unlawful delay in the implementation of the Act.

The Supreme Court expressed its dissatisfaction at this delay in implementing the NFSA despite three extensions.[129] The central government resorting to a series of time-extensions laid down in the law simply by the device of administrative orders represented a casual disregard by the central government for the law. In another matter related to failures of the union and state governments to respond to widespread drought, Swaraj Abhiyan vs. Union of India, the Supreme Court expressed surprise that even though the NFSA was passed by Parliament and it extends to the whole of India and came into force on 5 July, 2013, some States had not implemented it by the time it passed its order in May 2016. As remarked by the bench of Supreme Court:

> A State Government, by delaying implementation of a law passed by the Parliament and assented to by the President of India, is effectively refusing to implement it and Parliament is left a mute spectator. Does our Constitution countenance such a situation? Is this what "federalism" is all about? Deliberate inaction in the implementation of a parliamentary statute by a State Government can only lead to utter chaos or worse.[130]

It was only after this rap on the knuckles by the highest court, a full two years after the lapse of the time limit laid down under the law that the act (and that too only in relation to subsidized food) was finally rolled out by the union and state governments.

The central government has also notified rules to enable states to replace grain entitlements with bank cash transfers. This is being piloted in urban areas of Delhi, Chandigarh and Pondicherry. The union government's cash transfer rules provide that the money can be transferred to any household member's account, and not necessarily the oldest female member of the household. One of the strongest provisions of NFSA for promoting gender equity is to designate the eldest adult female member of the household as the head of household. These rules entirely erode this key progressive provision of NFSA. Moreover, it is likely that cash would in many cases go into the accounts of the male 'head of family', and is less likely thereby to be spent on food, as compared with if the cash went into the bank account of the woman head of household. A study conducted by Shikha Nehra at CES in 2015 also points to other difficulties with cash transfers.[131]

Chapter III Section 8 of NFSA provides for Food Allowance. The rules prescribed by the central government say that in case of non-supply from the central pool, grains should be purchased from the open market. The allowance that the central government would pay for this failure to supply is not at all punitive but only compensatory. In our understanding, in the spirit of the law defending entitlements this allowance should be paid to the consumers and should be high enough to be an exemplary penalty.

Also, the Central government is pushing for Aadhaar-based biometric authentication in the PDS, which requires the installation of 'Point of Sale' (PoS) machines in the PDS shops, and making it mandatory that the identity of the person who is drawing the subsidized food is verified by matching with their fingerprints against the Aadhaar database over the Internet. Dreze describes this as a 'juggernaut' which ignores rural realities.[(132)]

> This system requires multiple fragile technologies to work at the same time: the PoS machine, the biometrics, the Internet connection, remote servers, and often other elements such as the local mobile network. Further, it requires at least some household members to have an Aadhaar number, correctly seeded in the PDS database. This is a wholly inappropriate technology for rural India, especially in the poorest States. Even in State capitals, network failures and other glitches routinely disable this sort of technology. In villages with poor connectivity, it is a recipe for chaos.

This has led to a series of hunger deaths.[(133)]

It is acknowledged that one of the major causes of poor performance of ICDS and MDM schemes is lack of infrastructure in terms of schools, ICDS buildings and kitchens, and lack of drinking water and sanitation. According to the DISE 2015–16 data, [(134)] only 65 per cent schools in India have a boundary wall; 60 per cent schools have playground facilities; and 80 per cent schools have a kitchen-shed. The report also indicates that not all states have drinking water and sanitation facilities in their school premises. In Bihar 90 per cent schools and in Assam only 84 per cent schools have separate girls' toilets. Out of a total of 36 States/ UTs, only 33 have reported having separate toilet facilities for girls in more than 90 per cent of schools, 31 have reported having drinking water facilities in more than 90 per cent of schools. Further, according to Women and Child Development ministry less than half of the ICDS centres in the country have no toilet facilities.([135])

4. Failures of Enforcement

In the final analysis, what distinguishes a scheme or programme of government from a rights-based law, is the independence and powers of the institutions established under the law to enforce its provisions, redress grievances, and award deterrent punishments in case of violations by public officials. We also observed that the

NFSA did away completely with the National Food Commission; therefore there is no independent oversight and grievance redress institution at the national level. The NFSA further has left the appointment of the State Commissions, and the District Grievance Redressal Officers (DGROs) entirely to the discretion of the respective state governments.

From the information that we were able to collect until the time of writing from 10 states, only Bihar has appointed a State Food Commission. A party member of the ruling JD (U) has been appointed as the Chairperson for the State Food Commission, but there is no clarity on the role so far. In Jharkhand, the State Food Commissioner's appointment has been proposed. A separate set of rules will be prepared by the department for the Food Commission and the cabinet will approve. In Madhya Pradesh, currently the Consumer Commission has been given charge of the State Food Commission. In Maharashtra, for the present, a committee of state secretaries have been entrusted with this responsibility. In Odisha, the State Information Commission of Orissa has been entrusted with the charge for the present, and a gazette notification has been issued proposing the State Commission.

As far as the DGRO is concerned, in Jharkhand and Madhya Pradesh, the District Collector has been designated the DGRO. In other states, officials subordinate to the District Collector have been designated the DGRO. In Bihar, it is the District Supply Officer (DSO) or District Welfare Officer (DWO), in Gujarat it is the DSO, whereas in Odisha the Project Director of DRDA (District Rural Development Agency) has been given additional responsibilities for redressal of grievances relating to distribution of entitled food grains or meals and to enforce other entitlements under the NFSA. In this way, the officers responsible for ensuring the entitlements under the NFSA have also been made responsible for redressing grievances, which in effect give no independent recourse to persons aggrieved by violations of the Act. This is probably not surprising, because the Act itself simply left it to the discretion of state governments to appoint or designate any person for this role.

Conclusion: Making History?

India's Parliament did make history by finally passing the National Food Security Act in 2013. By this action, India became one of the few countries in the world in which it was now the legal duty of governments, enforceable in courts of law, to provision food for hundreds of millions of indigent men, women and children within its boundaries. Despite several infirmities of the law, the significance of this moment should not be lost in a land which for centuries suffered devastating famines, where chronic hunger continues to stalk more than two hundred million people, and which is home to every third malnourished child on the planet.

What has attracted most public attention are the provisions in the law for subsidized foodgrains under the Public Distribution System (PDS). Around three-quarters of all rural households, and half urban households, would receive highly subsidized rice, wheat or millets. The law still fell short of the demand that subsidized food should be a universal legal guarantee to all who choose to access it, because food is fundamental to survival. But it paved the way for the possibility of eliminating the discredited and divisive BPL identification as a qualification for securing subsidized food. The possible burial of 'BPL' did not come a day too early: Official poverty lines grossly underestimate poverty; and successive poverty censuses for identifying poor households have excluded many more impoverished households than those included. Instead, state governments were enabled by this law to identify not households which are poor but those which are rich, and exclude these from the PDS. However, as we have seen, most states have not adopted the path of relying only on the exclusion of rich households, and instead are preparing lists based on criteria for inclusion and not just exclusion. Sadly, there are also states that are choosing to use old and discredited BPL lists for the new NFSA entitlements.

The amount that the Bill guarantees, 25 kilograms a month per household of five persons, is below the scale of 35 kilograms mandated earlier by India's Supreme Court. With millions of tons of foodgrains rotting in government warehouses, this tight-fistedness could have been avoided. Guarantees should also have included pulses and oilseeds, to secure not just calories but also other elements of nutrition.

Another major failing of the law is its unconscionable neglect of the farm sector, ignoring the shameful irony that the largest population of food insecure households are precisely those which themselves produce food. The National Commission for Farmers chaired by MS Swaminathan had long ago proposed a Minimum Support Price Guarantee for all farmers' produce, which is equivalent to the cost of production plus 50 per cent. By including this in the Food Bill, not just the production of food but the income guarantee of food producers could have been legally mandated.

High malnutrition is related also to deplorable sanitation, open defecation, fouled drinking water, and denials of health care. The exclusion of these provisions from the law makes it so that even if it is implemented it will reduce hunger and food insecurity and denials, but not necessarily enhance the nutritional standards of the people.

But for me, the two greatest failings of the law are, firstly that it erased all protections for those who are most vulnerable to starvation. It should be self-evident that any food rights law must first protect those who are most gravely denied food. However it is precisely the provisions for these 'last persons' that have been eliminated from the law: The right of children who are out of school to eat from any feeding centre, pensions for the aged, single women and persons with disabilities, portable rights for migrants, feeding kitchens for the destitute and homeless, and legally enforceable protections and remedies for those who still live with starvation. I believe Parliament faltered when it lost sight of the poorest and hungriest—the malnourished child, children unable to enter school, migrant footloose labourers, the aged, single women, persons with disabilities and with stigmatized and debilitating ailments, the destitute, aged, infirm and starving. Only if they had been not just included, but also located at the heart of the law, would their hopeless hunger, unbroken through the centuries, finally begin to end.

The other profound (indeed potentially fatal) failure of the law is its unwillingness to establish robust and independent enforcement mechanisms at national, state and district levels, which are essential for the realization of any rights-based law.

On the other side of highly polarized public opinion, many were deeply dismayed by the law. Their unease stemmed from the high costs of the food law, which they feared would inflate deficits and fuel inflation; therefore they believed that the measure is profligate and populist. The deeper problem is that middle-class India, like in much of the world, remains deeply divided by debates about the most effective pathways to end poverty and want. One influential body of economists and policy leaders are convinced that it is only the rising tide of economic growth which will help overcome poverty, therefore the best contribution which governments can make is to facilitate private investment, while reducing government footprints of public spending and regulation. The alternate view is that even if economic growth is accomplished, those disadvantaged require substantial direct interventions of governments, for redistribution, protection, and state provisioning of basic human needs like food, education, health-care and social security.

Successive governments in India since the 1990s have placed central faith in private markets as the major vehicle for battling poverty. However at the same time, a combination of social democratic politics, judicial activism and civic mobilization have prevented the full dismantling of its welfare infrastructure. Instead

India has seen even its strengthening and backing by statute, especially during the last decade. India thereby struck a middle-ground by simultaneously pursuing two paths, of welfare and economic growth, probably unsurprising in a democracy with such high reservoirs of impoverishment and hunger.

The new government—elected midsummer in 2014, months after the passage of the food law and charged with ensuring its implementation—is even more emphatically and avowedly business-friendly. It began dismantling labour protections, and initiated writing down reforms in the compulsory land acquisition laws, to enable big business to both discharge labour and involuntarily acquire farmers' lands more freely. The latter had to be abandoned after extensive political resistance. Its policy to welfare and socio-economic rights such as to food, work and education, remains ambivalent. A significant section of the leadership of even the last government shared this ambivalence.

The law that was passed was opposed not just by those who were persuaded by market economics. Many supporters of the idea of the law were still contrarily concerned that the law does not go far enough: it is not universal, it neglects agriculture, it does not include provisions for the starving and destitute, and it ignores cohering dimensions of food and nutritional security, such as water, sanitation and health care, it ignores and excludes the populations which are most food insecure and deprived, and it does not contain reliable and independent institutions and mechanisms for its enforcement. There are many things that governments can—and some believe must—do to prevent hunger and malnutrition. These include growing enough food by sustainable technologies, promoting assured and decent work for all adults, ensuring clean water, sanitation and health care for all persons, and advancing greater economic, social and gender equality. In addition, the state must provision adequate food with dignity to those who are food and nutritionally vulnerable. Many believe that a right to food law should have contained all of these.

Still, they cautiously view it even as a potentially historic statute because for the first time legal duties on the state are in place which guarantee large populations assured and affordable access to food. They suggest that there is considerable scope for taxing the rich to ensure necessary investments in the nutrition, health and education of the working poor, as India's tax to GDP ratio is lower than most industrialized market economies, and India gives large subsidies and tax waivers to big businesses and the middle classes. The experience of states as diverse as Chhattisgarh and Tamil Nadu demonstrates that, given political will, the leaky and creaky PDS can be credibly fixed. There is no evidence that people work less if their stomachs are full: On the contrary, nourished workers are surely more productive. They also argue for the moral case for food provisioning in the context of the enormous avoidable human suffering imposed by hunger.

It is important to understand that a law is different from a programme or scheme of the government. It is entirely within legitimate powers of any democratically elected government to make, amend or withdraw any scheme. But once this becomes law, then this freedom of the executive is curtailed: It can choose to provision more than the law prescribes, but not less. This indeed is the rationale for creating a legal framework of enforceable social and economic rights. Just as the Constitution binds all governments, regardless of their specific ideologies and predilections to respect all democratic freedoms, socio-economic rights legislations like the food security law bind governments to be unwavering and steady in ensuring all that is necessary for dignified survival for all residents, regardless of competing priorities.

The device of socio-economic rights laws like NFSA therefore constitute critical protections for impoverished and vulnerable populations from possible neglect and deprivation by the state. India since the turn of this century, spurred by judicial and civic activism and political commitment in some quarters, had only begun to create a weak and incomplete welfare architecture of social and economic rights, albeit a weak one. The new government still has to demonstrate its real commitment to these laws and court rulings. Instead, by low budgets, lack of leadership for social sector strengthening, and some steps that threaten to erode these entitlements, there are fears that it is threatening to at least partly dismantle these incipient democratic protections of the poor by stealth.

As these contestations continue, hunger in India still persists on a scale unmatched in any other part of the planet. The right to food is the human right of every individual, to access with dignity, assured and adequate nutritious and culturally appropriate food necessary for an active and healthy life. Public action and public conviction must compel every government, in Delhi and the state capitals, to respect and realize this right, and to end the enormous human suffering associated with un-assuaged hunger.

The codification into law and constitutions of socio-economic rights is significant, but cannot in itself become a guarantee for these public goods to be equitably and assuredly accessed by all, especially socially and economically disadvantaged populations. Such laws are located in the tensions on the one hand of democratic aspirations and constitutional guarantees, and on the other of historical injustices and the pressures of neo-liberal policies. While many of the socio-economic rights have been trammelled within these tensions, it is important to remember that at least in part, they have also been realized. Democracy is simultaneously the site of egalitarian citizenship and of struggle. Socio-economic rights legislations are markers and enablers of equal citizenship, as much as these are instruments to battle inequality and injustice.

I end by asking why I am convinced that India must legislate and implement an even more robust food right law. Convincing economic arguments can be made for a food rights law. 'For those who transact only the language of growth...investments in people's bodies and minds would further compound the benefits of India's demographic dividend, with young workers healthier and better fed, and their minds more developed, better equipped to compete in the contemporary global knowledge economy. Progressive economists also remind us that there are alternative growth paths to the dominant economic paradigm of profit-led growth. Fitter workers and more money in their hands could also spur what they call wage-led growth'. Beyond economic arguments, I have argued that

> ...the paramount argument for a comprehensive right to food law is not economic, or even political (that it will generate more votes). The imperative is ethical... In a country which for too long is scarred by its absence of outrage about and suffering with desperate inequality, the greatest imperative for a right to food law is to breach our collective indifference. There is a great gaping hole in our collective souls, which we must mend. The people of this ancient land must push into history the enormous silent hopeless agony of generations, over centuries, of the inability to feed one's loved ones and oneself.

Mahatma Gandhi had counselled us to recall, in moments of doubt, the poorest and weakest person we know. I hope that it is their faces which our governments remember in the years that lie ahead when they implement a law which—if we still get it right—can alter the destinies of millions of our most dispossessed people.

NOTES

1. I am grateful for valuable research support from Raavi Aggarwal, Aditya Shrivastava, Shikha Nehra, Usman Javed, Vivek Mishra and Ambika Kapoor, and for advice from my colleagues Dipa Sinha, Sejal Dand and Biraj Patnaik. In the section on debates, I have drawn from my book, *State Food Provisioning as Social Protection*, published by FAO (2015), and for comments on the Standing Committee recommendations on an article I co-wrote with Ankita Aggarwal for EPW, 'Abandoning the Right to Food', published by

EPW (2013). The section about shortfalls in implementation of the law derives from the petition filed by PUCL in the Supreme Court of India (Civil Writ Petition no. 277 of 2015).

2. Mander, H. (2013). *Living with Hunger*. National Book Trust: New Delhi.
3. FAO (2014). *The State of Food Insecurity in the World Strengthening the enabling environment for food security and nutrition*. Rome: FAO.
4. Mander. H. (2012). *Ash in the Belly: India's Unfinished Battle against Hunger*. New Delhi: Penguin.
5. FAO (2003). *Trade Reforms and Food Security: Conceptualizing the Linkages*. Rome: FAO.
6. United Nations Human Rights Council. *The Right to Adequate Food, Fact Sheet No. 34*. Geneva: UNHRC.
7. Neoliberalism has been theorised variously as an ideology, in terms of Foucauldian political rationality, as an economic model based on principles of free market fundamentalism, etc. It is hard to find another term that is used so often without there being clarity as to what it means. This discussion, although important, is peripheral for the purpose of this paper. For our purpose here we consider it as a phase in the history of the development of capitalism that is characterized by the state becoming partisan in favour of property owning classes and fostering a model of economic growth that disproportionately benefits the better off and has resulted in a sharp increase in inequality. It has led to an acceptance globally of the need to reduce the role of the state, especially in favour of the marginalized, through the language of fiscal disciplining and by invoking the myth of the efficiency of the market in ensuring optimal provisioning.
8. FAO, n.d. *Methodology | The Right to Food around the Globe | Food and Agriculture Organization of the United Nations.* [Online] Available at: http://www.fao.org/right-to-food-around-the-globe/methodology/en/[Accessed 27 04 2018].
9. FAO, 2011. *Constitutional and Legal Protection of the Right to Food around the World,* Rome: Food and Agriculture Organization of the United Nations. p. 21.
10. In India, the Supreme Court said that the right to food is implicit as part of the fundamental right to life in Article 21.

11. FAO, 2011. *Constitutional and Legal Protection of the Right to Food around the World*, Rome: Food and Agriculture Organization of the United Nations. p. 22.
12. FAO, 2009. *Guide on Legislating for the Right to Food*, Rome: Food And Agriculture Organization of the United Nations.
13. Press Information Bureau, Government of India. (2013). *The National Food Security Bill, 2013 Receives the Assent of the President Published in the Gazette of India as Act No. 20 of 2013*. Available at http://pib.nic.in/newsite/erelease.aspx?relid=99309
14. Mander, H. (2012). *Food from the Courts*. Available at http://www.india-seminar.com/2012/634/634_harsh_mander.htm.
15. Targeted Public Distribution System (TPDS): Primary mode of distributing subsidized food and non-food items (such as rice, wheat, sugar and kerosene) to poor families, through a network of shops known as 'ration shops'. This system of distributing subsidized grains has existed in various forms since 1951. The Food Corporation of India conducts procurement and maintains the PDS, while the Ministry of Consumer Affairs, Food and Public Distribution and state governments jointly administer it. Further information is available at http://dfpd.nic.in/index.htm
16. The Integrated Child Development Services (ICDS) comprise a set of schemes aimed at improving health and nutrition of children below six years of age and pregnant and lactating women. Executed by the Ministry of Women and Child Development, the ICDS provides pregnant women health check-ups, education on health practices and supplementary meals for better nutrition. It also provides young children immunization and deworming among other health provisions, pre-school education and supplementary nutrition. Further information is available at http://icds-wcd.nic.in/icds/icds.aspx.
17. Full disclosure, the writer of this paper was a Special Commissioner to the Supreme Court in this case from 9th May, 2005, to the present day.
18. The Court ordered a phased expansion of the ICDS (pre-school nutrition programme), to include every eligible child under 6 years of age within its purview, which led to a budgetary expansion of 372% from the 10th to the 11th five year plan. Further, budgetary

allocations for the Midday Meal Scheme rose even more dramatically, by 713%, from Rs. 10 billion in 2002-03 to Rs. 80 billion in 2008-09. This information has been taken from, 'Food from the Courts', Mander (2012).

19. *Times of India* (2009). Congress manifesto. [online] Available at: https://timesofindia.indiatimes.com/india/Congress-manifesto/articleshow/4309391.cms [Accessed 21 Apr. 2018].
20. Government of India Planning Commission. (2013). *Press Note on Poverty Estimates 2011–12*. Government of India. Available at http://planningcommission.nic.in/news/pre_pov2307.pdf.
21. It is reiterated for full disclosure that the author of this paper was entrusted the responsibility of being the Convenor of the NAC working group for the National Food Security Bill.
22. Mander, H. (2015).*State Food Provisioning as Social Protection: Debating India's National Food Security Law*. Food and Agriculture Organization of the United Nations: Rome.
23. This data, taken from the Rapid Survey on Children, 2013–14, conducted by the Ministry of Women and Child Developments available at http://wcd.nic.in/sites/default/files/India%20fact%20sheet.pdf.
24. Food and Agriculture Organization of the United Nations. (2013). *The State of Food Insecurity in the World*. Rome. Available at http://www.fao.org/docrep/018/i3434e/i3434e.pdf.
25. The National Advisory Council (NAC) was a body constituted by the Prime Minister and chaired by Congress President Sonia Gandhi, mandated to advise the union government about all aspects of social policy and law, especially for disadvantaged groups.
26. Disclosure: The author of this paper was a Member of the National Advisory Council and the Convener of the Working Group of the National Advisory Council (NAC) mandated to draft the National Food Security Bill; therefore the opinion on the merits of this draft may not be fully objective.
27. Census of India Population. (2011). The Executive Summary. Available at http://www.censusindia.gov.in/2011census/PCA/PCA_Highlights/pca_highlights_file/India/Chapter-1.pdf.
28. Information on the number of Government and Government-aided schools as well as the number of children enrolled in primary

and upper primary schools is available at http://mhrd.gov.in/sites/upload_files/mhrd/files/statistics/SSE1112.pdf.

29. Census of India Population. (2011). Primary Census Abstract. http://www.censusindia.gov.in/2011census/PCA/PCA_Highlights/pca_highlights_file/India/5Figures_at_glance.pdf.
30. Press Information Bureau (2017). *Pan-India expansion of Maternity Benefit Programme (MBP) to benefit pregnant and lactating mothers across the country*. Available at: http://pib.nic.in/newsite/PrintRelease.aspx?relid=156094 [Accessed 23 Apr. 2018].
31. Jana, J., 2016. *The malnourished child – The Statesman.* [Online] Available at: https://www.thestatesman.com/opinion/the-malnourished-child-168095.html [Accessed 27 04 2018].
32. Dhume, S. (January 20, 2013).'New Delhi's Hunger Games'. *The Wall Street Journal.* Available athttp://www.wsj.com/articles/SB10001424127887323393804578557050745156758
33. Das, G. (March 31, 2013). 'Food Security Bill: Corruption by another name'. *The Time of India*. Available at http://blogs.timesofindia.indiatimes.com/men-and-ideas/food-security-bill-corruption-by-another-name/
34. Press Trust of India. (July 6, 2013). 'Volatile rupee hurts business: Rahul Bajaj'. *Business Today*. Available at http://businesstoday.intoday.in/story/volatile-rupee-hurts-business-rahul-bajaj/1/196508.html
35. Sinha, Y. (July 9, 2013). 'Food Security Bill is proof that PM is happy to go along with Sonia Gandhi's senseless welfarism'. *Economic Times.* Available at: http://articles.economictimes.indiatimes.com/2013-07-09/news/40469285_1_congress-party-finance-minister-fiscal-deficits
36. See for instance: Bhattacharya, P. (July 20, 2013). 'Everything you wanted to know about the Sen-Bhagwati debate'. *Mint*. Available at: http://www.livemint.com/Politics/zvxkjvP9KNfarGagLd5wmK/Everything-you-wanted-to-know-about-SenBhagwati-debate.html
37. Parsai, G. (May 7, 2013). 'Pass food bill even without amendments: Sen'. *The Hindu*. Available at: http://www.thehindu.com/news/national/pass-food-bill-even-without-amendments-sen/article4689314.ece

38. In the decade 1999–00 to 2009–10 while GDP growth accelerated to 7.52 per cent per annum, employment growth during this period was just 1.5 per cent, below the long-term employment growth of 2 per cent per annum, over the four decades since 1972–73. Only 2.7 million jobs were added in the period from 2004–10, compared to over 60 million during the previous five-year period. (See: Kompier, C. (2014). 'Labour Markets', in *India Exclusion Report* (2013–14). Centre For Equity Studies and Centre for Governance and Accountability).
39. Alkire, S. (July 29, 2013). 'This bill won't eat your money'. *The Hindu*. Available at http://www.thehindu.com/opinion/op-ed/this-bill-wont-eat-your-money/article4963938.ece
40. The tax-GDP ratio for 2015 stood at 10.3 per cent. Available at http://indiabudget.nic.in/ub2016-17/frbm/frbm3.pdf.
41. The Telegraph. (December 30, 2013). 'Dirty D-word & unspoken subsidy'. *The Telegraph*. Available at: http://www.telegraphindia.com/1131230/jsp/nation/story_17733538.jsp#.VBF4fvmSxqU
42. Bandyopadhyay, S. (2013). *Tax exemptions in India – issues and challenges: A discussion paper*. New Delhi: Centre for Budget and Governance Accountability.
43. von Grebmer, K., D. Headey, C. Béné, L. Haddad, T. Olofi nbiyi, D. Wiesmann, H. Fritschel, S. Yin, Y. Yohannes, C. Foley, C. von Oppeln, and B. Iseli. (2013). *2013 Global Hunger Index: The Challenge of Hunger: Building Resilience to Achieve Food and Nutrition Security*. Bonn, Washington, DC, and Dublin: Welthungerhilfe, International Food Policy Research Institute, and Concern Worldwide. Available at http://dx.doi.org/10.2499/9780896299511.
44. Ibid.
45. Mander, H. (2011). 'Ending indifference: A law to exile hunger?'. *Economic and Political Weekly*, Vol. XLVI(25). Available at: http://www.righttofoodindia.org/data/right_to_food_act_data/June_2011_ending_indifference_law_to_exile_hunger_harsh_mander.pdf
46. Morsink, J. (1999). *The Universal Declaration of Human Rights: Origins, Drafting and Intent*. Philadelphia: University of Pennsylvania Press.
47. FAO's 2004 *Voluntary Guidelines to Support the Progressive Realisation of the Right to Adequate Food in the Context of National Food Security*,

recommend inter alia constitutional and legislative action to achieve the right to food

48. The Constitution of India is available at https://www.india.gov.in/sites/upload_files/npi/files/coi_part_full.pdf
49. Human Rights Law Network. *PUCL vs. Union of India and others*. Available athttp://www.hrln.org/hrln/right-to-food/pils-a-cases/255-pucl-vs-union-of-india-a-others-.html
50. Vincent Panikurlangara v. Union of India, AIR 1987 SC 990: (1987) SC 990: (1987) 2 SCC 165; Unnikrishnan, J.P. v. State of A.P., AIR1993 SC 2178: (1993) 1 SCC 645; Mehta, M.C. v. Union of India, (1987) 4 SCC 463: AIR 1988 SC 1037; Rural Litigation and Entitlement Kendra v. State of U.P., AIR 1987 SC 359: (1986) Supp. SCC 517; Subhash Kumar v. State of Bihar, AIR 1991 SC 420 (para 7): (1991) 1 SCC 598; State of H.P. v. Umed Ram Sharma, AIR 1986 SC 847: (1986) 2 SCC 68; Bandhua Mukti Morcha v. Union of India, AIR 1984 SC 802 (para 10): (1984) 3 SCC 161. Sher Singh v. State of Punjab, AIR 1983 SC 465 (para 11): (1983) 2 SCC 344; Javed Ahmed Abdul Hamid Pawala v. State of Maharashtra, AIR 1985 SC 231 (para 4): (1985) 1 SCC 275; Sheela Barse v. Union of India, (1986) 3 SCC 596: AIR 1986 SC 1773; Upendra Baxi (Dr.) v. State of U.P., (1986) 4 SCC 106: AIR 1987 SC 191; Buffalo Traders Welfare Association v. Maneka Gandhi, (1994) Supp. (3) SCC 448: 1994 (3) Scale 1. ; State of J. &K. v. H.C. Bar Assocn., (1994) Supp. (3) SCC 708 (para 4): 1995 (2) Scale 239; Nilabati Behera v. State of Orissa, AIR 1993 SC 1960: (1993) 2 SCC 746; Sheela Barse v. Union of India, (1993) 4 SCC 204: 1993 (4) JT 558.; B.L. Wadehra (Dr.) v. Union of India, (1996) 2 SCC 594 (para 22): AIR 1996 SC 2969; Papaiah v. State of Karnataka, (1996) 10 SCC 533 (para 8); M.C. Mehta v. Union of India, (1997) 8 SCC 770 (paras 13 and 14)
51. This refers to the 'positive' obligation upon the State to uphold the expanded interpretation of Article 21's right to live with dignity, as decided in Vincent Panikulangara v. Union of India, AIR 1987 SC 990: (1987) 2 SCC 165; Unnikrishnan, J.P. v. State of A.P., AIR 1993 SC 2178: (1993) 1 SCC 645.
52. Pal and Ghosh (2007) show through NSSO data that, 'per capita food-grain consumption declined from 476 grams per day in 1990

to 418 grams per day in 2001, while aggregate caloric consumption per capita declined from just over 2200 calories per day in 1987–1988 to around 2150 in 1999–2000.'

53. Updated estimates can be found at the website of *The State of Food Insecurity in the World* (available at http://www.fao.org/hunger/en)
54. The NSSO (59th Round) report indicated that the average monthly per capita consumption expenditure of farm households was Rs. 503 in 2003. See: Bello, W. (April, 2007). 'Why Small Farmers Deserve Protection from Free Trade', *Global Asia*. Bello discusses how WTO trade liberalization, characterized by the removal of tariffs and quantitative restrictions in India, has resulted in what Utsa Patnaik calls 'a collapse of rural livelihoods and incomes'. According to reports of the National Crime Records Bureau, the total number of farmer suicides in India crossed 270,000 in the period 1995–2011. Also see: Sainath (2012)
55. Himanshu. (February 3, 2012). 'To Feed a Billion Mouths'. *Forbes*, Volume 4, Issue 3.
56. From interview with Dipa Sinha, Right to Food Campaign, (RTFC), August 2011. Ms. Sinha states that in the early drafting period of the bill, the RTFC had fought to include in access to land and natural resources as well as production and procurement reforms through a guaranteed Minimum Support Price (MSP).
57. NSSO surveys show that more than 40 per cent of rural households are landless and inequality in landownership worsened between the 48thand 59th(1992 and 2003–04) rounds of the NSSO.
58. See Parthapratim Pal & Jayati Ghosh. (July 2007). *Inequality in India: A survey of recent trends*, DESA Working Paper No. 45. The authors conclude that economic inequality increased in rural and urban India in the post-reform period due to 'the stagnation of employment generation in both rural and urban areas across states.' Employment growth in the 1990s plummeted in both rural and urban areas. With regard to factors relating to agriculture, rural employment growth rate was 0.67, and was directly attributable to the stagnation of agricultural employment in this decade. The authors site NSSO data, which indicated that total employment in the agricultural sector increased from 190.72 million in 1993–94 to 190.94 million in 1999–2000, an increase of 0.02 per cent, as

opposed to an increase of 2.57 per cent from 1987–88 to 1993–94. The authors also state that the decline in self-employment in agriculture—especially sharp for women—may have been related to changes in production patterns, which forced some peasants out of direct cultivation.

59. Ghosh, J. (2005). *Trade liberalization in agriculture: an examination of impact and policy strategies with special reference to India.* Human Development Report Paper.
60. Shiva, V. (2004). 'The future of food: countering globalisation and recolonisation of Indian agriculture', available online at www.sciencedirect.com
61. Based on interviews.
62. United Nations Children's Fund. (2009). *Tracking Progress on Child and Maternal Nutrition: A Survival and Development Priority.* New York, USA. pp. 10–14.
63. In 2010, the Government of India launched the Indira Gandhi Matritva Sahyog Yojana, a conditional Maternity Benefits scheme that provided an entitlement of Rs. 4,000 for the first six months after delivery to women aged 19 and above, for upto two live births. The objective of the scheme was to promote exclusive breastfeeding of children in the 0–6 months age group, by allowing mothers to take rest from work and feed their children. In 2013, in accordance with the provisions of the NFSA, the maternity entitlement under the IGMSY was raised from Rs. 4,000 to Rs. 6,000 for 6 months.
64. PDS (Public Distribution System), was geared towards attaining food sovereignty and towards ensuring food security for the entire Indian population.
65. Gulati, A. & S. Saini. (2015). *Leakages from Public Distribution System (PDS) and the way forward.* Working paper No. 294. Delhi: Indian Council for Research on International Economic Relations.
66. Basu, K. (2011). 'India's foodgrain policy: an economic theory perspective'. *Economic and Political Weekly*, Vol. XLVI, No. 5.
67. Office of the United Nations High Commissioner for Human Rights. (1976). International Covenant on Economic, Social and Cultural Rights. Geneva, Switzerland. Available at http://www.ohchr.org/EN/ProfessionalInterest/Pages/CESCR.aspx. Also see http://dfpd.nic.in/1sGbO2W68mUlunCgKmpnLF5 WHm/file1.pdf

68. Patnaik, P. (November 14, 2011). 'Why India Needs the Left'. *The Wire*. Available at https://thewire.in/196923/india-left-future-economy-social-policy/ Patnaik, P. (march 3, 2017). 'The Post-Neoliberal Conjecture'. *International Development Economics Associates*. Available at http://www.networkideas.org/featured-articles/2017/03/the-post-neoliberal-conjuncture/
69. The tax to GDP ratio in the U.S. is 31 per cent, *India Exclusion Report*, Centre for Equity Studies (2015).
70. Hirway, I. (2003). 'Identification of BPL households for Poverty Alleviation Programmes'. Economic and Political Weekly, Vol. *38* No. 45.
71. Sen, A. (1995). The political economy of targeting. In D. van de Walle & K. Nead (eds),*Public Spending and the Poor.*(pp. 11–24). Baltimore, USA: Johns Hopkins University Press.
72. Krishna, A. (2007). 'For reducing poverty faster: target reasons before people'. *World Development*, *35*(11), pp. 1947–1960.
73. Khera, R. (2011).'Revival of the Public Distribution System: Evidence and Explanations'. *Economic and Political Weekly*, Vol. 46, No. 44–45.
74. Castro-Leal, F., J. Dayton, L. Demery, and K. Mehra. (2000). Public Spending on Health Care in Africa: Do the Poor Benefit? Bulletin of the World Health Organization.
75. 15 per cent of children are estimated to be stunted at birth and 58 per cent at 23 months. See: Cronin, A.A., Rah, J.H, Ngure, F.M., Odhiambo, F., Ahmed, S., Aguayo, V. and Coates, S.J. 2014. *Water, Sanitation, Hygiene (WASH) and the Nutritional Status of Children in India: Understanding the Linkages and Structuring the Response*. A UNICEF and Ministry of Women and Child Development, Rapid Survey of Children, showed that under-five stunting was at 39 per cent in 2013–2014 (compared with 48 per cent in the NFHS-3, in 2005–2006) and under-five wasting was at 15 per cent (compared with 20 per cent according to NFHS-3 data).
76. Up until six months of age, exclusive breastfeeding provides total food security to the baby, WHO breastfeeding information (available at http://www.who.int/topics/breastfeeding/en).
77. Quisumbing *et al.* point to several studies from the 1980s and later that confirm differences in spending patterns of men and women. For instance, in the Republic of the Philippines, the share of female

incomes has a significant positive effect on calorie availability for the household, among other things. In the Republic of Rwanda, no female-headed households had severely malnourished children and a less than proportional number had calorie-deficient children, although men's earnings were greater by about ten times. In Brazil, women's incomes were found to have four times the impact of men's incomes on child weight-for-height. See: Quisumbing, A., L. Brown, H. Feldstein, L. Haddad and C. Pena. (1995). *Women: The key to food security*. Washington, DC: International Food Policy Research Institute.

Analysts posit that higher rates of malnutrition in South Asia compared with sub-Saharan Africa, despite higher income and economic growth, can be partly attributed to the lower status of women. See: Smith *et al.* (2003). *The importance of women's status and child nutrition in developing countries*. Washington, DC: International Food Policy Research Institute.

78. National Nutrition Monitoring Bureau (NNMB). (1975–2006). NNMB Reports, National Institute of Nutrition (cited in www.wcd.nic.in/research/nti1947/7.11.1%20Anaemia%20deficiency.doc6.2.08%20pr.pdf).
79. See for instance: Ramachandran, N. (2014). *Persisting undernutrition in India: Causes, consequences and possible solutions*. New Delhi: Springer. p. 52.
80. United Nations Children's Fund. (1990).*Strategy for improved nutrition of women and children in developing countries*. New York, USA.
81. Delhi Government's stipulated monthly minimum wage for unskilled workers is Rs 8,632 (available at http://delhi. gov.in/wps/wcm/connect/doit_labour/Labour/Home/Minimum+Wages)
82. Dand, S. & N. Agarwal. (2014). *Toward a universalist conception of maternity entitlements*. Centre for Equity Studies Working Paper, December 2014. New Delhi (available at http://centreforequitystudies.org/wp-content/uploads/2014/12/Maternity-Entitlements-Paper.pdf)
83. See for instance: SEWA Bharat and UNICEF. (2014). *A little more, how much it is—Piloting basic income transfers in Madhya Pradesh, India*.Available at http://unicef.in/Uploads/Publications/

Resources/pub_doc83.pdf; and SEWA Bharat. (2012). *An experimental pilot cash transfer study in Delhi- Executive Summary.* Available at http://www.undp.org/content/dam/ india/docs/poverty/Final-study-results-SEWA-PDS.pdf.

84. See for instance: NAC. 2011. Ibid.
85. For a case study on the nature of food provisioning by religious charities, see: http://centreforequitystudies.org/wp-content/uploads/2012/08/Religious-charities-in-Delhi.pdf
86. Rohit, P.S. (August 14, 2013). 'India's urban homeless increasing rapidly.' *The Times of India.* Available at http://timesofindia.indiatimes.com/india/Indias-urban-homeless-increasing-rapidly/articleshow/ 21822150.cms.
87. Deshingkar, P. & S. Akter. (2009). *Migration and human development in India.* United Nations Development Programme. Human Development Reports, Research Paper 2009/13. Available at http://hdr.undp.org/sites/default/files/hdrp_2009_13.pdf.
88. Government of India. 2013. *The National Food Security Bill, 2011.* Standing Committee on Food, Consumer Affairs and Public Distribution (2012–13). New Delhi. Available at http://www.prsindia.org/uploads/media/Food%20Security/SC%20Report-Food%20Security%20Bill,%202011.pdf
89. Mander, Harsh (August 26, 2013): 'Food security bill: why blame the poor and hungry?' *Live Mint.* Available at http://www.livemint.com/Opinion/LECvGhB8nDmWnX5i9OTL2H/Blaming-the-poor-and-the- hungry.html.
90. Mander, Harsh & Smita Jacob. (2010). *Eating Rough: Hidden Hunger on City Streets.* New Delhi: Centre for Equity Studies. Available at http://centreforequitystudies.org/wp-content/uploads/2017/07/Gender_REPORTS_AND_BRIEFS_community_kitchens_edit_Final_Report_4_Dec_2010-1.pdf.
91. For a detailed report on the socio-economic characteristics of the elderly population in India, see: http://mospi.nic.in/sites/default/files/publication_reports/ElderlyinIndia_2016.pdf
92. A survey conducted by an NGO on the condition of elderly individuals in India found that over a third had experienced some form of abuse. Verbal and emotional abuse was reported by 60–70 per cent of respondents in some cities, and physical abuse by about

a fifth of respondents in several cities. Available at http://www.helpageindia.org/pdf/surveysnreports/ elderabuseindia2010.pdf.

93. Studies on the effect of pensions report that while they help meet costs for food and other basic needs, they are inadequate for health and family needs (http://www.righttofoodindia.org/data/pensions/Old_Age_Pension_Scheme_in_Jharkhand_and_Chhattisgarh.pdf.) In this context, the direct provisioning of food would have a significant positive impact. In September 2014, the government of Uttarakhand announced a food security scheme for elderly women which proposed to provision free food grains to all women over 60 in the state. At the time, it was estimated that the scheme would target about 500,000 beneficiaries. It went on to instate a midday meal scheme for the group, to be implemented through the Anganwadi system.
94. For a discussion on the prevalence and particulars of disability in India, see: http://mospi.nic.in/Mospi_New/upload/disablity_india_statistical_data_11mar2011/Chapter%204-Dimension_Disability.pdf.
95. See for instance: Parulkar, A. (April 9, 2012). 'Starving in India: The forgotten problem'. *The Wall Street Journal – India*. Available at http://blogs.wsj.com/indiarealtime/tag/starving-in-India.
96. See: http://mohfw.nic.in/WriteReadData/l892s/file28-99526408.pdf.
97. Srivastava, A.K. & M. Tiwary. (2009). *Right to Food Case: Fourth Edition*. New Delhi: Human Rights Law Network.
98. Supreme Court Order of 27th November 2011 in *PUCL vs UOI* in WP(C) No. 196 of 2001 (available at www.righttofoodindia. org/data/2007nov11scorder.doc)
99. International Institute for Population Sciences.(2008). *District Level Household Survey (DLHS-3), India 2007–08*. Mumbai, India.
100. Dandona, L., E. Gakidou, M.C. Hogan, J.A. Hoisington, S.L. James & S.S. Lim. (2010). 'India's Janani Suraksha Yojana, a conditional cash transfer programme to increase births in health facilities: an impact evaluation', *The Lancet*, *375*(9730): 2009–23.
101. Hanlon, J., A. Barrientos &D. Hulme. (2010). *Just give money to the poor: the development revolution from the Global South*. Sterling, VA, USA: Kumarian Press.

102. Union Public Service Commission is basically India's central recruiting agency for All India Services authorized under part XIV, Constitution of India.
103. The Right to Public Services legislation (comprising statutory laws to guarantee the provisioning of certain public services, such as the issuing of electricity connections; ration and voter cards; land records; and caste, birth, marriage, and domicile certificates) has been implemented in a number of Indian states recently. Appeals against non-delivery or rejection of certain public services can be made before district and subdivisional administrative officials. The grievance redress mechanism does not, however, contain provisions on approaching authorities for the quality of services provided. Significant variation exists between states in how the legislation is actually implemented and monitored, and how grievances are addressed. For further details, see http://www.in.undp.org/content/dam/india/docs/report_on_national_consultation_on_strengthening_delivery_and_accountability_frameworks_for_public_service.pdf.
104. Ministry of Consumer Affairs, Food and Public Distribution, 2001. *PDS (Control) Order 2001.* [Online] Available at: http://dfpd.nic.in/pds-control-order-1.htm [Accessed 27 04 2018].
105. MDM (Mid Day Meal) entitles all children in the primary and upper primary classes of government and government-aided schools to free mid-day meals. As in the case of the ICDS, the Supreme Court order of 28 November 2001 not only universalized the MDMS in all government and government-aided schools, but also made its mandate a legal entitlement.
106. PDS (Public Distribution System), was geared towards attaining food sovereignty and towards ensuring food security for the entire Indian population.
107. G., Gupta, A. & Singh, T., (2011). *Women Working in Informal Sector in India: A saga of Lopsided Utilization of Human Capital,* Singapore: IACSIT Press.
108. Abel, C.H. (Ed.) (1996).Benefits and Systems of Care for Maternal and Child Health Under Health Care Reform Workshop Highlights. In National Research Council and Institute of Medicine,*Paying Attention to Children in a Changing Health Care System: Summaries of*

Workshops. Washington DC: National Academies Press. Available at https://www.ncbi.nlm.nih.gov/books/NBK233141/

109. Institute for Social and Economic Change. (2015). National Seminar on Women in Informal Sector—Issues and Challenges. Available at http://www.isec.ac.in/CWGS-Semian-brochure.pdf
110. Press Trust of India. (January 1, 2018). 'Maternity Benefit Scheme to be fully functional by Feb-end: Official'. *The Times of India*. Available at https://timesofindia.indiatimes.com/india/maternity-benefit-scheme-to-be-fully-functional-by-feb-end-official/articleshow/62326446.cms
111. This section has been assisted greatly by Centre for Budget and Governance Accountability.
112. Department of Food and Public Distribution. (2017). Notes on Demands for Grants 2016–2017. New Delhi: Ministry of Consumer Affairs, Food and Public Distribution. Available at http://indiabudget.nic.in/ub2016-17/eb/sbe17.pdf
113. Ministry of Women and Child Development. (2012). ICDS Mission: The Broad Framework for Implementation. Available at https://www.bpni.org/WBW/2013/Broad-Framework-of-Implementation-ICDS-Mission.pdf
114. Express News Service. (December 21, 2017). 'Maternity benefit scheme still not functional: Economists write to Arun Jaitley'. *The Indian Express*. Available at http://indianexpress.com/article/india/maternity-benefit-scheme-still-not-functional-economists-write-to-arun-jaitley-4992225/
115. Finance Commission of India. (2015). *.:: Finance Commission, India ::.* [Online] Available at: http://fincomindia.nic.in/ShowPDFContent.aspx [Accessed 25 04 2018].
116. Calculation: The increase in state share of the total revenue results in an increment of Rs. 1.78 lakh crores from 2014–15 to 2015–16. However, the Central Assistance in the same period decrement was Rs. 1.33 lakh crores from 2014–15 to 2015–16. Hence, the net increment in the state revenue from 2014–15 to 2015–16 was: Rs. 44,375.5 crores.
117. Centre for Budget and Governance Accountability, 2016. Budget Tract Volume 11, New Delhi: CBGA and UNICEF India. Available

at: http://www.cbgaindia.org/wp-content/uploads/2016/03/Budget-Track-on-Nutrition-Compressed.pdf

118. The State and UT Plan budget declined from Rs. 18,108 crores in 2014–15 to Rs. 8245.77 crores.

Ministry of Women and Child Development. (2016). *Notes on Demands for Grants 2015–2016*. Available at http://indiabudget.nic.in/budget2015-2016/ub2015-16/eb/sbe108.pdf

119. Krishnan, V., (2016). *Huge Budget Cut for ICDS | The Hindu.* [Online] Available at: http://www.thehindu.com/news/national/Huge-budget-cut-for-ICDS/article14133084.ece [Accessed 25 04 2018].

120. Centre for Budget and Governance Accountability, 2017. Mid-day Meal (MDM) – Union Budget Analysis Tool 2017-18. [Online] Available at: http://unionbudget2017.cbgaindia.org/nutrition/mid_day_meal.html [Accessed 26 04 2018].

121. Shrivastava, Saumya. (2006). *Public Spending for Nutrition in the New Fiscal Architecture in India.* CBGA Budget TRACK Volume 11, February 2016. Available at http://www.cbgaindia.org/wp-content/uploads/2016/03/Budget-Track-on-Nutrition-Compressed.pdf

122. The reference is this ASER Report 2014: PRATHAM. (2014). *Annual Status of Education Report 2014*. Available at http://img.asercentre.org/docs/Publications/ASER%20Reports/ASER%202014/4%20pagers/schoolreport2014english.pdf. However, there is no data on the number of schools compliant with all provisions of the Right to Education Act. Instead, we mostly have data on individual parameters.

123. Office of Registrar General. (2017). *Sample Registration System Bulletin*. New Delhi: Ministry of Home Affairs. Available at http://censusindia.gov.in/vital_statistics/SRS_Bulletins/SRS%20Bulletin%20-Sep_2017-Rate-2016.pdf

124. Ministry of Statistics and Programme Implementation. (2016). *Statistical Year Book India 2016*. Available at http://www.mospi.gov.in/statistical-year-book-india/2016/171

125. Press Information Bureau. (January 3, 2017). 'Pan-India expansion of Maternity Benefit Programme (MBP) to benefit pregnant and lactating mothers across the country.' Available at http://pib.nic.in/newsite/PrintRelease.aspx?relid=156094

126. Ministry of Women and Child Development. (2014). *Rapid Survey on Children 2013–14 National Report*. Available at http://wcd.nic.in/sites/default/files/RSOC%20National%20Report%202013-14%20Final.pdf
127. The data is compiled and calculated by the author from the data released by the Program Approval Board – Mid Day Meal 2017–18. Available at http://mdm.nic.in/PAB%202017-2018.html
128. These were Bihar, Chandigarh, Chhattisgarh, Delhi, Haryana, Himachal Pradesh, Karnataka, Madhya Pradesh, Maharashtra, Punjab and Rajasthan.
129. Vishwanath, A. (February 01, 2016). 'SC raps states for non-implementation of food security law'. livemint. Available at https://www.livemint.com/Politics/Q3O9ULySC2TgHRMHWAm3nI/SC-raps-states-for-nonimplementation-of-food-security-law.html
130. Supreme Court of India Civil Original Jurisdiction Writ Petition (Civil) No. 857 of 2015 Swaraj Abhiyan versus Union of India & Ors.
131. Nehra, S., (2016). *India Together: Ration to cash, a harsh transition: Shikha Nehra – 01 February 2016*. [Online] Available at: http://indiatogether.org/ration-to-cash-a-harsh-transition-poverty [Accessed 27 04 2018].
132. Drèze, J. (September 10, 2016). 'Dark clouds over the PDS'. *The Hindu*. Available at http://www.thehindu.com/opinion/lead/Dark-clouds-over-the-PDS/article14631030.ece
133. Ghosh, J. (January 5, 2018). 'Obscenity of hunger deaths'. *Frontline*. http://www.frontline.in/columns/Jayati_Ghosh/obscenity-of-hunger-deaths/article9998710.ece; Mander, H. (December 26, 2017). 'Jharkhand hunger death: A girl died crying for food. Her family is now accused of shaming India'. *Scroll*. Available at https://scroll.in/article/862338/jharkhand-hunger-death-girl-died-crying-for-food-her-family-is-now-accused-of-shaming-the-nation
134. National University of Educational Planning and Administration. (2017). *Elementary Education in India, Progress towards UEE*. Available athttp://udise.in/Downloads/Publications/Documents/Flash_Statistics-2015-16_(Elementary).pdf
135. Press Trust of India. (August 2, 2015). 'Not even half of anganwadi centres have toilets.' *The Times of India*. Available at https://

timesofindia.indiatimes.com/india/Not-even-half-of-anganwadi-centres-have-toilets/articleshow/48315281.cms

REFERENCES

Bryce, J, D Coitinho, I Darnton-Hill, D Pelletier and Per Pinstrup-Andersen (2008). Maternal and child undernutrition: effective action at national level', *The Lancet*, Vol 371, No 9611, 9 February.

Centre for Equity Studies (2015). *Report on the study of the Indira Gandhi Matritva Sahyog Yojana*. Available at http://centreforequitystudies.org/wp-content/uploads/2015/06/Maternity-Entitlement-Report_CES_29.05.pdf

Centre for Equity Studies (2014). *India Exclusion Report, 2013-14*. Available at https://dl.dropboxusercontent.com/u/29448893/India percent20Exclusion percent20Report percent202013-14_Ebook.pdf.

Mander, Harsh and Aggarwal, Ankita (2013). 'Abandoning the Right to Food'. *Economic and Political Weekly*, 23 February 2013.

Menon, S. (March 17, 2008). 'Don't serve biscuits in Anganwadis: Amartya Sen'. *Business Standard.* Available at http://www.business-standard.com/article/economy-policy/don-t-serve-biscuits-in-anganwadis -amartya-sen-108031701001_1.html.

Sen, A. (1982). *Poverty and Famines: An Essay on Entitlement and Deprivation*. Oxford: Oxford University Press.

Singh, K. (2013). *Separated and Divorced Women in India: Economic Rights and Entitlements.* New Delhi: IDRC and SAGE Publications.

www.ingramcontent.com/pod-product-compliance
Lightning Source LLC
LaVergne TN
LVHW030121160826
845673LV00019B/2903

* 9 7 8 9 3 8 2 5 7 9 7 2 4 *